ESSENTIAL BUSINESS VOCABULARY

THE MILLIONAIRE'S PLAYBOOK
1 OF 3

AT PUBLISHING

THE MILLIONAIRE'S PLAYBOOK: 1 OF 3

licensed professional before attempting any techniques outlined in this book.

By reading this document, the reader agrees that under no circumstances is the author responsible for any losses, direct or indirect, which are incurred as a result of the use of the information contained within this document, including, but not limited to errors, omissions, or inaccuracies.

Discover the meaning, benefits and practical ways to take advantage of 127 key business buzzwords. Knowing and understanding these vital words will force a paradigm shift in the way you see business.

If education is really power, this book is scientifically proven to give you superpowers.

⸻

It's one of the things we as humans hate to admit, that we don't actually know as much as we make others think we do. For the longest time I was living this dream that I was a businessman and an aspiring entrepreneur who will make millions in the future; 'watch me, I will'...was what I told people at school.

All I've ever wanted is to succeed, but although I was sure of it, I had no clue how it would actually manifest.

It was only when I started playing the game that is business and entrepreneurship, that I began to level up and move up the ranks.

What does 'the game' mean?

Well, I mean that business and entrepreneurship is a game both literally and figuratively - you might not know it yet, but you will. Unfortunately, it's not something that can be taught; only through your experience and practice will the game become more self-evident. Once you become conscious that it's a game with rules that must be understood, it's game over for the competitors.

Right now you're probably thinking:

"What the f*ck is this book all about? I've bought a book about business buzzwords and this guy is talking about business being a game! Show me some fancy words so I can learn!"

If you are thinking that, well done, you're learning already and although you aren't aware of it yet, you are already playing the game...you just haven't become conscious of it.

Why did you buy this book really? Don't worry this rant will all make sense shortly but for now, what are the main reasons you bought this book? To learn some new business lingo? Because you want to expand your knowledge? Because you want to be business savvy? Or is it because you recognize you need all the advantages you can get over your competitors if you want to be part of the 10% that succeed.

Maybe you've realized there's a hole in your game - a weak point, and that you lack the understanding of key business terms and principles, but, like me, you want to be a millionaire. You understand that education is quite literally the key to success. You know that the more you know, the more you can apply and the more you are able to communicate your business ideas, the higher the chance of you becoming successful. But, you recognize that you're still lacking knowledge and have no clue of some of the most basic business terms i.e. the meaning of having **ABSOLUTE ADVANTAGE.**

You don't have a major in business, and either you never went to university or didn't study business or entrepreneurship. You feel that you should be able to understand more business buzzwords to allow you to converse with other people in your business and during meetings. You want to feel and conduct yourself like a professional, not an impostor. This is a starting point.

You must put your ego to the side and learn and absorb knowledge if you want to become a successful businessman/woman. That's what your competitors won't tell you. People who are successful are constantly learning, they are constantly absorbing all the relevant information that will give them an edge.

That's part of the game.

Knowing more than others, but more importantly, applying and experiencing more than others by taking action.

So well done, you have started the game. You not only have taken action toward your goals, but you have also bought this book where you will discover all the key business buzzwords that are guaranteed to come up in a meeting, when listening to a podcast and when speaking to another successful business owner. You will also discover key business principles you must follow to ensure you become a success.

This is my selective pick of the business keyword I believe every entrepreneur should know.

Again, this is my personal selection of only relevant words. I am the owner of 2 six-figure online businesses and one seven-figure online business. I specialize in education and have done for the past 7 years. I only got to this point through the acquisition of knowledge and the application of it. Just knowing these words and principles changed how I viewed my business and I know it will change how you view yours too. I wish I had something like this when I was starting up, life would have been so much easier. But enough about me, this book is about you!

This book is about enabling you to acquire the relevant knowledge needed to dominate in your market. I'm not going to inform you of words you simply don't need to know, or irrelevant principles, as they won't take you closer to your goals.

By reading this book, you will gain a deep insight into business keywords and their benefits. You will also get a breaking of the fourth wall with certain words. I will provide you a personal BOSSNOTE on my thoughts and how you should apply yourself. As I said in the description, this is not a dictionary so don't read it like that, that's why there's no table of contents. This is (roughly) in alphabetical order and must be read chronologically. I would recommend you read it at night before bed so you can fully absorb and sleep on your newfound understanding of business terminology and lingo.

Of course, I have no control over how you read it, however I'll tell you the best way to get the most from this gold mine. This is book one of three of the millionaire play-books. After you read this, you are one step closer to your business goals. You will be able to confidently express and articulate yourself.

So, if you're ready to absorb wisdom, let's begin.

A/B Test

A/B testing is also known as split testing in the online world. It's a simple process where you test two variants of the same webpage, ad banner, cover, or title of an ad that you are going to promote.

Running an A/B test means you are identifying which variant drives more conversions. You can then use the winning variant in your scale campaign, with confidence the campaign will do well.

BENEFITS: *Optimize your promotion*, meaning *higher conversion rate* and *less money spent* on advertisement.

ACQUI-HIRE

When you are starting up a business and begin to build a team of devoted hardworking individuals, this acquisition process is known as acqui-hiring.
So, acqui-hiring is the process of building your team.

―――

BENEFITS: You can build *trust*, a great *support system* around you and a *collective shared goal* within your chosen team.

―――

ALPHA RELEASE

The alpha release is the release process of a product that remains incomplete. This product, whether digital or physical, is given to a group of people who act as 'testers' and use and examine the product before it's finalized.

———

BENEFITS: *Enables rigorous testing* of a product before it goes to the mass market. It *allows for quality control*, as the product developers can implement feedback given by the testers ensuring the optimum final product. If it's a software product, alpha release helps *identify bugs.*

———

ACCESSIBILITY

This just means how easily can your product, whether digital or physical, can be reached. Maybe through an app, a website, or at a physical store. Can your product be easily accessed?

BENEFITS: If you have a product that's easily accessible, this is great - it means your ***target audience can easily buy and use your product*** with ease, which means more sales and more money in the bank.

If your product is online, amazing - it means it's ***accessible to near enough everyone online***. This doesn't mean everyone will buy or use your product, it just means that anyone who is interested in your product can reach it if they have access to the internet.

ACCELERATOR

A business accelerator is a program that enables start-up companies to have ease of access to investors, mentorship from experienced business owners, and other support. This helps the business become self-sustained (no need for outside help in satisfying one's basic needs). These programs can last up to six months.

BENEFITS: Accelerator programs help businesses *move past the early stages of the start-up*, helping the business become *more established* in its respected field. These programs also help *connect businesses to the network* of their peers.

APPRECIATION

The general increase in the value of an asset over time.
This is the opposite of ***depreciation:*** decrease in value
of asset over time.

ANALYTICS

This is the evidence-based computational analysis of a business's collected data and statistics. This often means looking at the business's past data in order to gain a better understanding of how to improve certain areas.

Whilst looking at analytics are you looking out for stand out KPI (***Key Performance Indicators***) this is used by business to judge the performance, progress and targets.

Within analytics, the KPI which are examined are:

Acquisition cost:

Total expenditure when obtaining a new client, worker or asset.

Return on investment:

ROI aims to measure the amount a certain investment returns over time.

Customer lifetime value:

How much value a customer provides a business for the entirety of their relationship.

Monthly recurring revenue:

The recurring monetary value that a subscription-based business gets monthly. This definition works for any other time scale, such as annually - annual recurring revenue.

Units of product sold per day:

The amount of product sold on a daily basis.

Conversion rate of landing page:

The total number of sales divided by the total number of page visitors.

Advertising, marketing, and promotional costs:

The total amount of money spent on promotion of a product, or on increasing brand awareness.

Adaptive expectations:

This is the theory of how individuals shape their views about the future, using past trends and the errors of their own previous predictions.
An example of this would be predicting that 'the state of inflation has increased this year, therefore, it will increase next year'.

⸻

ABSOLUTE ADVANTAGE

This is the easiest way to determine the economical performance of a business company. If one business is able to produce more of something with the same amount of effort and resources as another business, then that business has an absolute advantage.

To make things clearer; let's say you have two fashion design businesses, **A and B.** Each has the same number of individuals in their teams and have access to the exact same information and resources. However, business **A** by chance, has a far more creative team. This means business **A** has an absolute advantage!

They are able to produce more high quality products with the same amount of resources.

Absolute advantage is relative to the respective business so the same principles which gave the business, for example, *'creativity'*, might not allow for absolute advantage in another market.

BENEFITS: I feel this one's self-explanatory...but I'll give you a hint it's in the name. ;)

ASSET

An asset is a useful, valuable thing that is the property of an individual person or company. ***Assets are characterized by growth,*** but not limited to financial growth.

Examples of assets:

Property/Land

Equipment

Trademark/Patent

Furniture

Inventory

ADAPTIVE INDIVIDUAL

A person who is able to quickly change their approach, behavior or techniques to meet the requirements of their business environment, conditions, and landscape. They are able to learn new skills relatively quickly and have the ability to take in new information and apply their knowledge.

BENEFITS: Once again, it's self-explanatory.

BOSSNOTE: *Being able to adapt is probably the most important characteristic an entrepreneur needs to succeed.*

⊏▭⊐

BOOTSTRAPPING

Bootstrapping is the process in which an entrepreneur uses their own savings in combination with their experience, skills and knowledge to start and grow their business without capital.

BENEFITS: Bootstrapping forces you to be *more creative* with your ideas. It puts you in a position where you gain *experience in how to handle money* within your business efficiently. You also have *complete ownership* of your company, so you don't have to answer to investors - or look for them.

BETA RELEASE

This is the next process of production, after your initial alpha release you then have beta release. This entails that you offer your product to your potential customer. They have time to use the product and will provide feedback. This feedback helps you understand where changes need to be made.

BENEFITS: Giving your potential customer your product to try before it's available to the mass market is amazing for *quality control* for your product. It gives you *confidence that you've got the best product*. It also means you've done testing, so you know whether your product is *consumer friendly*.

BOARD OF DIRECTORS

Board members are individuals who act as mentors and advise business owners on the best practices and ways to run their business, through experience and knowledge. Oftentimes, these select few are also shareholders in the business.

Board of directors can be people who help with the hiring process, business development and fundraising. This all general oversight management of the business.

BENEFITS: They can provide **_great guidance_** in what direction the business should go. If you have a great team and support system they can help you **_broaden your vision_** and help you **_attain your long term goals._**

DRAWBACKS: All these benefits are **_relative to the board of directors_**. If you have a great team then things are great. If you don't, then you are **_potentially halting the progress of your business_**. Finally, your board of directors may **_not be on board with your vision_** and **_increase pressure_** for you to deliver.

▭

BOSSNOTE: Think carefully about the people you let in your inner circle, make sure they are on board with your vision, your brand and have crazy work ethics. Make sure you constantly surround yourself with positive, hardworking, passionate people.

There's a saying: *'You are a combination of the 5 people you spend most of your time with'*. Well, your business is quite literally its own entity and the product of the team that makes it up.

BUSINESS DEVELOPMENT

This is the long term process of creation of value from an organisation, customer and market. This is essential to the role a business plays in its early stages of creation.

BUSINESS MODEL CANVAS

This is the template start up companies use to structure

their plan of action for the business and how they approach things. This is the strategic management of how the business will run.

This is also known as the BM template. Each business model has its own specialised model, with its own ins and outs.

Variables that dictate a business model

Source of revenue: *online business or offline business?*
Target audience: *young adults or the elderly?*
Product

These are the four types of business models:

BUSINESS TO CONSUMER

BUSINESS TO BUSINESS

CONSUMER TO BUSINESS

CONSUMER TO CONSUMER

BURN

This is a term which is often used by investors. 'How much will you burn in the upcoming months?' This term simply means how much money one spends within a given period.

BACK END

Back end departments or offices are functions in a business that provide the services that allow businesses to function.

This includes:

Administration

Accounting

Document handling

Communications data processing

Personnel (HR or human resources)

Sly comment: So for the most part the boring stuff. You can see this as the maintenance of your business. The things you absolutely should do but bore you to f*ck.

BUSINESS EXPENSE

Business expenses are costs incurred in the ordinary course of business. They can apply to small entities or large corporations. Business expenses are part of the **income** statement. On the **income** statement, business expenses are subtracted from revenue to arrive at a company's taxable **net income**.

BRANDING

Branding is seen as promotion of a particular product or company by means of advertising and distinctive design. Branding also means the message which you as a business owner are trying to send out. Brands represent things, even emotions. For example, one of the most recognisable brands in the world, Coca-Cola, tries to represent and is heavily associated with happiness and joy. Coca Cola literally translates to *'Tasty Fun'* or *'Delicious happiness'* in Mandarin.

Benefits:

Strong customer recognition

Competitive edge in the market

Immense customer loyalty and shared values

Drastically increase profit margins. A trusted brand will always win customers over one that isn't, even if the product is exactly the same.

Increases the credibility of a product and thus makes it easier to sell.

DRAWBACKS: NONE

BOSSNOTE: Building a strong brand goes a long long way. I know from experience, having started multiple businesses in different respected fields, I can strongly say the one myself and my customers are most connected to is the business with the strongest brand identity. People love to stand for something and be part of something great. I realised that they actively seek this out through brands.

Why do you think clothing brands are so successful?

They understand the power of branding and can charge ridiculous amounts for a piece of clothing. Most people buy not for the clothing itself, but for the feeling the clothing provides them - they are buying the brand! This same logic can be applied to near enough anything.

YES, IT WILL TAKE YOU TIME. BUT THAT TIME IS WELL INVESTED.
THAT'S MORE MONEY IN YOUR POCKET IN THE FUTURE.

BONDS

Bonds are a different way to raise capital and an individual. It's seen as a safer alternative to selling shares or taking out a bank loan. They're regarded as a lower risk investment. Like shares in listed companies, once they have been issued, bonds may be traded on the open market. A bond's yield is the interest rate (or coupon) paid on the bond divided by the bond's market price.

BENEFITS: Bonds are *less volatile and risky* when compared to stocks. If they are held for an extended period of time, they can provide a *stable* but more importantly *consistent return on investment.* Bonds also tend to have a *higher interest rates* when compared to banks.

BEHAVIOURAL ECONOMICS

This is the study of biases, tendencies and heuristics which influence individuals' decisions to improve, tweak or overhaul traditional economic theory. Studying behavioural economics helps us determine whether people make good or bad choices and whether they could be helped to make better choices.

BOSSNOTE: I would recommend you look further into

studies about this, analyse and reflect whether you're making emotive decisions or whether you are making rational decisions based on logic, facts and collected data, within your respective business.

Case studies have shown that people often overestimate the extent in which certain things in their business can be predicted. Studies have also shown that people are disproportionately influenced by a fear of feeling regret, and many people are engaged with business activities so they don't feel like they have failed.

BARRIER TO ENTRY

Barrier to entry is an economics and **business** term alluding to factors which may regulate,and prevent newcomers into a market or industry sector. This regulation can enforce limited competition.

What are different types of barrier to entry?

High start-up costs

Regulatory hurdles

Patent/trademark

Geographical barriers

Brand loyalty

Creative talent

BENEFITS: Barriers to entry helps regulate and protect the market. Barriers of entry are great as it means not everyone can succeed in a certain field. You need certain skills, knowledge, and backgrounds to enter certain fields. This might sound like a bad thing, but in all businesses, lower competition is always a good thing. If you have all the tools you need to enter a business then the barrier to entry helps you tremendously, if it protects your market from everyone else.

BOSSNOTE: View this the same way we are grateful for barriers to entry for doctors. You should be grateful that not everyone is able to start a business, as some businesses, even with a barrier to entry, are poorly run and looked after. You want a market which is able to produce the best functional business for society as a whole.

Before you enter any business venture, make sure to research the barrier to entry. The more niche you choose, if you join a business with a high barrier to entry, you'll have low competition. So, if you're successful, you'll be making a fortune, comfortable knowing competition is limited.

BREAKEVEN

Is the point at which both expenses and revenue are of equal value, cancelling each other out so there is no net loss or gain. One has "broken even".

Most start-up businesses typically take 2 years to break even.

Copyright is a type of intellectual property that gives its owner the exclusive right to make copies of a creative work, usually for a limited time.
The creative work may be in a literary, artistic, educational, or musical form.

BENEFITS: You get ownership. You are able to enforce copyright laws if someone uses your work without permission. It protects creators, and business men and women.

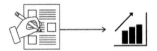

COPYWRITING

The act of writing text and copy for the purpose of advertising. Copywriting is seen in the entrepreneurial world as a skill which must be developed. This is essentially persuasive language/writing used to show a potential customer the benefits of a product and why they would be stupid not to buy it. Within the 'copy', they aim to hit certain pain points of the target audience, invoking strong emotions.

Things good copywriting should be:

URGENT: Buy now - discount price ends in 24 hours

UNIQUE: Should come from a different angle

USEFUL: It should be informative about the product and its benefits

ULTRA SPECIFIC: Give time frame, exact price and stats

EMOTIVE: It needs to hit the reader's pain points and resonate with them.

CLEAR: Simple words with clear communication. It should be very easy to read.

BENEFITS: Good copy, which means a good written advertisement, can *increase conversions* of landing pages, meaning more money, more sales, and more traffic.

CUSTOMER RETENTION

Customer retention refers to the actions and activities companies and organizations take to reduce the number of customer defections. Businesses tend to have customer retention programs in place subconsciously. They aim to help businesses retain as many customers as possible, often through customer loyalty and brand loyalty initiatives.

This could be giveaways, shoutouts, discounted prices for customers who have been with the business for a long time.

BENEFITS:

Your **brand will stand out** from the crowd.

You will make **more money** due to word of mouth referrals.

You will have an overall ***increase in individual customer lifetime value.***

You will ***receive better feedback***, which will enable you to make ***positive changes*** to your business.

You can ***build a strong, long lasting relationship*** which at times, can be the driving force of your business.

BOSSNOTE: That last point is so important, I say this as the owner of a publishing business and other online businesses. Although my passion takes me 50% of the way there, it's the built relationship with the customer that takes me the whole way there. I feel more obliged to work harder than ever, to produce high quality products as it's my customers and now friends who I care for that I am trying to provide with quality products.

It keeps me motivated, it keeps me focused, and it pushes me to go that extra mile and do some extra research to ensure everything is up to scratch.

CUSTOMER LIFE CYCLE

The customer life cycle is the process your customers go through when they are building a relationship with your business, from the point of initial contact.

CUSTOMER ACQUISITION

This is the process of a business getting a new customer.

CAPITAL

Capital is usually cash or liquid assets which are held or obtained by an individual of business for expenditures. In financial economics, this term can be expanded to include a company's capital assets.

CAPACITY

The capacity of a business is the maximum output level of products that can be sustained while delivering a product or service. Most businesses try to understand and manage their capacity.
Capacity of each business is completely different and unique to that particular business.

COLLATERAL

An asset which is seized from a borrower by a lender.
Lenders tend to cause collateral to retrieve the value of a
loan. This happens if the borrower fails to meet the
arranged interest charges or payments.

COMMODITY

A raw material or primary agricultural product that can
be bought and sold, such as copper or coffee.
Commodities are normally purchased in bulk.

Other commodities include things like, oil, cotton cocoa or
silver. It can also be things which are manufacturer
products like microchips and other computer resources.

CUSTOMER RESEARCH

Customer research is the process of spending time discovering what one's target audience likes, what their pain points are, why they would relate to the business, what motivates then, and what their buying behaviour is like. Customer research allows a business to deeply understand their client and consumer base. The clearer you are about who your target audience is, the better you can direct your efforts in product, advertising, marketing and pricing.

Here are some simple ways to carry out customer research:

Interviews

Online surveys

Living in the online environment your potential customer might be in

For example, if you have a business that sells products to dog owners, although dog owners are a huge variety of ages, the majority age range would be middle age or older, right? Now what platform would they most likely be active on?
Tiktok? Instagram?
Facebook?

So now that you have identified the platform they spend most of their time on. What next?

You can either join already existing dog related Facebook groups and begin networking, reaching out to people and connecting. You can see what sort of stuff they post and what gets the most likes which give you a better view on what they like and what they are like.

The next step would be to create your own Facebook 'Dog Lover's' group, maybe make it niche, 'Middle aged women bulldog lovers group' - the more specific the better. You only want **a piece** of the market, this makes things easier to handle. Anyway, now that you have that group, you can ask questions, interact and provide value. Over time you will gain a better understanding of your customer's behaviours, pain points, motivators and buying habits.

Trust me, I have done more customer research than you can imagine. It is a process that happens everyday. Business is never static. Things are always moving forward and if you slack just for a moment, competition will take over. A great way to get absolute advantage is by knowing your customer more than your competitors. Simple.

⊏━━⊐

Here are just a few benefits of customer research:

Minimises investment risk

Uncovers and identifies potential problems

Identifies holes in the marketplace

Better understanding of what the customer wants

Strategic planning for the future

THROUGH YOUR CUSTOMER RESEARCH, YOU CAN CREATE A CUSTOMER AVATAR.

CASH FLOW

Cash flow is the net amount of cash and equivalents being transferred into and out of a business.
When a business is able to create sufficient value and is able to generate positive cash flow, this tends to be the time that investors want in.

BENEFITS: Again, self explanatory.

CAP TABLE

This is essentially a spreadsheet which documents a business's shareholders, investors, ownerships, equity shares and similar.

CREATIVE MIND

This is the mind of a person that is able to see the world in a different way. In relation to business it refers to an individual's mind who is able to come at a business model with all the same information but is able to come at it from an entirely different angle which yields lots of benefits, whether that's making higher sales, making the system more efficient, or making customer acquisition a breeze.

A creative mind is able to solve problems quicker than the average person as they are not confined by rules. They can take a step back and think outside the box, they can see the bigger picture and make links others can't.

BENEFITS: This is a *skill which can be developed over time*, and gives you an *advantage over your competitors*. Creativity means you can *solve problems faster,* with less brain power.

Business is us constantly solving problems, and making links other people can't. When we do that, we succeed. When we do that, we get paid!

COMPOUND INTEREST

Compound interest is the interest you earn on interest.

Here's a quick example:

Let's say *$100* is in a bank account with an interest rate of *10% a year.*

At the **end of the year,** the account will contain **$110.**

If the **money is left** in the account untouched, **10%** interest will be **paid on the $110.**

Meaning in the **second year you will have $11** interest added, making **$121.**

BOSSNOTE: I'll leave you with a quote from **Albert Einstein:**
'Compound interest is the eighth wonder of the world. He who understands it, earns it; he who doesn't, pays it.'

DEBT

Debt is an amount of money borrowed by one party from another. Debt is used by many corporations and individuals as a method of making large purchases that they could not afford under normal circumstances.

BOSS NOTE: It's a common misconception that debt is

bad. This is wrong, debt is neither inherently a good thing or bad thing.

Debt is only as good or as bad as the person who takes it on. If you're an educated banker, businessman, corporation, government or real estate agent and understand the ins and outs of debt and how to use it to your advantage, then great.

However, if you're a person that lacks understanding of the ins and outs of debt but love getting the newest fashionable clothes and accumulating debt with the use of your credit card knowing you can't uphold the payback instalments, maybe debt isn't for you.

It must be noted that I am not a financial advisor, just a well educated, successful businessman.

Always do your own personal research. I would love to go into more detail about this topic but I simply can't as that's not the purpose of this book. The purpose of this book is to educate you as an entrepreneur on the most prevalent terms in business, equipping you with a solid understanding of the market and all the processes in running a business.

DIVIDEND

When a corporation earns a profit or surplus, it is able to pay a proportion of the profit as a dividend to shareholders. So dividend means the sharing/distribution of profits with shareholders of a business, once the business is well into profit.

Any amount not distributed is taken to be re-invested in the business, called **RETAINED EARNINGS.**

It's worth knowing that the owner of the business can also pay themselves a dividend!

DEMAND

The demand refers to the amount/volume of product that people are both willing and able to buy.
If a product is in high demand, it's a popular product and people want and are willing to pay the right price for it. In business we are always looking for products which are in high demand as this allows us to make the most amount of profit. It also means we can scale our business to the next levels.

BOSS NOTE: It is worth noting that the market chooses the demand of a product or service, and demand of a certain product can change over time. It's dynamic, not static. This just means the demand can increase or decrease at any time. However, there are certain things and evaluations that can be made to give you a clear idea of market trends and the direction things are heading in.

For example if you are working in Amazon FBA and you're selling Christmas products, understanding that the demand for your product is determined by seasonal changes, you are able to spot the trend that the demand for your products will increase from October onwards till the 24th of December at which point you expect the trend for the demand of your seasonal product to reduce.

Understanding trends will help you understand demand.

DEMOGRAPHIC

Demographics can be seen as the collection and analyzation of broad characteristics about groups of people and populations. This can include (but not limited to) **age, sex, class, nationality, geographic location.**

BENEFITS: Understanding your demographic goes hand in hand with customer research. The data collected through demographics helps businesses to ***understand how to market to consumers*** and ***plan strategically for future trends in consumer demand.***

DIVISION OF LABOUR

The division of labour is essentially what it says it is - the separation of tasks within a business. Having people who are specialised at a certain field working on that field and aspect of the business. For example, you would want a business manager to run and manage the business. You would want someone who is specialised in advertising to do marketing for your business.

BENEFITS: The business is *running effectively* and will perform so much better. You will have *increased group cohesion*. You are dividing the workload, which will *increase people's wellbeing*.

51

You are also ***utilising your team members to the fullest*** of their abilities.

BOSSNOTE: A lot of entrepreneurs believe they have to be the jack of all trades and spend their time trying to master a multitude of skills. This normally results in mastering none of them.
You are far better building your team of specialised individuals who play their own specific roles in the business. I appreciate when you're initially starting a business you're starting from the ground and a lot of the elements of the business will be run by yourself.

My advice is as soon as you can outsource, DO! It frees up more time for you to work on the things which will take your business to the next level, i.e the quality of your product or the quality of service which you provide.
You also have to accept that...**YOU CAN'T BE THE BEST AT EVERYTHING.**
Focused energy is better than scattered energy.

DEEP DIVE

When a business starts facing continual problems, it's time to take a deep dive into the business to identify, analyse and then to mitigate negatives in an efficient manner.

During deep dives, you will find **BLIND SPOTS** in your business, places that haven't been optimized and given the care needed to ensure the business is making maximum profits. Issues that have slipped under the radar.

BENEFITS: Deep diving allows the business to operate in the most *risk-averse way possible.*

BOSSNOTE: Although many businesses wait until problems start to arrive before they take a deep dive, you as an entrepreneur should be taking deep dives monthly! It will save you a tremendous amount of *time*, *money* and *energy*.

DISTRIBUTION

Distribution is the process of making a product and

delivery of service to the **consumer** or business user who needs it. Distribution can occur directly by the producer, service provider, or even by the use of indirect channels with distributors or intermediaries.

DELIVERABLE

A thing able to be provided, especially as a product of a development process. When you provide a deliverable, you are essentially providing a third party with the details of the service that they are going to provide you with or 'deliver' to you.

If you are in the online world, you would have or will come across this word. For example, if you want a graphic produced by a freelancer you will need to provide the deliverable, which entails, colour, size, time frame to complete the project, ideas of what you want the logo to look like. Then they will deliver you the product using the deliverable information you have provided them.

BOSS NOTE: This one is simple. Be clear, concise and keep things very simple.

EXIT CRITERIA

Exit criteria are the criteria or requirements which must be met to complete a specific task or process as used in some fields of business or science.
Exit criteria is mainly applied in software engineering.

⬛▭

Benefits:

Ensures *customers satisfaction*

It helps achieve ***technical excellence***

It make the development process ***simple and straightforward*** to follow

EVANGELISM MARKETING

Evangelism marketing is a fancy way of describing word-of-mouth marketing, which customers openly partake in constantly.

Certain businesses have an incredible relationship with their customers who believe so strongly in a particular product or service that they freely try to convince others to buy and use it. This is essentially a referral scheme without payment for the referral. The customers become voluntary advocates, actively promoting your business's service or product.

BENEFITS: Allows for cheaper marketing. You have people who are increasing your brand awareness. You are getting more sales, and an increased consumer base. Having an evangelist as a customer is simply one of the most powerful assets you can have in your business.

BOSSNOTE: This varies from business to business. Some businesses have more evangelist marketers than others. In my humble opinion, the best way to harness this amazing form of marketing is by focusing your energy on satisfying and solving your customer's deepest needs and problems, providing exemplary customer service, and finally, nurturing and building a strong relationship with them.

EVALUATION

A business evaluation is an analysis and review of a business entity. This tends to occur when a business owner wants to sell the business. The evaluation gives overall standing and operation. These are vital pieces of information a buyer would want to know, as it helps them gain a better understanding of what areas may need attention and what changes need to be implemented to get the results desired from the purchase.

Things included during the evaluation process:

Sales, products, services, marketing strategy, business activity, customer relationships (whether there's an established community or not), location...

BENEFITS: If you have a great evaluation = *LOTS AND LOTS OF F*CKING MONEY.*

BOSS NOTE: These are variables sensible buyers will look at. When I have bought a business, the main thing I'm looking at is marketing strategy, and whether or not the business has a strong community. The rest I have strong belief I can fix. If you have a strong community, believe me when I say you can monetize if you're ***creative.***

I'm grateful to have a team of extremely creative and passionate individuals.

So, how does this help you?

Focus on building relationships and communities.
Focus on the variables which are outlined above.
If you're building a business (which I assume you are as you've purchased this book), somewhere down the line you may want to sell it. Start now, to think about all the variables within your business and create value, and work very hard to increase the value of each aspect. Don't sleep on it, form it as a habit early on. Even if you never want to sell it, focusing on these variables is what makes the business succeed.

MAKE SURE YOUR BUSINESS IS BUYABLE.

EARNED MEDIA

Earned media this refers to publicity gained through promotional efforts other than paid media advertising.
Earned media included the publicity gained through advertising. Businesses have to spend the time and energy required to build strong relationships with your customers and brand advocates.

BENEFITS: Earned media is proven to have **_better_**
ROI and is also more **_cost effective._**

ENTREPRENEUR

YOU!

Write what this means to you.

FUNNEL

The sales funnel, also known as a revenue funnel or the sales process, refers to the buying process which customers go through when purchasing products.

The process of a funnel is as follows: find a buyer, qualify the buyer (make sure the product is sold to the right person), sell the product to the buyer (purchase).

An easier way to see this is as the journey the customer takes from point of entry (when they were first initially exposed to the product, to when they finally purchase the product and become a customer. Or, the sequence of steps the customer had to take to purchase the product. This process is almost always subdivided into different stages.

An example of a funnel for an online course could go as follows:

Sees an ad, clicks it

Get taken to online seminar and watches 'webinar'
End of webinar: gets taken to landing page
Purchases product at landing page.

It's important to note that the funnel process varies and is drastically different for each business and business models. So, like much of the processes outlined in this book, there is no one size fits all approach. Each sales funnel should be personalised and uniquely designed with appreciation of the business type, and the target market/ideal customer.

BENEFITS: *Every single activity is tracked* during the sales process which means you are more accountable. You can *easily spot weak areas* in the funnel process that need more attention.

If you have a great funnel:
Conversion rates drastically increase

More accurate predictions can be made about sales

Increases revenue of the business

Makes marketing easier

FOUNDERS

Founders are the individuals who established the business. They are the individuals who created something from nothing.

FREEMIUM

This is a common practice in which start-ups offer a free plan to customers which include product features, while trying to encourage subscribers to upgrade their plans to a more attractive offer.

An example of this would be Youtube; of course we have a free plan but they try to upsell us to their premium plan which means no targeted ads, more premium content made by youtube, offline watching, downloadable videos and music. Maybe even more.

Businesses try to make their premium offer as attractive as they can so it's a no brainer for the customer to buy the upgraded plan!

BENEFITS: The freemium model is a *great way to get the attention* of potential customers using the 'FREE TAG'. This of course *increases your product and brand awareness* as you have more eyes on your product. Freemiums also mean you are able to *upsell customers*, and is a great way to increase business revenue.

FINANCIAL SYSTEM

The collective bodies which make money move around the world. Governments, businesses, cooperations, banks, consumers and producer. We are all part and parcel of the financial system.

FREE TRADE

Free trade, also known as open trade, is the arrangement that countries are allowed to freely trade with each other without any legal constraints. The first free trade agreement was signed in 1860, between England and France.

Free trade is measured by the volume of exports and imports of countries.

BENEFITS: Free trade means we get *lowered prices for consumers*, it *increases economic value* of countries and you have a *wider range of goods* to choose from.

FINANCIAL PROJECTION

This is the process in which a business uses collected data and evaluation of external market variables to make a prediction of future revenues and expenses.

Most businesses account for both short term and long term financial projections. This gives businesses the forethought to better appoint their resources and allows for preparations.

FRANCHISE

Franchising is defined as an agreement or license between

two legally independent parties which gives: A person or group of people (the franchisee) the right to market a product or service using the trademark or trade name of another business (the franchisor). (**Standardised definition**)

Therefore, a business which allows the process to take place is known as a franchise.

Here are some common franchises:

McDonald's

Subway

Domino's

Taco Bell

BENEFITS:

Speed of growth

Increased capital

Increased brand equity

Limited risk and liability

Cheaper advertising and promotions

Decreased involvement in the day to day operation

Motivated and effective management

Benefits Of 'Joining' A Franchise Chain:

You have the advantage of **operating under the name** of a very **popular** and well **respected business.**

Most of the work has been done for you in terms of the **brand awareness** and **customer acquisition process.**

You have a great **support system.**

You **build strong business relationships.**

Defeats the odds that businesses fail within the first 5

years.

DRAWBACKS:

You don't have full control of the business

You are **tied to certain suppliers** which the franchise has formed.

You are **gambling that the brand reputation** will hold up.

Franchises require a **large** amount of **capital to start.**

You will be charged a **'franchise fee'.**

It can be **difficult to exit** the business.

FRANCHISE-ABLE BUSINESS

As we have already discussed what a franchise is, here are the characteristics of a franchise-able business.

Barrier to entry:

The business must be ***established***. The business must offer a ***unique idea*** or concept. The business must be teachable. This business must be able to ***provide adequate returns*** to the potential franchisee.

FULFILMENT

This is the closing achievement/completion of a deal, once it is agreed.

FUNDAMENTALS

This is the necessary foundation which must be built for a business to strive and succeed. Fundamentals of a business are tied to the business model, so they can differ from business to business. However, there are also overarching fundamentals to business as a whole, such as supply and demand.

BOSSNOTE: Depending on what business you want to start, make sure you assess the business fundamentals. Assess variables which need attention to ensure you have the best chance of succeeding in your particular business. Many people getting into business think it's a straightforward path, not fully understanding what makes their type of business successful. Is it customer service? Is it the product itself? Is it brand awareness?

Ask yourself the question: what are the most basic things that I need to fulfil every time with this business that if I don't, would lead to the collapse of the business?

Answer these questions and you have the fundamentals to your business.

FIRST MOVER ADVANTAGE

A first mover advantage is a term which is used to describe the inherent advantage a business or individual has over their competitors as a result of being first to market in a new product category. Due to the fact they are first in the market potential customers have one option to go to, to get the product or service which the first mover business provides.

This is also advantageous as the business is able to get a

head start in customer acquisition, customer research and branding.

BOSSNOTE: It must be said that this doesn't always guarantee success. The success of the business is down to the ability and execution of the first mover business. If a second business opens up in the same category and is able to provide a better service or higher quality product, they are more likely to succeed.

GOLDEN STANDARD

This is the reference point for the highest quality standard at which a service or product should be provided. Golden standard helps businesses consistently produce and deliver the best quality service.

GLOBALIZATION

Globalization is a term that refers to the trend for people, firms and governments around the world to become increasingly dependent on and integrated with one another. Globalization also refers to the process in which a business grows to a point where they gain international influence, meaning they can operate at a global scale.

There are three types of globalisation, *economic, cultural and political globalisation.*

We are mainly focusing on **economic globalisation.**

Benefits:

More money

Increased opportunity

Access to infinite market

An ever expanding brand awareness

Increased workers, customers, business partnerships, goods and services.

GROWTH

Simply put, this is the process in which a business increases in size.
Growth in a business is usually measured using certain metrics.

Sales, revenue, client base, number of customers, number of workers, increased cash flow and diverse audience base.

BOSSNOTE: The golden indicator of growth for you will be HATERS. Believe it or not, when you start to evolve and level up as an entrepreneur you will start receiving more negative reception. Ignore the haters and keep doing your thing. Haters unfortunately come hand in hand with progress and success! Trust me!

GOING PRIVATE

If a business is going private this means it is closing the door to all future potential.

GROWTH HACKING

Growth hacking is the process by which an entrepreneur uses unconventional strategies (these tend to be unique and creative) to drastically increase growth of a business at a cost that is significantly lower than the 'average' amount which would normally be required to attain the same results.

This is what a successful marketing campaign should aim to do.

BENEFITS:

Cost effective

Increased marketing effectiveness (scalable marketing)

Embraces the growth mentality

Encourages creative thinking

All of these benefits translate to ***more money***

BOSSNOTE: You as an entrepreneur should always be thinking of unique marketing strategies your business can incorporate. Doing so differentiates you from the market. It makes you unique, it also means your business will have absolute advantage over other similar businesses in your market. I personally am constantly thinking and encouraging my workers to think in this way. You need to stand out from the saturated market.

HAGGLE

Haggling is the process of negotiation between two parties on a fair price for a service or product.

BOSSNOTE: This is a skill which you will develop over time. Unfortunately, the only teacher on how to properly haggle is experience. Experience is after all our best teacher.

HALO EFFECT

This entails a consumer who now has a bias and favoritism towards a line of products due to previous positive experiences with the product or service. The halo effect strongly tied with a brand's strength and loyalty, and contributes to brand equity.

HUMAN CAPITAL

Human capital is the stock of habits, knowledge, social and personality attributes (including creativity) embodied in the ability to perform labour so as to produce value. Human capital can also be seen as the economic value of a worker's experience and skills.

BOSSNOTE: Make sure you invest in your worker, education, skills and health training. Doing so will increase the inherent value of your business. Although you should try saving where you can, it is also important to recognise the importance of spending and investing into your own education as well as your team's. So when that time comes, don't hesitate.

INBOUND MARKETING

This is a unique business strategy which aims to attract new customers by creating free high quality content that is valuable to the customer's experience and is tailored to them. Although inbound marketing can be very time consuming if you are just starting off a business, it is of the utmost importance as an extremely effective way of marketing which yields high returns long term.

Here are a few examples of different forms of inbound marketing:

Customer guides

Educational videos

Free training programmes

Podcasts

Infographics

To give a better overview of the method that inbound tries to follow: You attract your potential customer (via targeted ads, video, blogs, social media), following this you continue to **engage** with that potential customer (via, email, messenger, lead flows or marketing automations), then finally you **consistently delight** that potential customer giving and providing them with freebies and important valuable content which they would appreciate. For example, if your target audience was podcasters, you would frequently make video blogs on how they can solve the 'marketing problem' increasing their number of listeners, what the best practices are when starting a podcast.

BOSSNOTE: The very important thing about inbound marketing is that it is done **consistently over a long period of time**. You need to ensure you are **constantly pumping out great value**, and more importantly **helpful content** which your audience/potential customer is likely to need and engage with. You are trying to **build a strong relationship** with these individuals, so although **it is hard work** and frankly **tedious** at times especially when you're just starting off and you have no other people working in your team, it can feel overwhelming trying to keep up with things. Trust me, I know. Whilst acknowledging this, I must say that once executed, **inbound marketing yields tremendous rewards for** your **brand** and **customer base**.

Inbound marketing forms connections they are looking for and solves problems they already have.

INTERACTION DESIGN

This is the way your website is designed. Interaction design has the user in mind and tries to ensure that the website is as easy to use as possible. I.e, it's user friendly.

BENEFITS: Having a great interaction design **increases website activity** as people do browse through. You have a great design to your website and it gives it a ***professional feel*** which has been ***proven to convert more leads*** (potential buyers). Having a more user friendly design also ***increases traffic to your website*** and ***helps you rank*** well in search engines. Finally, having a great design is also one of the ***most powerful ways to market your brand.***

BOSSNOTE: If you're an entrepreneur looking to get into the online world, user interaction design is something that should be in the forefront of your mind. Scrap that, if you're an entrepreneur period, this is something you shouldn't overlook.

IMPORTS

This is the purchase of foreign goods and services and is the opposite of export.

INCUMBENT ADVANTAGE

This is typically a business term used to express the advantage that a firm/business already established in the market has advantage over a new business coming into the market. This is due to the fact the business which possesses an incumbent advantage has a settled place in the market.

BENEFITS: Having incumbent advantage means a business is *able to generate higher profits* than a new firm (an entrant) even if the entrant offers identical terms to consumers, or even better terms in terms of *price, quality, customer base, and opportunity* due to the already formed network/relationships with other businesses in the market.

INVISIBLE HAND EFFECT

'The unobservable market force that helps the demand and supply of goods in a free market to reach equilibrium automatically is the invisible hand.' This is the official definition of the invisible hand effect.

You can also see the invisible hand affect the forces which can't be directly seen but that are constantly working in your favour to get more sales or get more clients. For example, if you are constantly providing value for free to your audience, although there is no direct gain from this, in the background you are cementing your brand in their mind and if your product ever came up in conversation they would be the first to recommend it to their friend.

A perfect example of this is how you never directly see evangelists for your business, but they are constantly there in the background working, promoting and spreading the word about your business. It's important to note that the invisible hand effect using my definition can have a positive effect or negative effect, depending on how well you run your business.

If you run a great business, the invisible hand effect will be working in your favor. If you run a bad business, the invisible hand works against you.

INNOVATION

Business innovation is when a business or an individual introduces new processes, services, or products, which has a positive effect on their business. This can include improving existing methods or practices, or starting from scratch.

BENEFITS: This can give you a *competitive advantage* in the market. Innovation allows for significant improvement of systems and can lead to a large amount of *money being saved*, meaning more money for the business and increased capital.

INTELLECTUAL CAPITAL

Intellectual capital is seen as human ideas rather than physical ideas. Intellectual capital essentially means how valuable are your human assets in regards to creative process and problem solving.

Most of the time when you have intellectual capital you are able to get the ideas protected through a patent/trademark. This protects your ideas from being stolen, and gives complete ownership of that particular idea. Now, other businesses or individuals are allowed to commercially monetize this idea.
Intellectual capital is also seen as an **INTANGIBLE ASSET.**

INVENTORY

An inventory is the goods available for sale and the raw materials which are used to produce the goods, merchandise and material available.
Most businesses own an inventory which is seen as one of the most important assets that a business can have. If you have a high turnover inventory, you are able to clear your inventory quickly in a short period of time.

This directly correlates to the amount of revenue that your business is able to generate.

BENEFITS: A business can use the information which can be collected by the inventory turnover time (how long it takes for the entire inventory to be used up), to make an *educated examination/decision of pricing of product, manufacturing marketing* and whether or not they will need to invest in a new inventory. Having an inventory also *reduces your risk of over selling* as you have a knowledge of what you have left and are able to deliver to the market. Having this collected data also *improves your business negotiation* when it comes to building partnerships and eventually when it comes to selling your business.

INVESTMENT

In simple terms, an investment is the act of putting money into something in the hopes that in the future that money will grow and be of better value than the initial investment.

There are two forms of investment; direct investments which is spending on buildings, machinery, business etc... and indirect investing, where you are putting money in bonds and shares.

A keyword in this is that you invest in hopes. Of course there are ways to invest and reduce your risk of losing the investment; in doing so increases your chance of getting positive returns. The easiest way to manage risk is doing thorough research on what it is you want to invest into. This means you are able to make an educated decision on whether or not to invest.

BENEFITS:

Earn additional income

Beat inflation

Greater opportunity to make money through compound effects

BOSSNOTE: The best thing that you can invest in is yourself. So, begin to invest in yourself by reading books like these, which are vital for the success of an aspiring entrepreneur. Applied knowledge is power. You should also start investing in your health and mental wellbeing. These are all things which require no extra cost. I.e, begin to meditate for your mental wellbeing, and start choosing to exercise whether that is working out or going to a gym.

You have to be strong and healthy in mind, body and spirit.

☐

JOB

Definition: a thing all entrepreneurs hate and would never have permanently.

We don't work jobs, we create jobs.

KNOWLEDGE

Facts, information, and skills acquired through experience or education; the theoretical or practical understanding of a subject.

BOSSNOTE: The more knowledge which you are able to acquire in relation to your business, the better off you will be.

LEVERAGE

Leverage is seen as the acquiring of debt or the purpose of making an investment.

For something to be highly leveraged, the item has more debt than it does equity. The concept of leverage is heavily used by both investors and companies.

You are able to leverage assets.

LIQUIDITY

Liquidity is a term used to describe how easily an asset can be spent (converted to real cash), if so desired.

Cash is wholly liquid.

When an asset is converted to real cash or money in your pocket that means the asset is liquidated.

BENEFITS: If something has a high liquidity, it means it can easily be converted to cash. This is very attractive to a lot of people as some people in times of emergency can easily liquidate an asset if they need to. It provides convenience for the asset holder.

LIMITED LIABILITY COMPANY

This business is a separate entity to its owner, meaning that the owners are not personally liable for the business debt or liability.

General Process Of Forming An LLC:

Choose a name for your LLC

Choose a registered agent

Decide on member vs. manager management

Prepare an operating agreement

File biennial report

Pay your tax obligations

Comply with other tax and regulatory requirements

⊏▭⊐

LOGISTICS

The detailed organization and implementation of a complex operation.

This term is widely in the business sector and mainly refers to how resources are handled.

I personally view this as a breakdown of all the important aspects of a business, and how an operation is handled.

LONG TERMS

I'm sure you know the definition of long term, I just put it in here because this is how you should train your mind to think. Long term not short term. You must constantly be factoring the future to make decisions in the present far more manageable. You must have a long term view of your business and understand you should always act in accordance to things that will benefit you long term. This is a rule that applies heavily to all aspects.

Live not for instant gratification, but for delayed gratification.

Time can either work for you or against you. I am always excited about the future because I am spending my time wisely in the present. I have built the foundations and the more time goes by, the closer I get to my goals to my ambitions, the closer I get to becoming a fully realised entrepreneur.

A person who wants to be successful would be excited about the future, not worried or scared.

If you find that you are currently worried about the future and you are feeling unsure, take time right now to reflect and understand the deep rooted reasons as to why you feel worried.

We are problem solvers, that's what makes us so functional and adaptive. We solve problems whether that's business or internal problems we may face.

MONEY

Is not the root of happiness, living a fulfilled life is. Money is a means to live a more free life, whilst at the same time can enslave those who aren't careful. You should always make money work for you, not the other way round.

MONETIZE

This is the process in which an item that is non-revenue can be converted into cash, you can see this as the process of liquidating an asset.

To monetize is to liquidate an asset.

MANUFACTURING

Manufacturing is the process by which goods are created by hand or machine. These goods tend to come from raw materials or component parts of a larger product. This process occurs on a large scale, in combination with many machines and labour workers.

MANAGEMENT

The process by which you deal with people or things.

BENEFITS:

Deliver work on time
Produce higher quality of work
More productivity and efficiency
Decreased procrastination
Less stress and anxiety
Improved quality of life
More opportunities and career growth
More time for leisure and recreation

BOSS NOTE: I personally believe that having great time management is one of the most important things when it comes to being a successful entrepreneur.

This is a skill that must be developed over time and through practice, patience and experience.

I'm sure you would have heard the saying that we all have 24 hours in a day; it's what we chose to do with those hours that makes the difference.

Well this statement is true in more ways than one. When I was first dreaming about making millions, I would spend too much time thinking, when I should have been planning and acting. Through planning and acting you can gain a better understanding of what you are able to accomplish in a day.

As you go through your own personal journey, humans have a tendency to undershoot how long tasks will take, so always be conservative when you are setting goals and creating plans.

NETWORK

Networking is simply the exchange of information and
ideas among people with a common profession or interest,
usually in an informal social setting.
You can network with people who are in the same market
as you to find out information about things they do,
systems they have set up to make certain processes easier.

NETWORK MARKETING: This is a business model
which is heavily dependent on the one to one interactions
of individuals and representatives of a business who form

a network of people, mainly online, to try and generate sales. Although it can be great, in many network markets people only really get paid for each person who is recruited to the network rather than the sale of a product. Through these many network markets experience the **NETWORK EFFECT;** where by due to the increased number of individuals in the network, the group service or value see great improvement.

BOSSNOTE: Networking is part of our everyday lives. We are constantly involved with networks, with our friends, families, colleagues. It's just unconscious networking.

The real power comes from purposeful networking. When you first start a business, it is integral that you network heavy; I mean you have to reach out to hundreds of people each week (if not thousands); this can be done online, where you might have to live in your potential customer's platform and create a network, or even where your competitors or other business minded people are. Your aim should be to form a solid relationship with people by just being there, checking up on them and asking questions. This is how most businesses start. Once you form a network of people you trust, everything in your business becomes easier. You have the support for your customers and you have the guidance of your competitors who have walked a similar path to you.

OPTIMUM

Optimum means to perform at the highest quality, or for something to conduct at a favorable outcome.

For something to be optimized, changes are being made to the system or process to allow it to work in a more favorable way.

Optimizing can take different forms, which are all BENEFICIAL:

The introduction of a new more efficient method

Changes practices within the workplace

Creating automated systems that run faster

The reduction of cost whilst still maintaining the same or increased performance

BOSSNOTE: You are just coming into the entrepreneur space; just know that this is a word that will often come up and something that you should always be thinking about; what changes can you make to ensure your business is working as efficiently as possible? It's important to note that optimization mainly comes in the form of improving ad campaigns. My main optimization occurs with the ads I run, I try to get my cost down and either maintain or even increase performance.

You need to start identifying and implementing new things in your business which can bring it closer to the optimum.

Things might be going well, but can almost always be better. You should always have this progressive mindset. You should always be building momentum as an entrepreneur. It is those who master this skill, knowing they have much power to put on the gas are the ones who succeed. But just like a lot of things which I have mentioned in the bossnotes, it doesn't come without practice and nurturing of the particular skill, this is no different.

OBLIGATIONS

This is seen as a course of action which an individual has to perform due to morally or legally binding reasons. It can also be seen as a person's duty to perform a certain task.

BOSSNOTE: For you some obligations may come under planning, management, organization, representation and networking and of course, the development of your business.

Most start-ups have an obligation to give their business time and energy.

OPPORTUNITY

Opportunities are seen as a set of often unlikely circumstances that makes something possible.

An example would be an aspiring artist bumping into a record label that they have always wanted to meet and interact with.

BENEFITS: They provide us with a particular situations which we are able to seize and make the best out of. Opportunity gives us a chance to make our dreams, goals and greatest ambitions some true.

BOSSNOTE: You can create opportunities for yourself through taking consistent action. If you start, every action you take in your business will create an equal opportunity for you somewhere in the future if you keep working hard and staying consistent with your work. Too many people sit about waiting for the right opportunity to execute a business plan or to start working on a new project. The truth of the matter is there are no such things.

You create your own chance/luck in life, you are in control and no external forces enforce opportunity on you but yourself. You can train yourself to spot opportunities and it's a skill every person, not just entrepreneurs, should try to develop. I have gone through some transformative changes over the last year or two and being able to spot opportunities has become a thing that is more frequent. Then again, it's down to the fact I have trained myself to always see situations as an opportunity.

Each interaction you have in this world is an opportunity whether you know it or not - it might be made evident instantly, or it might take months or maybe even years.

It's important not to get caught up in opportunities; as I said, you can generate opportunity at any time, the important part is can you train yourself to execute once you're at that point.

Like the man Conor McGregor said: 'It's a beautiful feeling when preparation meets opportunity'.

OUTSOURCE

This is the process in which a business pays an outside supplier to produce goods, write books, design ad banners, or work on a service which the business themselves aren't directly linked to.

BENEFITS: It allows you to *keep your focus on the core business activity.* Outsourcing is also a great way to *help aspiring freelancers* make some extra money. It always provides a means for you to *grow your network and build relationships* with people outside of your close business circle, in turn potentially leading to the *development of your* *internal staff.* Outsourcing is an amazing way to **save time,** allowing you to focus on more important work that yields the most/best results for your business. Outsourcing always tends to be cheap, which in turn can **lower the cost of your business.**

BOSSNOTE: Outsourcing is a very important part of most businesses, and I truly believe if you are able to outsource things in your business you should, as it's mostly beneficial for both parties for the reasons stated above.

However, when you are starting a business, the initial thoughts are to save money and try to do these things yourself which is completely fine. Just have the recognition that once you are making enough money with the business to accelerate the process, you can outsource some services. This will help you in turn as you will get quality services through outsourcing which will help the quality of your business and the professionalism of your brand.

PROFIT MARGIN

This represents the number of sales in a business which turn into profit.

PROPERTY

A property is a thing which belongs to someone. If you have property, that is legally yours and you own it.

Here are the three different forms of property

Private

Public

Collective

PIVOT

To pivot means that a business is going to change and move to a new strategy, often meaning significant changes will be made in order to prompt positive improvement.

Different examples of what a pivot may entail:

Targeting a different demographic

Changing the main platform

The adoption of a new business model to increase monetization

The integration of advanced technology

The conversion of featured products as actual products and assets for a business

Bossnote:

Ways to effectively pivot:

Get on the *pivot early* on when you are aware of this being a possibility

Ensure that the *new goal* which you have for your business still *aligns with your vision*

You *don't have to completely eliminate your old model*, just take influence and inspiration from areas that did work and areas that didn't that you can scrap

Be an *active listener to your customer* and they will direct you in the right path. They have all your answers - again, this links closely to why knowing your customer is so important

Analyse and evaluate the pivot strategy to ensure that it *allows for scalability and massive growth.*

PRICE DISCOVERY

This is seen as the process in which the price of an asset is being determined by the market. This is a process which is heavily influenced by the interaction of buyers and sellers.

This is a word most traders will be familiar with.

PASSIVE INCOME

Passive income is earnings derived from a rental property, limited partnership, or other enterprise in which a person is not actively involved.

BOSSNOTE: Passive income is known in our community as the promised land.

PERCEIVED VALUE

Perceived value is your customer's subjective view of your product or the services which the business provides. Perceived value is formed by the comparison of your products/services quality to that of a competitor's.

Perceived value is measured by the price the public is willing to pay for goods or services.

BOSSNOTE: It is fair to say that at times, the perceived value of your product outweighs the actual value of your product. This is okay, as the aim is for the perceived value to be as high as possible to result in as many sales as possible, while still being genuinely valuable.

PATENT

A patent is the legal ownership of an invention, meaning no one else is allowed to take your idea and make money from it.

BENEFITS: Having a **patent** means you have the right to stop others from copying, manufacturing, selling or importing your invention without your permission. This means by law, you are able to protect your intellectual property.

PRODUCTIVITY

In a more literal sense, productivity is associated with the output and input volume. This essentially means the direct measurement of the efficiency of production input, including labour and capital used to produce a certain amount of output of a product.

In terms of productivity on an individual level, it still follows the same principles as the definition stated above. You can view productivity as how much quality work you are able to produce in a period of time. If you're being very productive in your business it means you are putting out the best quality of work in a highly time efficient way.

BENEFITS: You are able to ***complete quality work in a short period of time***. You are able to comfortably ***take on more challenging tasks*** with more confidence compared to a person who isn't as productive. Being productive also means you are ***moving on to your next task at a faster rate.***

BOSSNOTE: As entrepreneurs, we are always trying to find ways to increase productivity, to increase how much we can accomplish in a day. This is an ongoing process and one that requires time spent practicing different techniques and figuring out which one works for you.

Here are simple ways to increase productivity:

When you're working, get rid of your phone

Set a daily goal, weekly goal and monthly goal to help you stay on track

Tackle the most important tasks earlier in the day

Wake up earlier

Have routine breaks from work, e.g 20 minutes on, 5 minutes off

PYRAMID SCHEME

Pyramid schemes are chain referral schemes - marketing and investment frauds in which an individual is offered a distributorship or franchise to market a particular product. Profits are earned not by the sale of a product, but by the sale of new distributorships

BOSSNOTE: These are completely illegal and you should avoid them at all cost.

I very nearly fell for this in my early years when I was trying to discover what to do with myself.

QUALITY CONTROL

Quality control is a process through which a business tries to ensure that product quality is maintained or improved.

For great quality control, a business must create an environment in which both management and employees strive for excellence.

QUALITY OF LIFE

This is seen as the measure of a person's *health, wealth, comfort*, and the level of *happiness experienced* by a person.

BOSSNOTE: The benefits of this one are probably clear. We all want to be happy in life, this is probably the part where I express to you that money is not going to buy you happiness. I lie, it will buy you happiness, but only to the extent that it provides you with a good quality life in terms of wealth and comfort...and health if you use it correctly.

You have to understand your quality of life isn't dependent on money and it shouldn't be. Money is an added bonus and a means to experience new things that you otherwise would not have been able to.

What point am I trying to make?

In your pursuit for success via means of running a successful business, if you find that you are losing or sacrificing your mental wellbeing and have stopped enjoying your work, I urge you to reflect and understand that you should always put your quality of life first.

Remember that there **is** such a thing as toxic positivity.

REVENUE

Revenue is seen as the total amount of money a business is able to generate in a year. Revenue doesn't take cost into account, so it's not a reflection of profits.

RESIDUAL INCOME

This is seen as the income you will continue to receive once you have done the work for an income producing system.

Residual income include:

Building an online course

Working as an affiliate

Selling a design

Writing a book

Creating an app

Rental/real estate income

Interest earned from shares and bonds

Dividends paid to yourself from your business

BENEFITS: You do the work upfront and get paid continually month after month. It's thinking long term.

BOSSNOTE: I hope this example has made the idea and definition more clear in your mind. You can see residual income as the money you receive after you complete a piece of work that can continually pay you in the future - not just a one off payment, but an ongoing one that isn't completely passive, but let's say semi passive.

STOCK/SHARES

Is seen as quality which is held by an individual which represents the fraction of a corporation of business they hold.

STRATEGIC ALLIANCE

A strategic alliance is an arrangement which is reached between two businesses. This allows for mutual benefits to the projects they work on, individually or collaboratively. Strategic alliances are different to joint ventures.

▭

Joint ventures draw businesses' pooled resources to **create an entirely separate business entity.**

BENEFITS: Strategic alliance means you have access to a whole new client base and customers. You are able to easily insert yourself into a new business sector and advance your business prowess with the help of your alliance. You are able to create more income producing resources. You have increased risk management. You combine a pool of creative minds with your workers and allow for innovation to take place.

BOSSNOTE: Through networking, you are able to constantly form professional strategic alliances in whatever business you're in. I've said it through this book: the most important things in business are the relationships you build and form with people in your market space.

It's like the saying: 'It's not what you know, it's who you know'.

SYSTEMIC RISK

This underlines the possibility that a dramatic event can occur in a business which causes severe instability and can lead to the end of said business.

TREND

The general direction in which something is developing or changing.

BOSSNOTE: As an aspiring entrepreneur, you should be always looking for the trends in the market and seeing where you can jump in to make a profit.

TOXIC POSITIVITY

We define toxic positivity as the excessive and ineffective overgeneralization of a happy, optimistic state across all situations. The process of toxic positivity results in the denial, minimization, and invalidation of the authentic human emotional experience.

BOSSNOTE: I hate to say it, but this is heavily encouraged in the self-help community and by the image of what an entrepreneur should be like. It is overly popularised that you have to be constantly positive which naturally means mutes negative emotions. Studies have actually shown this can be detrimental to your wellbeing as suppressing feelings can cause more internal, psychological stress.

You also have to recognize that all humans go through some very tough patches in their journey to success. It's important not to withhold your emotions but rather give yourself time to feel the emotion, internalize it, then once you have reflected, thinking of an active way to regain control and to be proactive about your problems and move on. Having a positive attitude is important but at the same time, don't force positivity on to yourself all the time.

WEALTH EFFECT

This occurs when you become wealthier and consume more.

BURNOUT

Burnout is a state of emotional, physical, and mental exhaustion caused by excessive and prolonged stress. It occurs when you feel overwhelmed, emotionally drained, and unable to meet constant demands.

BENEFITS: This is clearly a negative thing.

BOSSNOTE:

This is a lot more common than you might think, and although you should have the hustle mentality deep in you, you also need to have a good gage of when burnout is creeping in. There is literally no point in getting yourself burnt out as it's counterproductive and a hindrance to you achieving your goals.

Here are some practical steps to take to avoid getting burnt out:

Have a healthy balanced work schedule
Take control back in your life (this can be done just by writing a simple timetable for your day, which has been proven to increase the sense of control in your life)

Having a nap. I know right, the only time you'll be advised to nap on a job ;) Seriously, naps are great for releasing tension and helping you stay focused and attentive.

Please do share with the group your story if you have experienced burnout and how you dealt with it. Spreading awareness can help us all move forward.

FINAL BOSSNOTE:

I would like to say thank you for purchasing this book. I hope you got a great insight and a broadened understanding of key business terminology.

On a more personal level, I want to let you know that no matter where you find yourself in life, no matter how good or bad the situation, always take time to reflect and always understand that you are in full control of your life.

Life will always challenge you, as will business - it's just the yin and yang. So when the going gets tough, make sure to keep going and push past resistance, as this is the barrier to entry of success.

Love from a fellow adaptive individual.

The Millionaire's Playbook.

Printed in Great Britain
by Amazon

10284569R00088

REINTRODUCTION

Published by
East Head Press 2021

Paperback   ISBN 978-1-7399297-0-1
.epub eBook   ISBN 978-1-7399297-1-8

Cover design and typeset by SpiffingCovers

REINTRODUCTION

DUNCAN J BROWN

PUBLISHED BY

1

The anchorman smirked as he dismissed Marjorie Lemming's reported sighting of a patch of blue sky. It had been twenty-seven years since the sun last appeared over London. The guest meteorologist agreed the claim was absurd. She was after all a Non-Worker, or simply a Non. Besides, Marjorie may well have had a drink or, worse, slapped on a sanctioned hit of heroin, before appearing via halo-screen on the show to make her ridiculous claim.

Ever since the Automation Revolution, fewer and fewer people had jobs or contributed to the system. The gradual classification and eventual segregation of people into Workers, Non-Workers and the Unregistered never received official approval. It was an organic process, and successive administrations across the globe adopted the terms and legislated accordingly.

Robert Corrigan was watching from his favourite armchair in his old ground-floor flat, a residence situated in a part of town avoided by people of value. He flicked his wristpad and the halo-screen dissolved, and his gaze naturally drifted across to the window and out onto the street. The suffused sunlight was constant, whether it was daybreak, midday, or dusk. Time and the sun had become less well acquainted with one another once the doldrums had settled in.

He had lived alone for longer than he cared to remember and, if called upon to do so, would have struggled to pinpoint when he first realised he enjoyed solitude. No singular moment sparked an epiphany; and it was not a construct or part of a wider strategy, it was a simple recognition of facts.

His flat bore its abject neglect well enough. The walls had been painted French-grey years before, a colour scheme chosen with the help of a virtual salesman. He liked the front room with its large windows. The room had a fireplace, and he'd spoken with the neighbour upstairs, who'd agreed to have the chimney cleared. She was a dotty old thing who had once been an Olympic gymnast. She'd returned from Beijing with a bronze medal and the locals had taken to calling her Miss Champion. The name had stuck. Sixty years later she struggled to negotiate the stairs or remember to lock her door.

An old grandfather clock marked each second with the resonance of age. The sound established a connection with an irretrievable past; a time Corrigan had read about in books and found a comforting distraction. The near-constant drizzle turned less well-maintained brick buildings green with lichen and moss. Corrigan could sense the damp as it crept closer. To keep it at bay, he periodically sent B4, his Mecha-Butler, up to Miss Champion's flat to treat her walls and ceilings. B4's reports included a schedule for the continued maintenance of their home and those belonging to Corrigan's immediate neighbours. It was not always easy for the little droid to organise the necessary activities as the neighbourhood was populated by Nons, political outcasts, or people who suffered from an aversion to androids. Corrigan acted as arbiter when required.

He scanned his bookshelves in search of distraction, skimming titles by Dostoyevsky, Kafka, Searle, Chomsky, Dickens and Dawkins, but nothing quite hit the spot. He'd read these authors many times over when he was younger. His mother had friends she referred to as her "bohemian butterflies", who'd read the same authors, and it was these bohemians who had recommended them to him. That was back in the day before the sun became fully shrouded and democracy faded, leaving a subtle mimic to reign over a categorised and controlled population. She thought it disadvantageous for him to associate with a crowd she had needed to distance herself from, however. Even owning titles such as these and stacking them on bookcases could compromise him. She pressed him to focus on more modern texts instead; books that would help him navigate the world of business, books recommended for program managers and anyone involved in IT or process transformation. The bone-dry texts bored him. He preferred something that engaged his mind, transported him to less hopeless times. The archaic writers, therefore, had been companions, even comrades, in a world where he remained an intruder: Nons who made their way up were slyly referred to as Floaters among the more established Worker class.

"Always a chance they might flush you," his mother reminded him incessantly. "If they think you're a commie *and* a homo, you can kiss your Worker status goodbye. They don't care who you do it with, of course, no, they're not religious or judgemental like *that,* but one wink to the idea of equality and down you go."

His wristpad pinged and he tapped the glass. A haloscreen message appeared: **Interview at DRT.**

Dennett and Reece Technology. What on earth would they want with me? he thought.

He clicked on the message and allowed the program to identify the sender and read the email with an approximation of her voice:

"Hello Robert

I received a job spec this morning. You were the first candidate I thought of. Please read it and let me know if you're interested. There's nothing about this online, so no point looking.

Program Manager Project Egret

The program is comprised of three projects, each with its own departmental lead. DRT is defining the cutting edge of Whole Brain Emulation (WBE), Artificial Intelligence (AI) and Genetic Engineering (GE). Each project spearheads one of these areas of research.

The successful candidate will have experience running multiple, complex projects simultaneously and be alert to potential synergies that might be nurtured and exploited. We are seeking the right personality to provide structure and order without undermining ingenuity or the flexibility that drives it, a natural leader to manage and support our team, someone with the vision to see beyond the probable and recognise the possible.

As I said, Robert, it made me think of you. I know you like a challenge. Sorry it's so vague.

Please get back to me ASAP. They're pressing for CVs.

Kind regards

Jill Waterstone"

The way DRT pressed keynotes made him groan. He scowled and said, "Type: Hi Jill. Please pass my CV to the client for review. You should have the latest version. I'm available any day next week. Kind regards, Robert." Then, "Send."

He had been out of work for nearly six weeks. Much longer and he would need to start searching, otherwise his status could drop back down to Non – and his mother would never forgive him. The unsavoury term Non was one he remembered from a childhood spent with a mother whose "employment" enabled connections with men in senior positions. These connections came with authority and influence, the kind needed to escape a place like Haringey. Hattie Corrigan had hauled her son up the ladder from Non to Worker through sheer exertion of will, and sliding back down would not do.

He wandered down to the split-level kitchen, instructing

his coffee machine to make a macchiato. The appliance acknowledged the request with a courteous, pre-scripted salutation, and whirred, the water gurgling as the coffee was prepared. He was about to take it through to the front room when his wristpad pinged again:

"Hey Robert

I sent your CV over and they've booked you in for 3pm on Friday the 17th. If that doesn't work, please let me know and I'll rearrange.

All I can say is someone's keen.

Kind regards and good luck.

Jill"

Corrigan took a sip of coffee and wandered back to the front room, back to his armchair and the large window. A family stood on the pavement on the opposite side of Harvey Road; a lean father, an exhausted mother, and two small children. He was a black man in his early forties, and she had ginger hair, freckles and a distended abdomen. She might have been pregnant or starving. The father's sharp beard made his features severe. His eyes were set back in their sockets, and when he stepped into the shadow of a doorway they seemed to vanish altogether. The woman appeared dazed for a moment, then she gathered the children about her knees. The little boy clung to her leg, while his sister toyed with her fingers.

What the family was doing became evident when two older boys arrived dragging a cart. The contraption contained some chairs, an old-fashioned halo-screen projector, and an assortment of open bin bags stuffed with clothes. A pillow fell out onto the street and the woman stooped to retrieve it, but her condition made it impossible. Her daughter grabbed the pillow, and the mother's eyes flashed with indignation.

One of the older boys was more attractive than the others. His skin had a healthy colour and he was better dressed. He avoided eye contact with the members of his family, as if not acknowledging them might make them disappear. Corrigan assessed the youth as a good-looking mixed-race boy.

Corrigan reclined in his armchair and placed his feet on the ottoman. He took another sip of coffee, and tapped his wristpad, opening up the previous screen. Jill's email conveyed nothing more than information. Her personable façade had always blocked any read of the woman herself.

He saw something move, placed his mug on the coffee table and leant forward. The father had shifted his position to stare into the deserted street. He turned to the left, then to the right, before rolling up a sleeve and affixing a patch to the crook of his arm. Mass-produced and affordable, the new form of heroin pad was called Belushi Grey, the latest drug of choice among Nons. News reports often reminded users the drug could trigger internal haemorrhaging and instant kidney failure, but Corrigan figured the manufacturers and marketers only wanted to ensure no one could file a complaint. After all, it was the only product whose customer base was more reliable than the world's military market.

The father craned his head back, staggered and slumped against the doorframe. In the dim light he appeared otherworldly, a vacated shell left behind while the real occupant ventured elsewhere.

A brown cat leapt up onto the window ledge and Corrigan jumped. The animal's eyes bore down on him with a face worn from hardship and cruelty. He gazed at the cat, and his heart gradually slowed. He looked past the ragged face to the doorway on the other side of Harvey Road. The street was deserted. Only the cat remained, like a windowsill sentinel.

2

Miss Champion woke Corrigan with her routine morning shuffle. He imagined her scuffing dry floorboards in threadbare slippers, white hair on end and her features fixed in an expression of bemusement. Her mouth hung open awaiting teeth she rarely collected from sideboards, armrests, or the edge of the bathroom sink. She was lost, adrift inside herself, and the world was a foreign shore upon which she found herself washed each morning.

B4 appeared in the room, eager if somewhat unsteady on its roller; its large doe-like eyes more irritating than ever.

"I thought I'd powered you down," Corrigan huffed.

The droid was approximately four feet tall. It coasted on a ball capable of negotiating stairs, had a pair of flexible arms, and a deep officious voice. It came with an automatic reboot system, one Corrigan would have to disengage if he wanted the droid powered down indefinitely. Although he had chosen it from a range of variants, he'd never warmed to it.

"You hibernated me," B4 said.

Corrigan instructed it to prepare tea and toast, and the droid sped off towards the kitchen. He called after it, "I'll have breakfast in the front room!"

He sat up, swivelled and placed his feet in his slippers. The droid struggled to remember its core duties, those Corrigan had programmed with the young technician who'd delivered the device. Corrigan recalled the quality of the young man's skin; how smooth and perfect it was. He'd found it difficult to focus on the matter at hand, and bungled the setup somehow.

He threw on his bathrobe and paced through the kitchen to the front room. The cat must have remained on the window ledge all night. Its eyes were unflinching and far too big for its emaciated head.

Corrigan sat in his armchair, but then returned to the kitchen to take his breakfast from the forgetful droid, and B4 followed him with a whir to the front room. He instructed the droid to clean.

"And don't forget the flagstones in the garden," he snapped. "I nearly slipped on some algae yesterday."

He placed the toast on the window ledge. The cat looked down at the melting butter and its tongue poked out. Corrigan called B4 back and instructed it to put some genetically engineered tuna in a bowl and bring it to him. He made his way to the kitchen and collected the tuna from the droid. B4 lingered, so Corrigan dismissed it and went out into the communal hall and unlocked the main door.

The cat saw him and recoiled. He raised the manufactured tuna, so the defeated animal could smell it. For a moment the cat remained wary, ready to creep away.

Then hunger overwhelmed trepidation and it dropped to the ground.

Corrigan placed the bowl on the floor, just inside the hall, and waited for the animal to venture in. Once the cat was fully engaged with its breakfast, he closed the main door and went back inside to eat his own. He left the front door open.

Corrigan ate some toast, drank his tea, and instructed B4 to make another cup.

The cat slinked into the room, stared at him and uttered a pitiful meow.

Corrigan placed his cup of tea on the window ledge and went down on all fours in front of the cat.

"I know just how you feel," he said.

He placed his hand over the cat's head, and it nudged him. He gently stroked the animal, which, no surprise, was ribbed with raised scars. Its fur was filthy; he would have to wash it. He called to B4 and instructed the droid to order cat food and a litter box. The droid acknowledged the request and Corrigan listened to it making computations and connections.

His wristpad pinged. It was an incoming call from his mother, which he elected not to answer, but clicked open his halo-screen and watched as his mother's message was typed out: "Answering a call from a dying woman might be an effort, but, when it's your mum, I figure you owe me. Give me a call. They've put me in bloody Intensive care and I'm anything but happy about it. Love you."

He chuckled.

Perhaps she really is going to die this time. Hypochondria's such a long, drawn-out but, I suppose, ultimately fatal condition.

Lazarus – for the name seemed to suit – watched Corrigan read the message and then wound himself figure-eight around his legs.

He took the animal through to the bathroom and placed it in the tub. "You're not going to like this," he said, "but you have to have a bath," and wet it down with warm water. "And I have to visit my mother," he added. "So, we're even."

Corrigan applied shampoo three times before Lazarus looked clean. The cat had limited energy and only summoned enough to manage a faint protest, beseeching his rescuer to stop with a series of fading meows. But he purred when wrapped in a towel. B4 was summoned and acted as a hairdryer – blowing hot air onto the animal via a manipulable hose – and the job was finished. Lazarus was transformed. His fluffed-up fur added several pounds to him. He followed Corrigan through to the bedroom, jumped up onto the unmade bed, and made himself comfortable.

The ache in his chest surprised Corrigan, and he marvelled at the possibility of loving an animal he had spent less than an hour with.

He tapped his wristpad and said, "Call Mother."

There could hardly have been a single buzz before Hattie Corrigan answered. She spoke without enthusiasm but not without vehemence. Her tirade included complaints about doctors, nurses, family and friends. He heard words, but his attention did not extend to absorbing whole sentences. The words collected in a list in the library of his mind, and he placed them, one by one, on the shelf:

Incompetence
Hurtful
Shameless
Humiliating
Pain

"Are you *listening* to me?" she snapped.

"Of course," Corrigan said, but he went on stroking and nuzzling Lazarus, and her vitriol remained as ineffectual as Marjorie Lemming's sun. When she had depleted her reserves, he assured her of his love and ended the call.

He raised Lazarus in his arms and said into the ragged, clean face, "That wasn't so bad now, was it?"

3

The following day was much the same as the previous one from a meteorological standpoint. Miss Champion had roused him with her mindless shuffling, and B4 had hovered before him. Corrigan instructed it to prepare porridge and tea and dismissed it.

Lazarus stretched out a paw towards his face. Corrigan wondered how he'd ever made it through a day without him. The empathy in the cat's eyes was more substantive than any of his human relationships. Those had been a string of failures and disappointments which were not worth revisiting. These days a quick tug to holographic porn was preferable to dating.

He got out of bed, retrieved his tea and porridge from B4 and instructed it to run him a bath. When he had lowered himself into the hot water, he called out and asked it to lay out his grey suit from Mailer's. The bath was too comforting to leave. He kept topping up the hot water and lingered for as much as an hour before he finally climbed out and dried and got dressed.

Lazarus appeared to sense Corrigan's imminent departure and watched him with a blend of curiosity and agitation.

"I often worry about the mouse in me," Corrigan mused. He leant down and stroked Lazarus's head. "Let me amend that," he said as he stood up and straightened his tie in the mirror. "I often worry that I'm *inside* the mouse which masquerades as me. I sit inside a furry suit watching the little vermin raising my paws, perfectly aware that I'll be overlooked. The best I can manage is a stray crumb and that, I assure you, is nibbled without hesitation or delay. I squeak my complaints down near the ground where my snout is usually positioned, sniffing out low-level opportunities for miniscule gains."

He enacted a scene of sniffing and searching, for the cat's benefit.

"Subsistence is the lot of us lesser rodents, and I'm certainly not vicious enough to be a rat or cute enough to lift my cottontail." He raised his backside in the air and frowned. "I've been struggling with my zipper, but it's around the back and I can't reach the damn thing. Every time I give it a go, it rides up my nape. One day my fingers are going to catch hold of it. I beg the Powers That Be to allow this moment to coincide with an uncharacteristic flash of bravery, for, when I tear it off, I'll stand naked before the world screaming, 'I'm a man, a man!'" He patted Lazarus again. "And that's quite a daunting prospect for a mouse."

He had seen a mouse at the underground station earlier in the week. It writhed on its sides, its legs running like those of a dreaming dog. He considered scooping it up and taking it home in his bag. It had either been injured or poisoned, and he might have given it comfort as it died from its injuries, or he may even have saved it. Instead, he stepped around it, his back brushing the wall so he remained as far away from the suffering rodent as possible.

B4 spun into the room and asked whether Corrigan would like a taxi. Corrigan considered his options and instructed the droid to place an order with Bluebird Taxis. B4 was about to leave when he asked what could be done about the droid's voice. B4 confirmed it could be modified as required. Corrigan wondered what would suit it better. Could the droid use a younger voice? The droid responded in a child's voice. It was an unsatisfactory, middle-class tone. He asked the droid to adopt a more working-class voice, but it was unable to comprehend the request. Corrigan mimicked the sound of his mother's voice, and the droid managed to echo the pattern. The result was sweet, and Corrigan asked B4 to make it melancholy. B4's eyes widened, and the droid asked what level of *melancholia* it should apply. Corrigan considered it for a moment, requested a level 3, which the droid demonstrated. He was satisfied with the result and instructed B4 to polish his shoes.

"Yes, sir," the droid said and moved off to comply.

Corrigan frowned and instructed the droid to adopt informality mode.

"Yes, Robert."

Half an hour later Corrigan was at the door and B4 was deployed to keep Lazarus from escaping. He leant down into the hover-cab and assessed the driver, a man in his mid-thirties in a much-worn brown leather jacket. The cabbie talked at a slow, considered pace about the weather and the most recent game of Elevator, a set of physical trials where Transients competed for food, medical assistance, or the reinstatement of their status as Nons. The cabbie assured him he thought it was nonsense and hoped he didn't mind if he called it cruel. Corrigan waved the man's trepidation aside, aware of the nervousness any Worker felt when questioning the way things had been arranged by Parliament. There followed a string of news updates borrowed from the latest broadcasts, including news that Marjorie Lemming had been arrested for political agitation.

Corrigan listened and placed words like undesirable books on an archaic shelf:

Dissident
Transient
Detainment
Strength
Freedom

The driver was an attentive listener and had absorbed the morning's propaganda without missing a syllable. The content and drift of his constant chatter were aligned with government policy, and it referenced no worrying texts, but his voice occasionally shuddered with suppressed emotion. It was as if the meaning he meant to convey – the covert message – was more emotional than intellectual.

His gaze settled on his passenger and Corrigan felt some dormant fervour stir and flit around the city where it rose around them. The cab hovered over the hospital before the driver brought it down beside the main entrance. Corrigan alighted and the driver smiled through the window at him. Much to his chagrin, Corrigan was immediately ensnared, and he scowled, turned away, and walked into reception.

The antiseptic scent of the place made him uncomfortable, and the receptionist barely registered him. He asked where his mother's room was, and she provided a set of instructions she soon realised he was incapable of following and summoned a Mecha-Assistant. The droid guided him to a lift, along several corridors, up a flight of stairs, down another corridor, and onto a ward.

His mother was sitting up in bed, pillows wedged behind her. She scrolled through pages on a halo-screen and tutted when she saw him approach. She told him to sit down, but as soon as he did, she barked at him to get up, make himself *useful* and bring her some water. He collected her jug and walked out in search of a place to refill it. The Mecha-Assistant showed him where to go and accompanied him back to his mother.

"Might have died of thirst," she said, "waiting for you."

He did not respond to her provocation but poured her some water and sat beside the bed. On second thoughts, he pushed the chair back, which scuffed the linoleum.

She glared at him with her keen eyes. "It's terrible in here," she said. "They've no idea how to handle an old girl.

All fingers and thumbs, specially round me Netherlands. They're a dreadful lot. And *you,* you let them do as they like. Leaving me in here, as much as rot before you'd notice."

Her monologue rolled on in a similar vein for half an hour and he listened patiently, once again storing away words rather than sentences. She admonished him, again, for reading writers who did nothing but stoke his sentimentality.

"We're all outside the clubhouse looking in like a bedraggled cat, Bobbin," she whispered. "None of us gets a say in anything that matters."

He nodded. He agreed, in a loose sense, with almost everything she said. And then she came out with a line that was a volume unto itself, "I never thought to suffer so as I couldn't make sense of it."

He wanted to take her hand, just as he had wanted to rescue the mouse and bring it home for a quiet death. She studied him, and her expression became something awful. There was regret in her eyes, but what Corrigan found insufferable was her pity.

She told him how the tumours had grown and blocked her, so she defecated into a bag that regularly split and spilt its fetid contents into the bed. The way she put it, the words she used, were calculated to provoke a reaction. He acknowledged what she said as if she were complaining about a domestic problem, a clogged sink or gutter. His dislocated response had a calming effect on her, and she reclined.

He poured her another glass of water and promised to visit the following evening. When she frowned, he told her about his interview at DRT. She perked up, laughed, and pointed at the equipment to which she was connected. The DRT symbol was apparent everywhere, and he was astounded not to have noticed it sooner. He wanted to know why they had attached sensors to her head.

"Nurse says it's to alert them to pain," his mother said, "but honestly, Bobbin, I can do that with me buzzer."

He felt memories tugging him into the past when she used her childhood name for him. Her collapse was in no way tethered to the things she had done to elevate her son. The cancer was as opportunistic as she had taught him to be. He wished her goodbye and made his way back to street level. He ordered a collection from Bluebird Taxis. After a moment's reflection, he requested the driver who'd brought him to the hospital. The hover-car descended not more than ten minutes later. He gave the driver an address. The driver looked taken aback and asked Corrigan to confirm the name of the establishment.

"Yes, Palais-Culo."

The cabbie shared a few more recent headlines and his thoughts regarding the latest version of a new line of genetically engineered eggs and poultry. Throughout, he kept his eyes on the passenger whenever he could.

Palais-Culo was a tall, thin, marble-fronted building. It stood on a roundabout near Billingsgate fish market. The peculiar, wedged shape of the architecture and the sheen of its wet, black stone made it ominous. The wrought iron gate was open, and an ornate entanglement of bronze arms caressed the gilded word CULO. Corrigan alighted and asked the cabbie to wait for him.

"Just a quickie, then," the younger man said.

Corrigan did not respond. There had been the slightest quaver in the Pole's voice, and the response made him feel like he was cheating. He walked up the steps into the house and was met by a Mecha-Butler similar to his own. The droid asked the client what he required. A menu was brought up and Corrigan scanned through it, rolling up one image after another with his finger. The young men were all fit, well made, and posturing. Corrigan selected 1232 for his eyes and the texture of his hair. The model was Polish in appearance, but perhaps not as rugged or interesting as his driver.

The Mecha-Butler checked their system and led Corrigan to a room. He opened the door to reveal 1232 kneeling on a bed. The prostitute's body was oiled, and he was fully erect. Corrigan closed the door and allowed his needs to be serviced. The encounter was swift and rough, as requested. He felt the young man unload himself, clung onto his shoulders and finished himself off.

Corrigan got dressed, hurried down the steps and returned to the awaiting car. The odour of sex shamed him, and he found eye contact awkward. The driver studied him for a moment and then lapsed back into repeating the results of the day's game of Elevator. Corrigan extracted keywords and placed them on a shelf:

Miserable
Desperate
Deplorable
Accidental
Painful
Denial

4

Denial.

The word lingered, and Corrigan had to wonder why. Yes, he told himself stories; yes, he indulged in daydreams and toyed with fantasies, but these were nothing more than respite from an otherwise interminable life. He did not agree with his mother's diagnosis that he was emotionally stunted, however. It was simply not true. He felt – had always felt – a great deal, but he could manage it and never felt overwhelmed. That was, after all, why she pushed him along such an enervating career path.

Lazarus stared at him from the end of the bed. He leant forward and stroked the animal, who responded by stretching full length and purring, like a woman might, he supposed.

At Corrigan's instruction, B4 unlocked and swung the double doors open onto the garden. Insect retardent screens folded into place to protect the flat from infestation. The material appeared to breathe, ready to respond to Corrigan's presence. As he stepped into the garden, the screen furled open and closed behind the homeowner and his cat. The light rain did not have the energy to fall, instead it floated, wafting horizontally at the slightest movement of air. Lazarus joined Corrigan on the bench beneath the awning. The out of work manager had taken An Exhale the night before, a slow-release insect repellent capsule. The mosquitos and midges which flourished in the wet climate subsequently left him in peace. A dragonfly fluttered into the garden and alighted on one of the hardy white roses that thrived in the humid conditions. Corrigan had always appreciated the design of these elegant insects. They reminded him of his youth when something resembling a summer with occasional interludes of sunshine still drew dragonfly nymphs from clear pools to metamorphose. They mesmerised him as a boy and they mesmerised him still even though their numbers had increased, and they were now as commonplace as hovercars and mecha-servants. He could hear the droid in the kitchen.

"Prepare lunch," he called, "and read through the WBE report as you do. Then lay out my Atelier suit."

The droid commenced reading the report on Whole Brain Emulation whilst it prepared one of Corrigan's favourite lunches. It was healthy and covered his needs, but it provided less comfort than Lazarus could with a single nudge. The ragged cat had woven itself into the fabric of his life, and made him feel secure in ways he could not define.

Certain lines from the report brightened Corrigan's imagination:

"Simulation mimics outward results. Whereas emulation mimics internal causal dynamics."

"Ah," Corrigan said, "a brain emulator is detailed and correct enough to produce the phenomenological effects of a mind. All very well, but we're decades from anything serviceable."

The roadmap proved DRT and its competitors had achieved no more than a brain database. None had yet managed a functional brain emulation, let alone anything species-generic, and that was necessary before individual brain emulation could be considered. Beyond this barrier lay mind and personality emulation.

His interview was at two o'clock, and Corrigan was aware the role was not on a path of least resistance. Yet something about the opportunity compelled him to consider it differently. It was a fascinating combination of research projects.

He'd wanted to read up on Caspar Ulmer, the CEO at DRT, but there was very little online. His family fortune had been amassed pillaging the rainforests for wood. Ulmer himself had moved to Montreal and had rarely spent time in Europe or America. He preferred online meetings but conducted final interviews in person.

He dressed for his interview and had B4 arrange his now ring-fenced driver. The cabbie arrived in torn jeans and a brown leather jacket. He had a strong, lithe build; his face a classically handsome shape under the rough. His blue eyes were a cloudy grey and gentler than the whole. This was a contradiction Corrigan not only appreciated but admired.

The driver's name was Bohdan, and his constant

reiteration of harmless headlines or small, largely inconsequential personal observations filled the silence. Corrigan rarely said more than a few words, but watched the driver's eyes in the rear-view mirror as the cab flew through the skies over London. There was something more than simple observation going on. It was clear since his trip to Palais-Culo the driver was taking an interest in the older man.

The cab settled on the tarmac outside DRT's central London office, a large building with well over a hundred floors. The plate glass was not segmented, and the tower appeared as a single block. It could have been an icicle, a diamond shard, or the blade of a giant knife. As he made his way through the revolving doors to reception, he caught a glimpse of Bohdan stood beside the cab. He had waited and watched as Corrigan climbed the steps and went into the building. He reminded Corrigan of a hero from an old Western, the kind of film he had hidden away on old archaic discs and secretly viewed when boredom got the better of his innate caution.

The receptionist greeted him by name and handed him a temporary pass. The panel was ready for him on the 128th floor, he was informed. He took the card-key and walked across the foyer to the lifts, where a woman of age dressed in a dark grey trouser suit waited in front of the doors. Her eyes were pouched in sacks of loose flesh and there was a yellow tinge to their underbellies. She smiled at him, and he had to wonder whether her fine white teeth were honest. She intuited something and shook her head.

When the lift arrived, he allowed the woman to enter first.

"One hundred and twenty-ninth," she said with an American accent, her imperious drawl almost unbearable. Corrigan wanted to slap her old chops but realised she could be a member of the interviewing panel.

He observed they were going to the same floor. Or were they? *Damn. What did the receptionist say?* He watched the floor numbers as they sped by, hoping for a recall.

The woman dug around inside her handbag for something, then pulled out a leather-bound notebook with a metal clasp and clicked it open. The pen inside was gold with a diamond stud. She scribbled, and Corrigan glimpsed the word *presumptuous*. He admired the curve of its letters, how smooth they were, like the contour of a blade. But he regarded the woman and her leather-bound notebook as one might observe roadkill.

Presumptuous.

The ascent was fast, tranquil, and Corrigan was relieved the lift offered no external view. Lifts that ran up the outside of buildings always made him edgy.

"Floor 129."

The doors opened. He allowed the woman of age to leave first and watched as she made her way towards a desk. The receptionist was a pale-skinned young man who acknowledged her with a polite nod and, "Good morning, Belinda." He had a somewhat distant quality about him, as if he would rather be anywhere else.

"Afternoon, Michael," the woman said. "I assume the others are here?"

Michael assured her the board was assembled.

Corrigan met the receptionist's steel-blue gaze. Nothing about his presence appeared to impress the pale-skinned young man in any way, but he asked how he might assist, his tone heavy with disdain. Corrigan squared his shoulders and told him he had an appointment at 2pm. He was asked to confirm his name. Michael then flicked open a halo-screen, scanned various files, and eventually opened one containing Corrigan's details. He tutted. "Your interview is on floor 128 not 129."

Corrigan nodded, and the young man indicated the stairs, his tone heavy with condescension. Corrigan considered descending to street level.

Good God. He grabbed the handrail between 129 and 128.

How the hell did you fail to recognise Belinda-bloody-Reece?

He had just stared at one of DRT's founding members like a carcass on a highway. He broke out in a sweat. Less than a flight of stairs separated him from his interview or the full descent to Non; from a path of much resistance to an armchair in a large window overlooking a street.

A woman in her early twenties, with long hair and fingernails, confirmed Corrigan was expected and asked him to please take a seat, and someone would be with him shortly. She then frowned behind the large mahogany desk and admonished him for being late. He apologised, but she had no interest in hearing him finish his story about going to the wrong floor, and he had no time to dwell on his tardiness, as a tall, thin man with greying blond hair marched along the hall and surveyed him with cold eyes.

"You're late," the man said in a clipped German accent. "My name is Professor Draseke." He offered Corrigan his hand and his skeletal fingers made the handshake unpleasant. "If you will follow me, please."

Draseke's heals clipped the polished tiles of the corridor and Corrigan watched him from behind as he kept pace behind him. Through a glass wall, a droid could be seen preparing a tray of instruments, and it greeted them with a familiar voice when they entered the room. Draseke noted how Corrigan registered the cranky New York drawl with a raised eyebrow.

"The company's voice is modelled on Belinda Reece's own inimitable lilt," Draseke said. "She is more than just our founder; she is sewn into the very fabric of our IT estate." He gathered some papers. "I will leave you with Constance."

"Constance?" Corrigan asked.

"Our Mecha-Medic."

The professor swivelled on his polished shoes and left the room without further interaction.

The droid was efficient and immediately directed him to a toilet, where he was asked to provide a urine sample. Although he needed to urinate, it was initially impossible to entice even a drop from his bladder. In his mind, he moved all thoughts and images of Belinda Reece into a storage file – the shiny bathroom was reminiscent of the lift he shared with the founder – and the sample was complete.

He handed the vial to Constance, who thanked him and directed him to roll up a sleeve. He looked away as the blood was drawn.

"Completed," Constance said. "You may open your eyes, Mr Corrigan."

Constance then took his pulse and temperature, and led him to a simulator booth. The room was empty and, when the droid switched off the lights, very dark. He allowed the tranquillity of those precious seconds of darkness to buoy him, like the warm waters of the Mediterranean he had read about in books no one ever mentioned.

His precious seconds of calm were then shattered by several halo-screen projections. The visitors arrived and disappeared randomly. They barked questions at him, made unpleasant observations about his appearance, and rebuked him for being late. The questions were fired at him with such rapidity he struggled to answer any of them at first. By degrees, however, he managed to regulate his breathing and focus. A broad-shouldered man appeared to be the political questioner. He wanted to know what Corrigan made of recent regulatory changes within the Asian market, what he thought of the UK government's plan to build, build, build, and the US president's views on the climate crisis. Another face, young and female, obviously an HR person or a recruitment scout, wanted to know how he would cope with disharmony in teams.

The others, when they appeared, were also all white professionals of different ages. One rarely saw other races represented in more senior roles in European business settings. Maintaining Worker status was harder for non-Caucasians given the bias of recruitment engines and their underlying algorithms.

Once he managed to assign a role to each of the visitors, he was able to answer a much higher percentage of their questions and he began to see a logic to the structure of what was being asked. He realised, for instance, that the *difficult team members* he was being asked to hypothetically manage were engaged remotely, working in China, and therefore the questions regarding recent regulatory changes – particularly relating to channels of communication between the various nations – were relevant and must be taken into consideration. He made a game of it in his mind, and by the time the room was plunged back into darkness he was in his stride and could have gone another hour of bombardment.

Constance collected him from the booth and directed him to a desk set up with a virtual monitor. He was required to absorb a case study and provide a response – the kind of managerial nonsense he'd been doing for twenty-five years. This was followed by a virtual interview, during which he was queried about the approach he adopted in response to the case study, followed by a series of questions regarding his CV, and why he thought he was the right choice of not only program manager for Project Egret, but as a potential employee of Dennett and Reece Technology.

His heart rate, blood pressure and brain activity were monitored throughout and, on completion of the evaluation, Constance returned him to reception where he was asked to sit and wait; the panel would be ready for him shortly. A halo-screen displayed the latest news above the receptionist's head, and he found himself distracted by the subtitled content. Bohdan had misheard a current news item. Apparently, Marjorie Lemming had not been arrested for making a false claim regarding her sighting of a patch of blue sky in Tooting, she had been demoted to Transient status pending a trial. Her domicile had been requisitioned for a more deserving person of age, who had recently been demoted from Worker to Non due to failing health.

"The panel is ready for you now, Mr Corrigan," the receptionist said, and she directed him to room Z001.

He hurried along to the appointed "room", a glass booth designed to seat six. Four young people sat around a circular table in a joint stupor. He pressed his hand to the door, pushed, and offered a tentative hello.

The chunkier of the men emerged from his trance.

"Mr Corrigan! Please come in!" He stood and shook Corrigan's hand, somewhat tenderly Corrigan thought. "I'm Tony Reece."

The more athletic man stepped forward. He spotted Corrigan's blush and said that meeting Belinda's grandson often put people off-guard. "I'm Steve, by the way. Steve Dennett."

The women introduced themselves as Nancy

Carmichael and Linda Harris. If Tony was a grandson, were these girls nieces?

"We're not related to anyone important," Linda chirped. Her face was fixed in an expression of genuine or fake ecstasy. It was impossible to gauge. "I'm from HR, and Nancy's part of our People Team."

Corrigan told them how nice it was to meet them. The four laughed appreciatively and sat down. He remained standing until Tony requested he, please, take a seat. The New York accent made the request sound more like an order, but his smile diffused the edge.

Steve asked whether Corrigan had ever worked for DRT, and he explained he had once worked for Clockwork, who was a subsidiary, but never for the mothership. He wished he could retract the term as soon as he'd used it, but Steve seemed to appreciate it.

No mention was made of the program or the individual projects in what was an informal sort of exchange. They did not ask him to discuss his skill set or to elaborate on his experience. Instead, they asked questions about where he lived, if he had any hobbies, pets, or played any sports. What was his favourite tipple? Restaurant? What did he think of President Downey?

"We just want to get to know you a little," Nancy from the People Team chuckled. "The company never hires anyone without first seeing whether we *like* them," she added.

Linda grinned, obviously still in the throes of ecstasy, and said something about them needing to know if a person was the right *people fit* for the company.

Corrigan nodded seriously, and followed with a weak smile. When Tony returned the smile he released a pitiful excuse for a laugh.

Steve Dennett turned to Corrigan in earnest. "Anyone who works for the firm has to demonstrate a real can-do attitude, Bob," he said, and the familiarity of the shortened version of his name was somehow made even more uncomfortable uttered in an American accent, and Corrigan shrank from it. Steve put on a mock frown. "You don't mind being called Bob do you, Bob?"

"No," Corrigan said. "That's absolutely fine, Steve."

Corrigan was then taken to lunch. He smiled throughout the inane conversation; he nodded appreciatively at their banal observations; he even laughed at the *funny* bits in their trite stories. Eventually Steve and Tony had to *make tracks,* and Bob was left with Nancy and Linda, who escorted him to the main reception area.

"Terrie," Linda said, "could you please book Mr Corrigan in for another interview next week? It's role 78009." When the receptionist confirmed the booking, Linda said, ecstatically, "You're such a *superstar,* Terrie!"

The girls then followed him out, and Nancy took his hand and told him what a *pleasure* it had been. Corrigan gestured towards the waiting taxi, the revolving doors behind them still in motion. "OK! You take care, Bob, and we'll see you next week!"

The women hurtled back through the doors and disappeared.

Corrigan collapsed onto the back seat of the cab.

"Should I drive you home, *Bob*?" Bohdan asked.

"Don't *ever* call me that again."

An expression of hurt shadowed the Pole's face. It remained only fleetingly, but it was an honest twinge. A mosquito alighted on his cheek and injected its stinger through the driver's skin.

"You forget to take an Exhale?" Corrigan snapped.

"I don't take synthetic poison," Bohdan said. "I use homeopathic stuff."

"Obviously, an effective product. You must share your secret."

Bohdan asked where they were going, and Corrigan asked to be taken to Eastbourne. The driver kept his eyes on Corrigan whenever the skies were clear of traffic, the hover-cab hugging the coast and accelerating where able. Grey mist wet the windows and Corrigan peered down at the broken teeth of old England. The dirty chalk wall always made him melancholy, and he asked whether Bohdan was hungry.

Bohdan caught his gaze in the rear-view mirror and held it. "The company wouldn't approve," he said, scratching the spot where the mosquito had drawn blood. "And I'm on the meter."

"Leave it running," Corrigan said, "and join me. I won't tell."

They found a small fish and chips place down near the beach. The smell of hot fat and batter allowed Corrigan to discuss the interview in an altogether more useful perspective. "But," he declared, without restraint, "the people at DRT are idiots."

"Americans," Bohdan said, and put a large chip into his mouth.

Corrigan smiled at that. He wondered how Lazarus was doing; whether he was laid out on the bed or following B4 around in hope of scraps.

Turning, he caught his reflection in the window and recognised not only the worn-out man sat there, but the worn-out man's phony face. He looked at Bohdan, and the driver gave him a knowing smile. It made Corrigan uneasy. Was it that obvious he was a sham, a masquerade of a man?

5

Corrigan held Lazarus out at arm's length and said of Belinda Reece, "What an old *witch*."

Yet how he had ingratiated himself with the Fab Four, fawning and feigning interest, his smiles as real as the old witch's fine white teeth.

His wristpad pinged. He put Lazarus on the floor. An email had arrived, along with a text from his mother: "Dying, if you're bothered. Love Mum."

He flicked the irritating message aside and clicked open the email entitled **Tier Two Interview**. It was direct, simply providing the time and location for his next interview, and was signed "Kind regards, Blake Adler".

Corrigan accepted the invite and scrolled to a navigator page. He typed in the name Blake Adler. No media results were returned for the executive. There was nothing on the man anywhere. So he typed in the name Caspar Ulmer again, and it seemed the CEO was just as media-shy. There were pictures of the founders everywhere, just not the big guns.

"But they're just figureheads, these days," Corrigan muttered. "The real power sits with Ulmer and his leadership team. And what a shadowy bunch *they* are."

B4 arranged a taxi for the morning of the interview, and Bohdan collected him with his customary Polish punctuality. The cabbie mentioned having tried a lab-reared egg, and other than a slightly meaty taste to the yokes, he considered them first-rate. Corrigan had worked on a project for Origination Produce. Although real eggs and poultry were expensive, he could not stomach the thought of eating genetically engineered products once he'd seen how they were produced. Row after row of headless, featherless, legless hens puckered eggs out every thirty minutes, the disembodied birds connected to a program that regulated homeostasis for the lab-grown mutants. The same protein and carbohydrate gloop – a kind of porridge – was endlessly recycled and passed time and again through the digestive tracts of these purely functional, non-thinking or feeling organic machines. As Bohdan was talking, he studied the back of the driver's head and his eyes in the mirror and wondered why they had not pounced on one another.

The cab landed in front of an inconspicuous glass dome in Hoxton. Bohdan leant out of the window. "Good luck," he said, and when Corrigan did not respond he put the cab in flight gear, hovered and headed for the horizon.

A door slid open as Corrigan approached the dome and he stepped inside the protective bubble. Fine oak stairs led down to an open-plan reception with wooden floors and a broad mahogany desk. The receptionist seemed inordinately beautiful, and there was something vaguely familiar about him. His parents had to be as attractive as one another to have produced someone quite so flawless. Corrigan assumed he must be a graduate, but wondered why he'd felt a flicker of recognition.

The receptionist smiled and wished him good morning. The expression was genuine, and Corrigan responded in kind. He noted the name tag when "Jonathan" asked him to sign in. There was a degree of bashfulness in Jonathan's face that Corrigan found heartening. He was asked to take a seat. "Adler will be with you shortly."

Corrigan watched the receptionist. Something about the name Adler had made Jonathan blush and sit upright in his chair. The faintest of lines furled his forehead beneath his neatly cropped afro. It was unusual to see even a lighter skinned black man working for an operation like DRT. As was the case with all larger corporations, algorithms were deployed to ensure an exclusively Caucasian and Asian employee base. Of course, barriers could be breached as his mother had managed to do on his behalf, so Jonathan must have connections.

It was a short wait, less than a minute, which Corrigan was thankful for. The exec arrived, a heavyset-to-overweight, sweating, heavy-browed man, with hand extended. Their shake was evenly distributed, neither weaker nor stronger from either party, and Corrigan was satisfied with the impression of that. Adler directed him to his office and sat behind a large antique desk. He gesticulated towards a Chesterfield armchair, and Corrigan sat.

Alder eyed Corrigan for over a minute before he

spoke. He had read Corrigan's CV and conceded he was competent. What he could not gauge, however, was the candidate's commitment level. The exec spoke loudly, with an accent Corrigan found difficult to place. It could have been New York or Boston. It was certainly east coast, but it felt weighted down beneath a layer of snow, perhaps Maine or even Canada.

"How're you, Corrigan?" Adler asked, with a detectable wheeze. "The weather treating you right?"

"The weather?" Corrigan smiled. "I'm no Marjorie Lemming." When Adler failed to respond, he added, "The woman who recently claimed to have seen a patch of blue sky over London."

Adler nodded but his eyes revealed nothing. "Who's to say she didn't see something?"

"She's mad."

"That would be the official line, but maybe this Lemming woman saw more than just a Belushi blur."

Corrigan studied the executive for a moment and considered his answer. Perhaps there was a strategy underlying the thread, the way the questions in the simulation booth eventually revealed a pattern.

"Why demote her if she actually saw something?" he asked.

"Hope is a tricky business. It can be a useful tool when applied appropriately, but there are situations in which it can be more disadvantageous to our goals than anything," Adler said. The prospective manager remained silent. "I suspect you think she might have seen something." The executive's interrogatory eyes continued to bore into him. "Caution will only ever get you so far, Corrigan."

Corrigan sweated under Adler's stare. Perhaps he should have agreed there was a possibility of Marjorie Lemming having seen *something,* but the threat of demotion was ever-present, and Adler held a position where decision-makers of that order were within reach.

"I see you've been in for your Stage 1 assessment and met Happy and Clappy from the People Team."

"They were…"

"Intense, I know." Adler assessed Corrigan again. "You also met Tony and Steve, our princes in waiting." He held up his hand when the interviewee attempted to speak. "Born to an unending smorgasbord, those boys have to attend one tedious soirée after another, and they love it. The kind of envoys needed to hold the money in one place. Effective networkers and diplomats but operationally they're useless."

"I found them polite and…"

"I'm sure you did *Bob*…You've skipped around," Adler then said, "and I can't see an intentional career path. It's like you're some kind of opportunist."

"All good management is a mixture of diplomacy, opportunism and exploitation," Corrigan said.

Adler indicated the projected CV. Corrigan had managed teams and led a string of successful IT projects, but he wanted to know how he felt about leading something research-based, where outcomes were not fully defined.

Corrigan had a ready answer but coloured it with a

hint of cunning. He explained how fascinated he was by the three research fields, but added his cunning: a comment on the undefined, the unimaginable.

Adler leant forward, placed his elbows on the desk and asked, "How'd you define that?"

"Keeping an open and yet incisive mind," Corrigan said. "A willingness to dig deeper; to go off plan and seek something altogether different."

"It's impossible to go *off plan* when there isn't one." He shook his large head at his interviewee. "You're going to be running through a jungle where no trails have yet been blazed. DRT employs the finest minds. What we're doing...no one has any idea. Secrecy is...well, it's like cleanliness to a goddamn puritan down there."

"Down where?"

"The facility's two miles down. What we're doing hasn't yet seen the light of day. Not that we get any goddamn real light."

"I assure you," Corrigan said, "I'm as discreet as a mouse."

Adler observed him following that. The scrutiny was severe. "If it'd been my decision, I'd say you weren't up to the job. The role's as undefined as the research domain. It proved too much for Malcom Mercer. Did you know him?" Corrigan shook his head. "Mercer was a runt, but he was determined and resilient. The little bastard wasn't up to it, though." The scrutiny continued. "You'll spend a lot of time underground. There's a need to bury what we're doing and keep it down in the hole."

Corrigan was aware of a trickle of nervous sweat between his buttocks, yet he fixed his gaze on Adler and remained motionless in his Chesterfield armchair.

"Ulmer wants you for some reason I can't fathom," Adler then said. "It might be the snake in you. But I suggest you stop riding around on your goddamn belly and stand upright. The team won't accept a man who isn't up to it." The executive eyed him as if he were on trial. "Maybe it's something in your blood, eh, Corrigan?"

An image of vials of blood and urine placed on Constance the Mecha-Medic's trolley revisited him.

"My blood?"

"You know, something innately managerial." Adler put his feet up on the desk, with no little effort, and tapped his wrist implant. A halo-screen shone from his eyes and he scrolled through a series of CVs. Their team meant business, and he expected Corrigan to get under their skin and force the best out of them. Perhaps Corrigan could use his Non background to motivate their reluctant genius.

"Privilege sometimes fails to breed talent," Adler said.

For some reason, Corrigan felt compelled to stand. "I can deal with–"

"I'm not asking you to *deal* with anything," Adler cut in with another wheeze, viewing the standing man from under his brow. "You gotta keep a grip without anyone noticing. That's what real leaders do. They don't get offered a role, they live these positions their whole lives, are born to it, no matter what some bohemian butterfly might have to say on the subject."

Corrigan was startled by Adler using one of his mother's phrases. DRT must have set up surveillance alongside the provision of Hattie's high-end medical equipment. All the same, it was an extraordinary program, but it wasn't unique from a managerial point of view. He had a way with people; he managed to nurture and get the best out of any team. He held Alder's gaze and said, "I'm a far better leader than you'll ever be. And I must say I'm used to more diverse teams."

"Diversity could be advantageous at an operational level," Adler said, "but here at the decision-maker tier, it just won't wash. There's only so much room in the clubhouse."

Adler curled his lip, shut down the halo-screen and escorted Corrigan back to reception. He would send him some material to look at, he said. CVs, so he could get his head around the key team members. He also wanted Corrigan to come to a demonstration the following Thursday. "Goeth's showing off the latest A Class Guardian. It'll be an opportunity to meet him and a few members of the board." He then shook Corrigan's hand firmly and was gone.

Corrigan smiled a tease at Jonathan on the way out. He decided not to summon Bohdan. What he needed was a drink.

The Merry Slaughter was on the corner. There was a covered travellator pavement ahead, but he stepped out into the street to avoid having to use it. Traffic flew through grey skies above his head, mingling with swarms of tstese flies, the latest migrants from Africa.

Corrigan entered the pub and ordered a whisky. The barman poured Glenfiddich into a squat glass.

"That'll go on your tab, Mr Corrigan," he said.

When Corrigan shot him a curious look, the barman assured him DRT would cover it, so he ordered a second and went out into the garden. The awning was up, and a gas heater warmed the air at the table. He sipped his whisky.

"How the hell am I right for this post in terms of a *people fit*?" he chuckled.

6

On the Tuesday of the following week, his mother messaged and said this was it. Death. She was so insistent he rushed to the hospital and found her sitting up in bed eating a cream cake and sipping tea. She looked at him, and there was sufficient contrition in her gaze to prompt a smile from him. She held up the cake and told him how good it was. When he rolled his eyes she insisted even the condemned were allowed a final meal.

"You've not been condemned," he said.

"I'm one of those awful people who look their best when most unwell, Bobbin, me luv," was her response.

She patted the bed. He weighed his options and decided to sit on the chair. She put down her tea and inspected him. One of his contact lenses chose this moment to fold in the corner of his eye. He dug around in the watering socket and cursed. Having managed to pull out the errant lens, he held it up to the artificial light.

"It's ridiculous wearing bits of old plastic in your eyes when a surgeon could sort you out," she reminded him. "And he could implant a halo-screen for you while he's at it. You mustn't live in the past like you do, in that old flat of yours. Why you don't get a nice modern flat, I'll never grasp. You can dump that old bookshelf full of dodgy writers while you're at it. I mean, look what spouting that kind of nonsense did for me bohemian butterflies. No one's seen hide nor hair of them for over twenty years. Demoted to Transients...or worse...the disappeared."

She rearranged herself on her pillows and winced a real wince.

He regretted his interminable irritability with her. It wasn't her fault she was dying. He decided to stay with her for an hour. She obviously craved time with him, and it was a small sacrifice for the peace and quiet of her reluctant gratitude. He brought up a halo-screen and they watched her favourite reporter interviewing a senator.

"He's such a wanker," his mother said.

He agreed, and they shook their heads in unison. The US had suffered the same problems for decades – the political elite continued to distance themselves from the masses, and the environment had essentially been written off – and they never made any progress.

"The world's been through any number of wet patches," the senator insisted.

His mother declared that the senator was a *wet patch* if ever she'd seen one.

He agreed, and she laughed. As soon as the segment concluded, he gave her a kiss on the cheek and retreated for home.

Ten minutes after he walked in the door the hospital called to say she had died quietly in her sleep. There must have been a level of incredulity in his voice, because the nurse kindly explained, "No, she hasn't nodded off. We can't pop along the hall and rouse her."

He demanded to know how they had not been alerted this was going to happen, and *done something*, hooked up to all those sensors as she was. The nurse explained the data went directly to DRT, and reminded him they had gone through the arrangement with him at the time, as advised by the gentleman at DRT who had drafted the terms.

"What gentleman?" he asked.

"A Mr Adler," she confirmed.

Corrigan asked if his mother had suffered. The nurse reiterated that she had just nodded off, and... He flicked off his halo-screen and lay out on the bed. Lazarus stretched out along his left leg and looked at him. He could see his mother's face wrinkled in a giggle and hear her calling the senator a *wet patch*.

It did not strike like a truck. It was more slow-motion. He went to sit in the garden with a bottle of brandy, for something to do. The first few drinks went down easily enough, and then he went for a wander along Harvey Road, bottle in hand, his grief a new weight under the fog and drizzle. The liquor removed all remaining sharpness from the dull edges and ill-defined structures of the long street he lived on.

He had forgotten just how derelict the real world was. It sprawled around the outskirts of the more well-maintained city centre. His flat was an oasis from the squalor, rundown yes but a home managed and cared for by B4. The surrounding houses were stained green, windows broken here and there, boarded up with old bits of wood from discarded packing crates and pallets. His neighbours were Nons or Transient squatters whose children played in the streets after dark. The older kids quickly progressed to acts of violence and many became early adopters of Belushi Grey. The manufacturer ran a scheme allowing children under thirteen years of age free access to the government sanctioned drug.

Corrigan slipped on a wet paving slab and stumbled as two adolescent boys crossed the road ahead. They clocked him and waited for him at the top of the street. One of them had a neatly cropped afro indicating he came from a family who still considered appearance a matter of pride. The other was a scrawny boy with pale skin, a gaunt face and large hands dangling at the ends of undernourished arms. The scruffier of the two whispered something in the other boy's ear and they nodded in unison. They might have been armed with knives but Corrigan had nothing to steal.

"Nice weather," he grunted as he came level with them.

The boys stared at him, their surly expressions fixed and hardened. They made no move and he felt them watching as he plodded on toward Finsbury Park. Perhaps they intuited something was wrong, that he was suffering some private misery. He grunted, realising they would not risk interfering with a Worker. The way Corrigan dressed set him apart and although life was undoubtedly harsh for the boys, it could always be worse or brought to an abrupt end.

The cruising ground was only a short walk and as he lumbered along, his thoughts drifted to childhood memories. He recalled how his mother used to gather her butterflies together over bottles of cheap synthetic wine. They pondered books no Worker would dare open let alone own, sharing thoughts and ideas as they divided what little food they had. He watched her change, distancing herself from her real friends and turning her charm onto men who could help them escape the ghetto. The idea of Hattie informing on her old friends had occurred to him and although he had no evidence, it was a common form of advancement. Whenever she looked at him, a mixture of disappointment and aspiration burned in her glare. He would never know exactly what she sacrificed to elevate him, but it couldn't have been easy.

He kicked a jagged paving slab as the rain fell like the breath of an out of fashion deity, Neptune living hand to mouth. Corrigan's hair was wet and his teeth were numb. He plodded on, determined to engage in an act of intimacy so anonymising it would purge his conscience and make him forget.

Now in the park, cruisers slipped through trees and shadows, and he was soon bent over in a scrum. They abused him, took turns with him, and when he cried out it increased their pleasure. When they tired of him, they slipped away again, and he reeled from the drink and vomited into a ditch.

The vulnerable man was set upon by a cloud of hungry mosquitoes. He had forgotten to take his weekly

Exhale and without the slow-release repellant he was fair game. He let them alight and drink their fill and as their translucent bellies swelled, he recalled a report regarding the danger of a new, hybrid species of tsetse fly. A swarm of the aggressive predators had brought down and killed half a dozen Non children who had been playing in an abandoned, unsupported council estate.

He called Bohdan, and the cabbie used Corrigan's wristpad signal to find him and arrived ten minutes later. He asked him whether he wanted to be taken home, but Corrigan was slumped on the back seat. Bohdan reminded him of his interview in the morning.

"No," Corrigan said, "it's a...demon...a demonstration."

As the cab hovered over Finsbury Park, Corrigan imagined his mother rising from the redundant confines of her body. He looked to the rear-view mirror, where Bohdan was watching him cry.

"She was a terrible old thing..." Corrigan said. "*Terrible*. But she was mine. *Mine*. I apologise...oh, for fuck's sake...no I don't."

When they arrived at Harvey Road, Bohdan helped Corrigan inside, through the kitchen and into his bedroom. Lazarus observed them as they entered the room from where he was sitting on a chair by the bed, all four legs tucked away under him. Only his tail moved. Bohdan lay Corrigan out on the bed and went looking for his Mecha-Butler.

B4 was in the front room and insisted Bohdan identify

himself. Bohdan laughed when he heard the droid's female cockney accent. He identified himself and requested that the droid hydrate its owner.

Bohdan stood sideways in the doorway. One of his buttocks jutted out as he rested his weight on one leg, the contour round and full in the twilight of the hall.

"You don't have to go," Corrigan said.

"I do," Bohdan replied. But he would have stayed if he could.

He said goodnight and switched off the light.

7

"Bobbin," B4 said, "you will miss your appointment."

Corrigan focused on the droid's flat face. He made to wave it away but got caught up in an intravenous line feeding into the back of his hand.

"You needed hydrating," B4 explained. "I also included pain relief, something for them bug bites and a top for your weekly Exhale. We don't want you being eaten alive like those poor little blighters who wandered into the old Broadwater Farm estate. That's where the Transients and other damaged butterflies end up."

Corrigan stared blankly at the odd little droid. What *had* she called him? He must have been hallucinating or dreaming, because he was sure she'd called him by a name only his mother ever used.

"Run a bath," Corrigan said and wrenched the needle from his hand. "And lay out my Westwood suit. Then order me a taxi. And clean those damn flagstones again."

The droid confirmed she had already booked Mr Bohdan. He could not remember having requested the droid do this, but had no objections. The little droid handed him a packet of Serenity lockets as he made for the door. The painkillers also acted as mild sedatives. He read the familiar label, *Serenity, a Beatitude Product,* and tucked the packet into a pocket. The company was a subsidiary of DRT who also produced Belushi Grey. Corrigan had resisted taking them in the past as they were known as a pathway drug to the harsher, more addictive product. Given B4 was also a DRT product herself, it wasn't so surprising to find her pedalling their other merchandise. There was no time to question her now, but he'd have to think about what to do with her when he got home.

In the cab in his suit, Corrigan looked at Bohdan closely and thanked him.

"No worries, Mr Corrigan."

"I didn't do anything I should be ashamed of..."

"You did not. Where to?"

Corrigan told him the address, and they sped towards the city, but as they approached Bohdan brought the cab up to 800 feet from the average 350 feet, into the bottom edge of heavy grey clouds. Corrigan light-heartedly asked how high the taxi could go, gripping the armrest, but Bohdan was concentrating on the cab, which groaned as it began to rise further still. As they broke the cloud layer, Corrigan gripped harder. What was Bohdan doing? The intensity of the sun was blinding, and the blue of the sky startling. Corrigan muttered something about what could have been, as an airliner roared over them and they were tossed on waves of turbulence and a layer of fine, filthy soot. The nostalgia was as painful as the light.

"Anything could happen in a wasteland," Bohdan said.

Corrigan nodded, but asked the cabbie to, please, take

him to his meeting. He noted the fleeting look of hurt on Bohdan's face, again, and regretted being the cause, but he must not be late.

Bohdan began the descent, fast. Corrigan inhaled and held his breath. Larger aircraft were heard in the distance, but they were otherwise alone.

The cab returned to recognisable altitude, where London huddled for warmth below and settled beside the address in Hoxton. Corrigan stepped out onto the covered pavement and started walking. He stopped, turned back, and Bohdan opened his window.

"Thank you," Corrigan said.

"It was nothing."

"Nothing to one man," Corrigan said, "is everything to another. Let me buy you dinner."

"Not necessary."

"Make you dinner?"

It was agreed Bohdan would join him for dinner at Harvey Road.

The beautiful graduate was at reception.

"Good morning, Jonathan," Corrigan smiled.

The receptionist smiled back, with a flicker of new confidence. He explained Corrigan was to go down to level six, where someone would meet him and pointed in the direction of the lift.

The lift descended far too quickly, and he inhaled and held his breath, his go-to safety mechanism for control of his stomach. Seemed like it was going to be a day of rapid descents. When the doors opened a thin, sly-looking man in his early sixties was standing sentry. Corrigan recognised Draseke immediately from the day of his first interview.

"I'm Draseke, we met," the man said in his tight German accent, and they shook hands. Again, Corrigan noted the skeletal fingers. "Professor Goeth has not surfaced and here I am. The longer I wait, the longer you take."

Corrigan apologised and explained the driver had lost his way. Draseke assured him there was no need for explanation and said he hoped he had not had breakfast. Corrigan was still in possession of his tea and toast and wondered about the mention of breakfast.

"The hell with toast! There's sausage!" Draseke exclaimed, and took him by the arm and escorted him towards a large hall alive with conversation and elegant young servants with white gloves and silver trays. "Try it!" the scientist said, grabbing a skewer. "And careful you don't impale yourself." He pulled a metal toothpick from his pocket and grinned. "You can do so much damage with one of these. Imagine the pain."

At the front of the auditorium stood what Corrigan assumed to be an A Class Guardian. The android was still and was evidently powered down. It had an anthropomorphic form sheathed in a flexible black skin. Its head was a large oval, the surface of which gleamed beneath the overhead lighting. The body and limbs reminded him of an insect, a very large, upright ant perhaps, or a wingless dragonfly. Corrigan approached it and reached out to touch the machine.

"No, no," Draseke said, "try the sausage, Mr

Corrigan." He held out the chipolata on a skewer.

Corrigan took it and frowned. He tasted it. It was rubbery, but pleasant.

"Ladies and gentlemen," Draseke then announced, and the rumble of conversation quietened. "Herr Professor – Mr Goeth, I mean – is unable to attend this morning, and has asked me to introduce our latest A Class Guardian model."

The rumble resumed, and there was a polite surge towards the front of the auditorium. Draseke powered up the android and it walked out amongst the crowd, which parted here and there as it progressed. The scientist instructed the Guardian to perform a series of tasks, which included running, climbing a ladder, carrying one of the waiters across the room, relieving the waiter of his tray and pouring coffee and tea for the guests. Its agility was remarkable, and Corrigan was impressed by how refined its movements were and by its overall elegance, even though he could not deny its insectile qualities. The head reminded him of the dragonflies he once caught when he was a boy. The Guardian's head had the same translucent surface and the matter contained within the glassy dome was dense, impenetrable and dark. He asked Draseke who was controlling it.

Adler wheezed from behind Corrigan's shoulder, "It operates itself, although it's not exactly a thinker."

"No, it's a doer," Draseke confirmed.

Adler introduced Corrigan to several board members, which was pleasant enough. While they were in between introductions, the exec took a moment to lean in and whisper, "Draseke is useful. Try and stay on his good side. He's involved with the military – US, that is – and he's got connections. Knows more than he should about what happens to Transients like Marjorie Lemming." Adler stepped back, tapped the side of his nose with a finger, and added, "Just so you know who you're talking to. The man works for us, but he's got a number of government projects on the boil." With this, the exec wandered off and mingled, leaving Corrigan to ponder the precariousness of his position.

And then he came face to face with Belinda Reece.

"Good to meet you," she said, dental implants on full display.

"We've met," Corrigan said. "I mean, we shared a lift."

The baggy-eyed woman regarded him. "Yes, you're right. You followed me to the wrong floor." She leant in and he lowered his head to hers. "The one hundred and twenty-ninth is where the board meet. No one else gets past Michael. He's such an unpleasant boy."

"Lovely pale skin, though," Corrigan observed.

"I wouldn't recommend him, dear, he lacks enthusiasm."

She wandered off, and an unpleasant image soured his sausage.

"Someone will get hold of you soon to arrange an interview with the CEO," Adler said. "It's a formality but has to be done in person. You can hang on here and have a few more sausages, or head home and plan dinner for your cabbie. Makes no difference to us. After all, you never voted us in, eh, Corrigan. That's what your Mr Chomsky writes, isn't it?"

A tray appeared before him. Corrigan looked at the A Class in charge of the tray, and the Guardian tilted its head and righted it several times in quick spasmodic jerks. He had watched the captured dragonflies of his childhood do this as they reacclimatised to new environments. He asked the machine for its recommendation. The android righted its head and pointed at a mushroom vol-au-vent.

What most intrigued Corrigan was how silent the Guardian's movements were. He marvelled at it, and would have stayed longer were it capable of conversation. He was about to leave when the android placed its tray on a table and touched his arm.

"Perhaps he's smitten," Draseke said to Corrigan.

The A Class made a series of gestures Corrigan assumed to be sign language, which Draseke observed with wide eyes. He leant in and whispered in Corrigan's ear, "Someone's passing you a message."

The android signed another line, and Draseke interpreted it as: *Our reluctant genius is always cooking.*

Corrigan stared at the android and asked, "And who is this reluctant genius?"

The machine signed: *It is always good to have a chat with a clever fellow.* The A Class then retrieved its tray and resumed serving guests.

"Extraordinary!" Draseke exclaimed. "Someone is – as you say in England – pulling our legs. Every single one! Like a naughty child with a spider."

Draseke tried to introduce Corrigan to a pair of stakeholders, but he was unsettled by the encounter with the A Class and said he wanted air. The thin, mealy-eyed scientist helped manage the disappeared, he recalled, and Corrigan imagined himself being transported to Cairo on a CIA plane. He also recalled the advice he'd been given, swallowed a Serenity and shook Draseke's hand as warmly as he could, all the while nodding and apologising as he made his retreat. He hurriedly pressed the button to call the lift, waves of panic sweeping through him.

When the lift finally returned him to the surface, he glanced into Adler's office on his way out. The exec was deep in conversation with a halo-image of Draseke. The projection poured from the American's eyes and the German stood gesticulating. Corrigan hurried past to find the air he now genuinely needed.

"Mr Corrigan," Jonathan said.

Corrigan startled but smiled at the lad. "I've a final interview with the CEO, Caspar Ulmer. Adler said someone would be in touch about that."

"A date and time have not yet been agreed," Jonathan said, "but I'll let you know ASAP." The young man lowered his gaze. "I'm off in a minute."

Corrigan felt guilty even considering it, but suggested a spot of lunch would not go amiss. What he really needed was a drink.

"Have lunch," the exec called from his office. "There's a nice place around the corner. Give him ten minutes and he'll show you the way."

"I can wait outside?" Corrigan offered.

"Please don't. I don't like being alone with that man."

8

Corrigan took Jonathan to The Merry Slaughter and ordered them a pint of beer each while they looked at the menu. The food was simple; the kind of no-nonsense fare he preferred. They ordered fish and chips, and Corrigan instructed the publican to put it on his DRT account, and they walked out into the garden. Corrigan glanced at Jonathan and again marvelled at his skin. Life had yet to write a single signature on it.

"Been with the company long?" he asked.

"Nearly three years."

Corrigan nodded, too seriously, caught himself and smiled. The smile was reflected in the young man's eyes. There was a light there which had not dared to shine during previous interactions.

A ruddy barman brought their food and asked if they needed anything else. Corrigan requested some water. When the man left he turned to Jonathan, "Why have you remained a receptionist so long?"

"Could I be taken for white?"

"No, not quite and I realise that recruitment algorithms remain as biased as the men who designed them."

Jonathan smiled through the awkward moment.

"Yes," he said. "The odds are stacked against me, so I'm studying, and the company sponsors me."

Corrigan pursued this as they ate, and Jonathan revealed his fascination for AI. DRT was researching the field from several angles and allowed him to work flexible hours so he could attend courses and study in the evenings. The young man was articulate and clearly intelligent, but Corrigan drifted awhile his interest waning.

"I prevaricated over where to specialise," Jonathan said, "which is why I'm a twenty-seven-year-old receptionist for Corp America. For now."

"Ah...you're twenty years younger than me." Corrigan noticed the sigh that accompanied his maths.

"Guys your age always say it like that...you know... as if the gap were some twenty-year-old twink sat between us. I enjoy the company of older men. Guys my age are immature." Whilst Corrigan pondered Jonathan continued, "I thought you were handsome...the minute I saw you." He threw a quick look around to make sure they were alone. "Mr Adler also noticed."

Corrigan asked whether anything had been said, and Jonathan assured him Adler did not need to *say* anything. "Has Adler ever tried it on?" Corrigan then asked, pushing his empty plate away.

Jonathan shook his head. "If he likes boys, he doesn't like me. He does, however, enjoy games."

Corrigan felt something twist in his chest, and he could hear his mother's laughter somewhere from the other side. "Well," he said, "I'm sure your studies await."

Something happened to the young man's face, and the older man thought he might cry. "I'm as far from a prize as anyone could get," he said. "You'd realise that given time." He stood up, and Jonathan followed him through the bar to the street.

"If you didn't like me," Jonathan said, "you might've said. I thought...I thought you'd been looking."

Corrigan avoided eye contact and explained looking was no longer the same as touching, not at his age. He apologised.

Jonathan stared at Corrigan for a moment, the air of expectation still there, but when Corrigan did nothing he turned and walked back towards the office. Corrigan watched him retreat, the way his shoulders slumped yet his buttocks rolled in his neatly pressed trousers. Relief, regret and longing tumbled about beneath Corrigan's ribs, so he tapped his wristpad and ordered a cab, Bohdan his driver of choice. He looked up the road and saw Jonathan, hunched over in the mist. Two clicks and he deselected the Pole as his preferred driver. Four minutes later he climbed into a cab and was hurried through the drizzle towards Hornsey. He typed a quick message to Bohdan explaining he had eaten and they would have to take a rain check on dinner.

He stepped out of the cab at the station so he could walk up the hill. The climb placed a strain on his calves and he welcomed the exertion. Drizzle wet his face and collected in his hair. He thought of his mother. On the wave of loss he plodded on, his heart lolling on the seabed with the bottom feeders, the oceanic rats and mice. He was at home here; it calmed him. He walked along Harvey Road where the junky-father had slumped in the doorway. He was back, and Corrigan looked at the man, at his blank eyes and parched parted lips.

"Can I help you, man?" the stranger growled.

Corrigan ignored the threat, but could not dismiss the resemblance to Jonathan. He let himself into his flat. It was dark, but he did not turn the lights on. He walked through to the front room and sat. The junkie opposite lit up a joint, his face illuminated for a flickering second.

9

Confirmation of his interview with Ulmer arrived via a generic email rather than from Jonathan. He would likely never see the young man again. And although it was highly unlikely he would end up with Bohdan as a random driver, he decided he would use public transport as a precaution in the future.

He sat in his front room, his feet up on the ottoman with Lazarus on his lap. B4 brought him a cup of coffee and he scrolled through the team's CVs.

Goeth was an extraordinary engineer whose designs had been used domestically for years. He was now working on DRT's Guardian models, which had obvious military potential. Goeth's skin had the same unhealthy pallor in the bio photo, and he'd combed a few greasy strands of hair over a pallid scalp for effect. The overall impression was one expected from a man whose life-long pursuits had been mechanical.

The professor's assistant was an engineer called Jun Fuse, who was born in Japan but had grown up in London. Corrigan pulled up a three-dimensional photograph of the man and spun it around. The engineer was as beautiful as he was handsome, but his dark eyes were impenetrable. He searched for more images of the engineer and found several on social media sites. He was not smiling in a single photo. There was a brief section on his younger brother Arthur. They had different fathers, the younger having been the result of his mother's affair with a Transient. Corrigan felt an urge to tap the word *Transient* where it sat beside the word *Unknown,* but it would have been a futile gesture, so he resisted.

He took a sharp breath when he opened Tierney Harding's profile. Her expression was flabby but severe, and she seemed to judge him over the rim of her glasses. It also suggested a disappointment never satiated by work. He read her CV and wondered if she had written it herself, "A neuroscientist who helped define what a mind is and might be."

Katherine Meregalli's CV represented a woman in her early thirties with white-to-translucent skin, blue eyes, high cheekbones and thin lips. Her blonde hair was cropped short, which gave her the appearance of a convict. She was acknowledged as a world leader in genetics, and her work at MIT led to ground-breaking organ cloning. In fact her list of accomplishments was impressive, and he thought she would be an asset to any team. There was a link, however, to a psych evaluation. Her son had died earlier in the year after contracting a respiratory infection while on holiday in Venezuela. The report concluded her current psychological state could be "advantageous to the company". Corrigan wondered what he was getting himself into managing this team. He toggled back to her profile picture. He was certain it had been updated since her son's death. There was something penitent there that did not rest easily with her otherwise determined gaze into the camera.

Having two women in senior positions on the programme was unusual. Of course, they were both from high-ranking families and there was no disputing their experience or knowledge. At the same time, even Belinda Reece was known to frown on advancing women into senior roles. They must have had or made connections as he assumed Jonathan had been forced to do in order to breach the firewall on anyone who wasn't white or Asian.

Finally, he arrived at Ramon Lopez, the man who would serve as his PA. Lopez was not unattractive. His hair was jet-black, his skin a warm brown. His expression could not be read, though, and this unsettled him. Lopez had spent months in Ulmer's direct employ, having been a manservant before the CEO promoted him to his PA, a station the South American had retained for three years before being assigned to the program.

Clearly been placed for a reason. But he was assigned to Mercer, not me...

Lazarus looked up at him, and there was something in the cat's eyes. The animal appeared wary, if not afraid. Corrigan patted its head, but its dread was not alleviated. Then the cat went stiff under his embrace. Aborting his searches, he leapt up and rushed him through to the bedroom and laid him on the bed. The cat's breathing was laboured, and it paddled with a paw.

He called B4 and instructed the droid to find a vet who made house calls. The machine whirred into action, and he had to resist the urge to kick it where it balanced, running its search. The droid's eyes widened when contact was made. It was standard for the conversation to be withheld, and Corrigan knew it was over when B4's eyes resumed their normal size.

Within the hour a vet arrived and B4 brought him through to the bedroom.

The professional examined the patient. "These old cats," the vet said, "Putting the animal down's the only thing for it."

Corrigan called the vet a charlatan and ordered him from the house.

B4 rolled over and her eyes softened as she studied Corrigan. "I am sorry the vet proved inadequate." The droid moved closer. "He really was a bit of a wet patch."

Corrigan blinked at the familiarity of the phrase, yet couldn't place it.

He lay beside his faithful friend. There was nothing to be done, but he would comfort Lazarus nonetheless. His wristpad pinged, and he struck it to silence, but it had instead accepted the incoming call.

"Mr Corrigan?" He recognised the voice and almost cried out. "Mr Corrigan, it's Jonathan."

Corrigan held onto Lazarus and kissed his fur. "It's not a good time."

He was about to switch off his wristpad when a halo-screen opened, and Jonathan appeared in the room.

"What's wrong with your cat?"

"He's dying!" He felt humiliated weeping over a cat, but he could not control his emotions.

Jonathan told him not to worry, a team would be with him in the next fifteen minutes. "Give them five minutes with…what's his name, your cat?"

"Lazarus."

The young man placed a hand to his forehead. The image then flickered and disappeared.

Corrigan told Lazarus how sorry he was, and the cat placed a paw on his nose and uttered a struggling meow. He buried his face in the animal's belly and stroked his back.

When the DRT team arrived, Corrigan instructed B4 to let them in. They ushered him aside and administered medication and placed sensors on the cat's head, their tasks completed quickly and quietly. One of the technicians told him the cat would go peacefully now.

"Goodbye, gents," the droid said, "and thank you for dragging a reluctant man into the present age."

Corrigan ignored the verbose droid, focussed as he was on a vial of blood in one of the technician's hands. It mattered not what they had taken, as the cat no longer appeared afraid or in pain. He was breathing heavily, but it was not as desperate. Lazarus purred as Corrigan stroked him, and the sound lulled him to sleep.

When he awoke, the little corpse was dry and stiff. Corrigan kissed his cheek, and then laid a towel on the floor and put the cat on it. He fetched candles and placed them around him.

He would question the Mecha-Butler regarding her speech malfunctions later, but for now, he sat grieving for his ragged cat.

10

Jonathan came to Harvey Road and helped Corrigan dig a hole in the garden. They performed a simple ceremony, during which a clipping of Lazarus's fur was taken and placed in a jar. B4 prepared tea and they sat in the front room. The man across the street took intermittent drags on another joint.

"I wish he wouldn't do that," Jonathan observed.

"The family appeared a few weeks ago, moved in," Corrigan said. "The father's using Belushi Grey." He rolled up a sleeve and mimicked slapping a patch to his arm.

Jonathan agreed he looked the sort, but he seemed to be considering a question. His face tightened, and his eyes no longer focused on the world outside the flat.

"What is it?" Corrigan asked.

"I'm working on a research program at DRT," Jonathan said. "There's a fair bit of interplay between departments and fields of inquiry. Adler's not as close to some of the research, but he reminds us we've a duty to identify opportunities." When Corrigan frowned Jonathan asked, "You're aware of DRT's cloning program?"

"Katherine Meregalli's heading that."

"Yes, but she's not alone. We're working on non-human

subjects. I'm on a research project in Hoxton. I'd have said it was an accident – I mean my becoming involved – but for Adler."

Corrigan placed his cup down. "Having given him a name like Lazarus, I must've hoped for a resurrection, but a clone would never be *my* Lazarus."

"Which is why the team downloaded a copy of his brain," Jonathan said. "It aligns with company policy on exploiting opportunities... I mean, taking a prototype out of the office. I– "

Corrigan held up a hand to halt his companion. He understood what had been done. "It might one day be possible," he said, "and for that I'm eternally grateful."

Nothing further was going to develop between the two men, but Corrigan felt they had established a friendship. He expressed as much to Jonathan, who confirmed a similar belief. Friendship was more important and valuable than anything, they agreed.

Corrigan studied Jonathan's face. Although they had uttered the right words in the right way, he felt certain there was no future for them. They were parting, and Corrigan had no doubt the younger man would soon forget him.

11

Corrigan was summoned to DRT's central office to meet Ulmer. He had B4 arrange a cab and was pleased when Bohdan arrived to collect him. It had been absurd to remove the Pole as his preferred driver and even more absurd to consider public transport an option. He apologised for his temporary radio silence, and the cabbie told him not to worry.

"You're a busy man, Mr Corrigan."

"Not so busy as to be discourteous," Corrigan said. "I have this interview, and I don't even know quite what they want me to do." He apologised again and segued into a change of subject. "What do you think of cats?"

"I liked yours," Bohdan said. "He seemed sad somehow."

Corrigan told the driver Lazarus had died, and accepted his condolences.

"I had a dog when I was a boy," Bohdan said. "He was a dumb old thing, and he followed me everywhere. We'd walk through the woods near Rajsko and the older boys would leave me alone because Lenin was with me." Corrigan chuckled at the name, and Bohdan explained the old mutt had a bearded chin.

The cab flew through the mist and its wipers slugged back and forth over the windscreen. Corrigan could see his reflection in the window, a man passed his prime.

"You look dapper in a suit," Bohdan said.

Corrigan didn't acknowledge the compliment the driver voiced into the rear-view mirror. He continued to study his own reflection and, as he considered it, his heart stung. The cynical creases and sweeping yet scoffing eyebrows; lips as thin as earthworms and the nostrils flared unimpressively. Bohdan swung the cab down to street level. He disembarked, and asked Bohdan to wait for him.

"I'm on the meter."

"I'll expense it."

Corrigan was directed up to the 129th floor. He stepped into the lift and pressed the button. The interior was a mirrored fairground maze: he was surrounded by bisected reflections of himself. He hadn't noticed that before, distracted as he had been by Belinda and her word *presumptuous.*

"Good morning, Michael," he said.

The receptionist glared from behind the counter. His face was as pale as ever; his blue eyes too bright beneath a shock of black hair, as if Katherine Meregalli had engineered him. Corrigan was instructed to follow the corridor around to the right and past the boardroom, where he would find Ulmer's name plate on his office door. He was told to knock and await acknowledgement before entering.

Corrigan thanked him, but before he left he beckoned

the receptionist to lean in closer. Michael remained rigid, but on a second beckoning complied. When he was close enough for Corrigan to whisper, he said, "Belinda says you lack enthusiasm."

The receptionist snapped back, his eyes fixed, too bright.

Corrigan smiled and turned away, and felt a stir of power as he did.

He located Casper Ulmer's door and knocked. A conversation was being wrapped up.

"Come in," a loud and familiar voice then called.

Behind a vast mahogany desk was the man he had come to know as Blake Adler.

"Sorry for the subterfuge," Ulmer said.

He assessed Corrigan the way a magician might do; the prospective program manager the punter, and Ulmer the mesmeriser.

"Why *should* I give this role to you, eh?" Ulmer suddenly asked. "And for Chrissake stop fidgeting and take a seat."

The question was one Corrigan had asked himself. He knew nothing about the science other than what he had picked up from the pre-interview documentation and B4's additional research, but the concept of whole brain emulation had an allure, one he was disinclined to dispute.

"I suppose," he said, "humanity is driven by a need for continuance and, in this age, we're travelling nowhere fast. People may not sit still long enough to register the fact, but it squats on us like the weather. Other avenues for our continuation have become essential."

Ulmer leant over his desk to study the prospective manager once again. "And the lights could go off at any time," he said. "We're travelling a highway to hell. Sometimes wonder if it wouldn't be wise to cut to the end, but surely nothing's more compelling than self-preservation?"

Corrigan took a moment to reflect, attracted by a paperweight on the desk, an orange porcelain frog perched on a fallen log. Behind this was a well-groomed bonsai tree. Beyond was a display case full of winged creatures; an array of beetles and dragonflies by all appearances caught in mid-flight, pierced by pins and heading towards an arrangement of similarly impaled butterflies and small birds.

"Circumstances," Corrigan ventured, "oblige humanity to step into the unknown, and had circumstances been–"

"More compelling," Ulmer interjected. "*Yes*. We'd move at *greater* velocity! Right now, however, we're stuck, pinned down like that dragonfly you keep staring at." The CEO stood up and his booming voice rolled off the walls. "Reece Tower is situated behind the Tate Ultra-Modern. You shouldn't have any trouble finding it."

When Corrigan failed to respond Ulmer sighed. The air-con hissed, but sweat dappled his forehead, even though the room was chilled.

"And don't take any of our *scientific beauties* at face value," he then stated. "Meregalli's a tangle of neurotic nerve endings; Goeth's a Kraut first and foremost, and

Fuse's a first-rate technician, but he's a mystic when you take him to task. And don't mention his brother, that's a sore spot. Though, from all accounts, the boy's a whizz, so might be worth getting to know him. Then there's Harding – a manipulative, downright masculine type."

Corrigan stared at the CEO.

"You have to be inducted," Ulmer continued, "before you join the team underground. Secrecy is of utmost importance, and you'll be thoroughly checked and tested before you're allowed anywhere near our facility. We need to be sure your reading list hasn't distorted your view of the order of things. Us capitalists can be a bit wary of elevating Floaters to positions of authority, but I trust you're intelligent enough to understand that no one ever voted you in either. That's not how the system works, Corrigan."

"Those old books of mine are more mementos than anything."

Corrigan fidgeted in his chair, sweating more as he made his excuses. The invasiveness of the CEO's knowledge made his heart pound. Ulmer must have eavesdropped on his latest conversation with Hattie. *Floaters can always be flushed, Bobbin.*

"Even a bit of Dickens could get you perceived as a commie," Ulmer said. "But that's partly why I *want* you for the role. People management is more your forte than mine. The team isn't working together optimally. I want you to get in there, get *connected.*"

"Yes, teaming is one of my core skills."

"Don't feed me your consultant bullshit," Ulmer growled, which triggered a brief spell of coughing. "What I *want* is a connection to our team down there. I want you to be my eyes and ears as much as anything."

"Yes, of course."

Corrigan then found himself dismissed with a wave of a hand. He returned to reception and told Michael to arrange an induction. He was satisfied when the receptionist called him Mr Corrigan. But the man refused to look at him and navigated to a layered schedule. Lines of longitude and latitude lay on top of one another, and he reached in and pulled dates and time slots from various calendars and wrapped them up in bundles. When a green loop encircled two clusters of names, Michael tied them together and moved them to the right of the screen.

"We can fit you in Monday the 15th," he said. "Casual attire is acceptable and I'll forward the details. Given it's an NDA, no agenda can be provided."

"Thank you, Michael. And, just for the record, I'm sure you would be enthusiastic," Corrigan said, "given the proper conditions." He was rewarded with a slight discolouration of the receptionist's pallor.

Corrigan stepped into the lift, avoided his reflection, and made his way back to street level. Bohdan was beside the car, and he opened the door for his passenger. They rose to 350 feet and levelled off in the drizzle, where a rumble of thunder could be heard.

"Don't hear that much these days," Bohdan observed.

"Just fate moaning in the distance," Corrigan said.

"Jupiter's an old man now. He can no longer deliver anything as magnificent as a storm."

There were no cyclones, or even decent downpours anymore. The skies remained laboured but unable to drop their payload. Ulmer's words repeated on him: They *were* on *a* highway to hell.

12

Corrigan decided to power B4 down and package her up for return. The droid's familiarity mode had overstepped, and he could not help but notice the way she mimicked not only his mother's voice but also her attitude. This, he assumed, was some form of augmentation algorithm designed to seek other associations. Corrigan had frequently impersonated his mother to amuse the cat. No doubt the droid had saved and implemented some of what it had heard.

As a final act as her master, he had asked the droid to investigate a refund. The droid explained Mecha-Servant. co had been acquired by DRT and a full refund was available to him as an employee. The annoying little droid also advised him an upgrade model was available at no additional charge.

"An upgrade," Corrigan said.

"Yes," B4 replied, widening her eyes. "You may order an upgraded Mecha-Butler with a number of new features, including lifelike face and hands. You may also order a Mecha-Child or Mecha-Partner. Honestly, though, if you'd only get your eyes seen to, you'd soon find a real man."

Before he set off, Corrigan sealed B4 up in her box.

He thought of this as the funeral he never arranged for his mother. Hattie's bohemian butterflies had disappeared many years ago and her more current friends were no more than opportunistic connections, people who would never deign to attend a service for a woman who had done what was necessary to haul herself and her son up that impossibly tall ladder from Transient to Non and from there to the elevated position of Worker. He would arrange collection and return when he got home.

Bohdan collected him on time and conveyed him to the office in Hoxton, stepping outside of the cab as was his custom. Corrigan patted his arm and headed towards the bubble. He was relieved not to find Jonathan behind the desk, but another young man. He did not smile at the receptionist or even acknowledge him other than to announce his name. He was instructed to take the lift to sublevel seven.

The descent was unkind to his stomach, but at least there were no mirrored surfaces. The doors slid open and, to his surprise, Jonathan stood waiting, wearing a lab coat and an open-necked shirt.

"I know I shouldn't have," he said as he guided Corrigan by the elbow along the corridor, "but I requested it." Jonathan registered the incredulity on his face and added, "There are technical steps to the induction. I thought it might be nicer if someone familiar... I mean, with your recent loss."

Corrigan attempted a smile, but was still floundering around in the incredulity.

"I don't want to alarm you," Jonathan said as they walked, "but this is a psych evaluation. You mustn't worry, though, the procedure's painless."

A woman in a knee-length grey dress and a lab coat was waiting for him. Her hair was dark red, which Corrigan figured was bottle-fed. They shook hands and she introduced herself as Regan Thorn. "I have you for today," she said. Her accent was possibly north of Manchester, although it had been eroded by years living in London. "We'll be going through a series of questions and scenarios designed to highlight any concerns from a psychological standpoint." She gestured towards Jonathan and added, "My assistant will attach sensors to your head and take readings."

Corrigan was invited to sit in what resembled a dentist's chair. He leant back and rested his head while she opened a halo-screen and studied his CV. Jonathan busied himself attaching sensors.

"Ouch!"

Regan spun around. "Oh," she said. "I'm sorry. That shouldn't hurt."

The particular sensor on his crown continued to irk him, but the pain was not significant. Regan sat down on a chair by his side and clasped her hands. Her questions were a combination of situational and personal, and he did not find them particularly difficult or uncomfortable. Even questions around the recent death of his mother did not distress him. It was only when she asked him to provide a history of his sexual encounters he began to feel warm.

"I wouldn't ask," Regan said, "if it weren't part of the assessment." She clasped her hands again. "I tell you what, just give me the headlines." Corrigan stared at her. "First sexual encounter?" she suggested. "You know, was it comfortable, in any way dangerous? And then perhaps a quick run through your partners and any, well, peculiarities or fetishes."

Corrigan imagined DRT already knew his first sexual experience had taken place when he was fourteen. He had told enough shrinks and it had probably done the rounds. He had gone swimming and stayed late at the pool because he disliked getting changed with other boys. On this occasion, he went into the shower room and found a teenager towelling himself down. He must have stared at the boy, who insisted he take a closer look if it fascinated him so much. A few slaps had been administered. Corrigan tried to look away, but was forced to his knees.

"So," Regan said, "you were orally raped."

Corrigan never thought of it like that, which was why his mother insisted on taking him to so many shrinks.

"How'd she find out?" Regan asked.

"Hattie, my mother..." Corrigan said, "wanted to know why I was late home." When Regan smiled at him, he sighed and said, "I told her I'd been sucking cock."

Regan, just like every therapist who'd proceeded her, wanted to know why Corrigan expressed it in those terms.

"She annoyed me. I wanted to upset her."

From there, the section on sexual history became easier. He found himself laughing his way through his escapades, and was pleased to see Jonathan smirking behind a virtual monitor. The pain at his crown receded and he expected the session would soon be over. Regan wound up her questions and excused herself. Jonathan did what he could to minimise the pain of removing the awkward sensor, and Corrigan rubbed his head as he was released.

"I'm sorry," Jonathan said. "It's not supposed to hurt."

Corrigan extracted himself from the chair and stretched to free his discomfort. "There are a great many things in life that are not meant to hurt, but do nonetheless."

He asked Jonathan to accompany him back to street level. They walked past the exec's office and Corrigan watched him. He avoided looking into the vacant room. Once back outside in the drizzle, the look of expectation appeared once more on the young man's face. Corrigan recognised it for what it was. All he had to do was lean forward and kiss him and a bond would be sealed. He shook Jonathan's hand.

Bohdan was watching, leaning against his vehicle, and Jonathan waved as they sped off towards Hornsey.

Corrigan smiled at the driver's eyes where they were framed in the rear-view mirror, but Bohdan wore his familiar look of hurt and did not engage him in conversation.

"I'll be off to my new post," Corrigan said when they reached Harvey Road, "and I don't expect I'll have much need of a driver."

"I enjoyed our conversations and, who knows, the world sometimes opens paths no one can predict. I hope ours will cross again, and perhaps we will get a chance to share dinner."

Bohdan stared at Corrigan, the drizzle shiny on their faces, and his expression was not difficult to read. Corrigan felt a rush of emotion he could not contain, and suddenly his face was wet with tears that trickled through the drizzle. Neither man spoke again, both bearing the moment.

Anything could happen in a wasteland.

A green dragonfly flitted past and danced in courtship for a another of its kind. A smaller red insect perched on a white rose petal, its head flicking as it assessed its suitor's ballet. Corrigan marvelled at the simplicity of their interaction and retreated into his flat and stood behind the closed door. He listened to the rumble of the engines as Bohdan took the cab up over the house. It hovered for a moment before speeding off. He walked through the kitchen to the spotless front room, where B4 waited for him with her dilating eyes.

"I hope you're pleased," the droid said.

"I thought I packed you away."

"You can't keep an old girl down."

Corrigan observed the droid, and although he knew the machine was referencing its memory banks as part of an augmented familiarity mode, it still annoyed the hell out of him. "Power down!"

Her lights went off and her eyes disappeared.

Miss Champion shuffled across the silence. Corrigan visualised her white hair, like a naked birch at midnight, her loose skin and her eyes as vacant as space. What had happened to her family? Most likely they had all died, or left her to ruin. She was as alone as a creature could be, yet he thought himself more so.

Let me go down in the hole and remain there.

13

He decided to keep B4 and never put her in a box again. He even gave her a set of instructions for the daily maintenance of the flat while he was away.

It was early morning when he set off and he could see the droid's blue eyes through the front room window. It felt ridiculous, and yet he raised his hand and waved. B4's eyes widened as she absorbed the new experience…and sought an appropriate response. Corrigan waited, and the droid raised a metal hand. He could not dismiss the bizarre notion he had forged a relationship with her. A mechanised substitute for his mother, perhaps? It seemed the memory of her had been preserved on some perverse level by the little domestic unit.

He had not ordered a cab, and did not take the underground or a tram. He'd planned his journey on foot, deliberately. The drizzle wet his hair, which he found pleasant, aware it would be the last surface experience he would have for some time. Of course, he would come up for air on occasion, from two miles beneath the city.

He stood on the crest of Crouch Hill and surveyed London, reluctant to own his part in the tragedy of its unrelenting depression. The city's hover-trams, covered

95

treadmill pavements, and eight-lane motorways remained rammed, as if any reduction in traffic would be a form of capitulation, an acceptance of ecological responsibility. Hover-cars flitted as the dragonflies he caught as a child had done before he tore off their wings. Dull lights flickered on and off on the Thames, its black water as telling as Grimhilde's mirror. Clouds bent double, unable to muster more than the wretched drizzle.

He crossed the river via Millennium Bridge, wading harmlessly through a swarm of tsetse flies. He recalled B4 reminding him to take an Exhale the night before in readiness for the journey. He patted his pocket and felt the reassuring presence of the Serenity lockets she also insisted he take as he passed the malfunctioning droid on his way to the door.

The DRT building was barely distinguishable from the surrounding towers aside from the red light on its roof, a marker for wayward aircraft, and employees. He fixed on this, passing row upon row of unoccupied buildings.

Ulmer had only mentioned Project Egret's previous manager, Malcom Mercer, once by name, otherwise it had been 'the runt'. It had been the runt who slowed progress and failed to sow the seeds of unity. The runt was apparently as short on ingenuity as he was in stature. He reached up and scratched his crown where the drizzle had dampened the scab on his head, and thought of Jonathan.

It's not supposed to hurt.

Reece Tower was encased in plate glass and he approached the entrance via a concrete walkway. The paving slabs were heavy with moss, like fallen tombstones, and he chose his footing with care. Perhaps the uneven surface may have been designed to trip a man up. Perhaps that is what had happened to his predecessor.

Two dark-haired women sat behind an oak desk, their hair pulled back so their faces were tight and severe. The navy-blue suits and white cotton shirts were equally as austere. They wore gold DRT pins on their lapels. They swivelled their leather chairs as Corrigan approached, and he was confronted by a complete lack of anything. His querying look was greeted by one pair of eyes only, which flicked to the right.

The snub struck, and stuck.

He had succeeded in life, many times, and had been a better manager than most, despite his mistrust of ambition. *Always good to increase your skill set,* he mused, his thought submerged beneath dark waters, the Thames perhaps, rippled by the breath of an exhausted god. It had been the current of necessity that had conveyed him downstream, gaining experience in the waters that bore and bored him. Yet the humiliation of the snub. He prickled with it. He wondered whether he had become addicted to the burdens of authority, or perhaps there were other forces at work.

The great god Avarice and his minions.

A security officer, he assumed, stood beside a door at the far side of the lifts, his attire more funereal than corporate, his gold pin in place. Yet he appeared to be a healthy mourner. The young man opened the door, a single, silent movement. When Corrigan glanced back over his shoulder, the man's features clenched, and he dropped his eyes and pulled the door closed.

After four long flights of stairs, he arrived at a concrete cell, where a redhead in a grey suit said, "Good morning." She stood, her skirt tight around her thighs, but she did not look at him.

The humiliation prickled again. Why would no one look at him?

"This is your designated entrance point. The security operative is upstairs because it is your first day. In future please use your ID."

She held a red card-key out on a gold chain, which she deposited in the palm of his hand when he held it out. The card was standard, representative of various other positions where he had been reduced to an account number and password. He slipped it over his head. The wisp of a card had the weight of a pair of manacles.

"This will open the upstairs door," she said, "and allow you to use the lift." She sat and tapped into her virtual keyboard. "DRT requires absolute secrecy as per the NDA you signed. Many of our employees not only work in the subspace but live there. An apartment has been prepared for you." She gestured towards the service lift.

He tried to catch her gaze, but it seemed to be something separate to her skull rather than emanating from it. She pressed a button beneath her desk, and the metal doors parted to reveal a glass lift. He stepped over the threshold and was sealed inside.

The transparent bullet plummeted through sedimentary

layers of silt and clay peppered with prehistoric flint and bone. The pressure built as an orange marker loomed out of the darkness, bold white letters announcing the first mile. The lift was controlled by air pressure, and no sound accompanied its movement. His heart beat in his throat and his stomach ached as it curled in on itself. Sweat trickled between his buttocks, as it had when seated in Adler's Chesterfield.

"Brain emulation," he said.

When the doors opened, a slim woman in a white knee-length lab coat was waiting: Tierney Harding. Her shoulders were soft and round under the coat, and spectacles hung from a chain around her neck. She fingered the chain in quite a delicate way and smiled at him. Her long nails were painted a pale shade of pink. Her face seemed deflated somehow, as if youth had blown it up firm but the passing years had had the effect of an invisible puncture, a slow leak. The whole was bright with an expression of keenness, but also the self-satisfaction he had seen in her CV photo.

"I'm Professor Harding," she said. They shook hands, and one of his prejudices was confirmed by the firmness of her grip. "You can call me Tierney. I was never one for formality, dear, and its *whole* brain emulation." She looped arms with him. "We don't just grab the content, we mirror the functionality, decoding the data traversing those inscrutable synapses, creating independent mechanical brains – more than just temporary accommodation for homeless human minds."

Her Bostonian accent was a drawl he found less irritating than other American inflections. The rapidity with which it was deployed, however, lessened its appeal.

Harding manoeuvred him along the corridor to an office.

"Harbours are what we're constructing," she said. He nodded the way sociopaths are meant to do. "Ports of call; dry docks for weary passengers who can alight until new, stronger vessels are made ready for their eventual reintroduction."

"Reintroduction?"

Harding frowned. "I'll go through it in more detail later but, suffice it to say, the more solvent among us will soon be able to buy extended tickets for the playground."

Corrigan made an on-the-spot assessment, although it was no basis for a professional appraisal: her heart was not in her well-prepared speech. The woman was also unattractive.

"Try and settle in," Harding said as she turned on her low heels and walked away.

14

Corrigan stood in his new office, the full weight of two miles of earth, rock and history pressing down on him. Somewhere between him and the open sky, Lazarus lay in the ground, his body feeding worms and grubs. The aloneness, never far away, settled in.

The man he recognised as Ramon Lopez appeared in the doorway with a pewter tray, his eyes impassive in his boyish, serious face, his black hair combed into a corporate shape. He placed the tray on the desk, stepped back and introduced himself.

Corrigan noted the beautifully carved wooden handles, and the Japanese style reminded him of the bonsai tree in Ulmer's office. He passed his hand over the polished wood of his desk and offered his PA a smile. "What's *this* about?" he asked.

The PA appeared irked as he explained the CEO's family fortune was rooted in the logging industry.

"Yes, I know. The Ulmers spent years deforesting Brazil, Honduras and all those other little countries, like *Venezuela*." He waited a moment to see if Ramon would respond. The PA's lack of comment was emphatic.

Corrigan was pleased to see the tray did not include

a sugar bowl. Although he resisted most temptations, he struggled with a hankering for sweet things. "You take milk?" He looked at the South American, but did not wait for him to respond. He did not like the PA's formality and suggested he call him Robert. Although Lopez still maintained the expression and deportment of an embalmer when he nodded, Corrigan thought the PA was a sweet thing and made a mental note to take care.

He poured for them both and sat down. Peering at the PA over the rim of his cup he asked, "How often do the departments interact?" and gestured for Lopez to take a seat in the armchair opposite. Lopez considered the request before sitting down. "Walk me through the infrastructure, starting with Professor Turner."

"Do you mean *Tierney*?" The sneer slightly altered the man's smooth face.

Corrigan laughed and apologised for having confused the professor's surname. He gestured for the PA to continue, and Lopez explained the professor's name was Tierney Harding. There was no ignoring the severity of his response – a momentary flicker in the black eyes – or the notable twitch of his lower lip as he added, "I thought you'd been briefed, Mr Corrigan."

"I've a terrible head for names," Corrigan said. "I retain detailed accounts of situations from years ago but forget names ten minutes after hearing them. I'll rely on you in that regard." Lopez nodded, and the flicker went out. "I'm sure Malcom must have had similar weaknesses." To the blank eyes he said, "Mercer, my predecessor..."

Ramon Lopez stared at his boss. "I do not recall Mercer having any specific weaknesses." For the first time, the PA picked up his coffee and took a sip.

"That's a *good* answer," Corrigan said.

Lopez appeared to assess the creases of Corrigan's face, the crow's feet and the grooves on either side of his nose. Something akin to a smile flirted with his lips, barely discernible, and vanished. Corrigan asked how Harding fit into the overall structure, and the PA adjusted his body in the chair, which uttered not a creak, as if unable to register its occupant's weight.

"She designed the company's WBE prototypes."

"Is she arrogant?"

"I don't think so. Professor Goeth tends to steal any limelight."

"Where are we in terms of budget?" When the PA stared at him, Corrigan frowned. "I need to know our spend to date and where we are against what we've been allocated. If you can't measure it, you can't manage it."

Lopez studied the new manager for a moment before replying. "There is no limit on spend, no budget restrictions. Of course, we *do* keep an eye on spend, but the assumed value of the end product...anything required is provided."

These words triggered Corrigan's acute imposter syndrome, and he imagined Belinda Reece muttering the word *presumptuous* to herself. Who was this upstart? This Floater who did not know his place? He nodded, just to do something while he considered a better response.

"I've never managed anything with no upper limit," he

then conceded. "I suppose we're all here to give Mr Ulmer what he wants, no expense spared."

Ramon Lopez seemed to shrink momentarily on mention of the name Ulmer, but he soon reasserted his ironclad defences. "Perhaps the focus should be on galvanising the team."

"Yes, better collaboration." Corrigan smiled. "And there are just the three departments: Brain Emulation, Robotics and Genetics?"

"Professor Goeth prefers to call his team the *Design Pod*."

"Of course he does."

Ramon eyed the manager closely. "Well, they design anything from office chairs to androids."

Corrigan nodded, thinking yet again that he had no idea what role he was supposed to fulfil. *Get connected.* That's what Ulmer had said. He must get around and figure out what the team was working on, assess what they needed, why they were so siloed.

"There are sub-divisions beneath each of the main teams," Ramon said.

"Tire me with that later. What I need is background; insights into why the divisions haven't been integrated." Corrigan stood up and Lopez watched as he moved towards the door. "The head of Genetics is Professor Meregalli?"

"Correct." He pushed back his chair. "Meregalli's in control."

"That's not what I heard." Corrigan opened the door.

Lopez placed his coffee cup on the tray and joined him.

Corrigan observed Ramon's face in the long second that passed before they moved into the corridor. There was no agitation whatsoever; the implacability was a formidable defence. No one would build walls so high, camouflage and fortify them so well, without having something to protect.

15

Lopez struck Corrigan as sharper than average, not someone who would fail to realise when he was being played. Of course, he hadn't mistaken Tierney Harding's name for Turner and only deployed the tactic to lull his PA into a false sense of security. Although Corrigan had a good head for names – he retained the detail of everything from employee records to financial statistics – his sense of direction remained irreparably poor. Luckily, Ramon was well acquainted with the facility.

An A Class Guardian came up to greet them in the corridor leading to Robotics. It was a similar model to the one demonstrated by Draseke, but it moved differently. Its head was the same, translucent as a dragonfly's, dark matter undulating within like a foetus or a tumour. The android greeted them and tilted its head.

Corrigan turned to Lopez. "They *speak* now?"

"*I* speak now," the Guardian said. "My name is Gregor. Professor Goeth asked me to look out for you."

Corrigan stared at the smooth reflective surface where the android's face could have been. The machine righted its head and the manager enquired as to whether it could see.

"I certainly can."

Corrigan followed the Guardian and Lopez along the corridor.

"The head of an A Class Guardian is also an eye," Lopez explained, dropping back in step with Corrigan. "These provide a one-hundred-and-eighty-degree field of vision."

"There are no audible hydraulics, or unpleasant pings or whirring?" Impressed and yet a little bemused, he turned to Lopez. "Gregor is a far more advanced model than the one Draseke presented to the board."

"He is a recent experiment," Lopez said, his face assuming an even greater severity.

"A successful one," Gregor added.

"Why has it been given a name?" he asked, catching up with the android. He reached up towards its featureless dome. "Are you a bedbug, Gregor?"

"No, I am *not*," the Guardian said and grasped the human wrist, which it restrained only for a moment. "In answer to your question, I named myself, and I did not need the help of *Mr Kafka* in doing that."

Corrigan's chest tightened, and he reminded the presumptuous machine it was an A Class Guardian, a clockwork *ant* or a wingless dragonfly. It would do well to remember its place. He rubbed his wrist where the metal digits had left their mark. They walked on, and the corridors of the underground facility seemed to close in around him.

As they walked he noticed a length of black cable dangling overhead. It ran on a set of tracks built into the ceiling. The android was attached via a rectangular box on its back.

"It's an umbilical," Lopez said.

"And does Gregor have an emulated brain?" He tried to repress his concern, but his inflection betrayed him.

"No one shares project details with me," Lopez replied. "This model's not so different from the A Class presented by Draseke."

Goeth laughed as he came out of his office to greet them. "The latest A Class cannot be compared with that marionette," he drawled. "As for Gregor, may I tell you what I really think?" His large belly grumbled, and he patted it. "He's a *being*."

Corrigan shook Goeth's hand and conceded Gregor was a clever device. Holding up his hand to halt Lopez, he followed Goeth into the office. The professor left the door open, an oversight perhaps, less noteworthy than his untucked shirt.

"You mustn't insult him," Goeth said. "He thinks in much the same way as you and me. The latest brain emulation program is a near-perfect simulation. As I explained to Harding, there's no point creating a mirror image of an organic brain. It cannot be done. It's preferable to embrace the mechanical attributes and create something different."

"I believe the directors would be disheartened to hear you say so..."

"Yes, they would," Goeth agreed. "That's their nature. They need to acknowledge we're moving towards a bastion; a space where minds can rest until they're ready to be reintroduced to organic recipients. The emulated brain's not necessary for this purpose. If Professor Meregalli can provide donors, the emulated brain becomes a by-product. All this work Harding has undertaken to map and decode synaptic interfaces becomes redundant."

Corrigan suddenly felt tired and struggled to follow everything the scientist said. He reminded Goeth their brief was to enable whole brain emulation and integrate it with AI. He looked around for a place to sit, but every surface and chair was a chaos of storage.

Goeth winked. "Are you interested in knowing what I really think?" He allowed no time for a response. "Science rarely follows a program."

Corrigan insisted it was reliant on rigour. The German countered it was more organic, and went on to say Mercer understood the nature of the program and it was a shame to have lost him. Corrigan stated there must have been performance-related reasons for Mercer's dismissal. The German cut him off and insisted Corrigan's predecessor had been lost, but had not been dismissed.

"Lost?" Corrigan repeated.

"He disappeared, and that was both inconvenient and conspicuous," Goeth said. "Ulmer was forever dropping breadcrumbs in his path."

"Why on earth would he do a thing like that?" Corrigan asked.

"Mercer had a theory about Ulmer. Saw him as a criminal mentality who on some level wanted to be caught." Corrigan stared at the scientist. "One cannot take credit for a thing if no one realises one is *doing* it, Mr Corrigan. Perhaps that is why our CEO plays these games of his, creating characters like Adler to get closer to us and scatter his crumbs before we even know he's the hunter himself."

Corrigan scratched his head, dislodging the scab. Blood wet his fingertips.

Goeth stared at the man the company had chosen as their manager. "Have you ever watched a dung beetle rolling a ball of shit through a desert, Mr Corrigan?" Corrigan could not fathom what the scientist wanted to convey. "The insect can carry an enormous burden and make it look like light work. Sheer dogged persistence got our CEO a long way across that desert, but if Harding delivers the program, those directors of ours will be paralysed, as we have been."

"The board are only interested in bottom lines..."

"And that's why their hair will stand on end! Imagine trying to sell a thing like *that*. Who'd willingly enter complete darkness? If we downloaded your mind to one of Harding's holding tanks," Goeth said, "that being would be severed from your existence immediately."

"I received an education," Corrigan said, "and surely some things go without saying."

"Be wary of making uninformed assumptions. This business is murkier the deeper we dive into it. The new being would awake – if we can be so bold as to use such mundane descriptors – in a space that is absolutely empty."

Goeth paused so his words could percolate. "Dis*lodged* from sensory organs, the mind receives no input. Being used to senses of sight, hearing, touch, taste or smell it may even go insane. It would not be dissimilar to locked-in syndrome, only the mind would be completely locked in, without so much as a clouded perception of the world it inhabits."

"And this had not been foreseen?"

"It has only ever been tacitly acknowledged," Goeth conceded. "No one has been willing to consider the consequences."

"Because it's unachievable."

"*No*! *Being* achievable is what sends shivers down their spines. It's *undesirable,* Mr Corrigan." Goeth rearranged his trousers over his stomach, which growled again. "For a spell, those trapped inside Harding's metal boxes would be completely reliant on the strength of their imagination, which remains an essential deception required to stop the emulate devouring itself. Some of our finer minds will argue..." Goeth dropped his voice to a whisper, and stepped closer to Corrigan. "They'll tell you an emulated mind is unable to *feel*."

Corrigan had been watching Lopez in the corridor, speaking with Gregor. Two other Guardians had approached, and he intuited from Gregor's gesticulation that the android had instructed them. They righted their heads as they took their leave again.

Goeth took another step, and this time Corrigan stepped back. "Gregor is our first experiment," Goeth whispered, "and I assure you he's a sly one. I believe he *does* feel. Perhaps not exactly as you and me, but he's a product of our ingenuity, devotion and love." Corrigan recoiled at that. "Yes, our *love*. Our first apple has not fallen so very far from the tree. He may be disinclined to own these sensations, may even be coding to block them out, but–"

"Can that thing control its own coding?"

"I believe Gregor is seeking a form of independence. I spoke with Professor Harding about this, but she dismissed the idea as if I were an idiot." The professor chuckled, and there was a hardiness to it. "I showed her the anomalies in the program, and–"

"She failed to acknowledge the problem?"

"The professor did not consider it a problem, but a development, and an interesting one." He frowned. "Harding was not the one to *fail,* as you put it."

Corrigan wanted to know whether in the professor's opinion Gregor was a prototype the company could ship out. Goeth advised against it, and Corrigan agreed. He observed the company could not be left without a product.

"No, of course not," Goeth said. "They knew what they were doing when they placed us down here. Our assumed independence was a clumsy ruse. We met to discuss our work almost immediately, but it was and remains a fractious argument. We're all striving towards a common, unspoken goal."

"Immortality," Corrigan said. What a relief it was to have spoken their goal aloud. *That* was what he was there to do. Motivate the team, get them to collaborate as only he could. They must deliver "extended tickets for the playground", as Harding said. As long as Ulmer and the other members of the One Percent Club could attain greater longevity, they could all sleep better at night. The idea infuriated him, of course, made him think of Hattie's bohemians and all the disappeared, those demoted to Transients, people without name, address, or entitlement of any kind. Where they went, no one asked, Broadwater Farm or a ditch, but it was the dread of every Worker, Floater or Non.

He headed towards the door. Humankind's continuance was Egret's *raison d'etre*. The German was fully aware of the facts, and had been from the minute Ulmer tasked him with designing the complex, and Corrigan told him so. Goeth stood open-mouthed, and his hand returned to his stomach.

Corrigan then marched up to Gregor and instructed the android to take him to Genetics.

"Have Harding meet me in her laboratory in half an hour," he instructed Lopez, and followed the android further into the bowels of Earth.

16

Once again Corrigan admired the Guardian's sensual design. Its skin bulged as it moved, stimulated by powerful synthetic muscles. The android paused at an exit and said, "Please excuse me a moment," and reached up behind its back, unplugged the overhead cable and removed a small box from the wall, which it inserted into the empty socket. "I require a transmitter whenever I leave the lab."

"Must be debilitating."

"A minor inconvenience."

"Has the change been scheduled?"

Gregor stopped and turned around to face his questioner. "Development here is so rapid, one might call it ungovernable."

"Good answer. And I *am* the governor."

"Indeed, Mr Corrigan, a role for which you are eminently suited. I had a look at your emulated file. Such an intriguing construction."

Corrigan stared at the android. "My emulated–"

"Everyone's mind is now emulated to the degree possible during induction, Mr Corrigan." The android paused and allowed the manager to regain his composure. "I am sure there is more to you than meets the eye."

The uncomfortable revelation made sense. That bloody sensor hurt as it did because it had to go deep enough to take root in his brain. He hoped they hadn't taken a high-level approximation of his mind, and that a rudimentary simulacrum had sufficed. He realised he had stalled and felt a need to change the focus of their conversation.

"What became of my predecessor?" he asked. "Seems careless to have *lost* him."

"I know very little regarding Mr Mercer, save what I gleaned from Gregory Meregalli."

"Did Mercer make an impression on the boy?" Although he attempted to make his inquiry sound matter of fact, the curiosity was unavoidably apparent.

"Boys are by nature impressionable, and men of integrity and talent are impressive."

"So what did become of Mercer?"

"I am afraid he vanished."

"That was conspicuous, if not *inconvenient*," Corrigan observed.

"It was convenient for *you*, Mr Corrigan."

Corrigan felt the pressure of his compressed lungs. "Has Professor Goeth programmed you to be impertinent?"

The Guardian bent down so its dome was level with Corrigan's face. "I have not *been* programmed."

"Then kindly explain how you came to be." Corrigan's heart rate accelerated, and the scab on his scalp throbbed. It required resolve not to scratch it.

Gregor tilted his head. "I'm Professor Meregalli's son. More correctly, I suppose I am the remnants of the child.

The boy was an inferior physical specimen, gifted with a fine intellect."

Corrigan recalled looking at a photograph of Gregory Meregalli, but the image failed to come into focus now, when he needed it the most. "I never understood how he ended up in what's left of the rainforest."

"The boy was frustrated living underground and wanted to see the world."

"Venezuela's a very specific part of the world."

"Ramon was visiting his aunt and agreed to take the boy with him."

Corrigan raised his hands. "And she allowed her son to be downloaded?" he said. The interrogatory tone seemed to stall the Guardian. Gregor did not move or speak. Perhaps the transistor was no longer able to interact with the ghost in the machine. Corrigan moved closer to inspect the device, and its head jerked as it rebooted. "Professor Meregalli approached her colleagues. She was insistent Professor Harding salvage what she could. Given Harding's work remained incomplete, and the child was feverish, it might have been a disaster if it had not been managed so well."

"There are those who'd call it a miracle."

"Only when I was a child, did I speak of childish things, Mr Corrigan. The professor was desperate, but the others might have dissuaded her had they been so inclined."

"And the board authorised the procedure?"

"Everything is monitored by the company. Any activity left unhindered carries assumed sanction."

Corrigan felt his authority slip, and it would slip further if he remained passive. One flush away from Transient status; disappeared like Mercer. He ordered Gregor to take him to Professor Meregalli.

"Or do you call her mother?" he asked, his voice fully loaded.

"Professor Meregalli will have nothing to do with me."

17

They were met at the Genetics lab by two plastic-clad technicians in gas masks and led to a chamber where Corrigan was instructed to remove his clothes. The Guardian watched the human undress and tilted its head as he assessed the man's body. "You have aged well."

Corrigan tried to convince himself the android merely absorbed data, and analysed and commented upon it, but it seemed an unlikely assessment. Corrigan and his mechanical companion entered the shower and were sprayed with a fog of disinfectant which hissed from stainless steel nozzles. Corrigan was, quite naturally, reluctant to inhale. He was then dried under streams of hot air, and a door opened onto a second chamber where he put on the protective clothing provided. The gas mask seemed draconian, but he accepted it.

Katherine Meregalli was parading the facility in a white boiler suit that clung to her contours, making her small breasts more prominent. Although her cropped hair was severe, it did not diminish the beauty of her features. When she saw them, she marched up to Corrigan and demanded to know why he had brought *that thing* with him.

Corrigan held out his palms to assuage her. "I was only

made aware of the situation with the two of you en route."

Meregalli folded her arms sharply across her breasts. "It can't resist the urge to share."

Gregor approached them with a hand over the space where a human heart would be. "You are unjust. I can still access the part of my being that has a biological connection to you."

"Don't you dare!" Meregalli snapped. "You stole his heart, but you can't make it beat."

Gregor turned to Corrigan and adopted a regretful and conciliatory tone. "Professor Meregalli has failed to make an organic copy of her son."

Corrigan watched as they argued over whether the boy was lost, or if he was in the Guardian, and whether his desires and aspirations were still active or had been archived. Regardless, the Guardian asserted the boy's thoughts remained fascinating from a psychological perspective. Gregor continued to bate the professor, who insisted it was impossible to archive a living being.

They looked at Corrigan as if he could provide the answer to the riddle of their predicament. The manager's back straightened and his expression darkened. He concluded that whatever had been done fell outside agreed procedure.

Meregalli threw her hands in the air. "Procedure has never been defined. For all his strengths, Mercer never insisted on documented processes. He embraced the organic nature of what we're doing. The project's been floundering without him." The severity of her glare intensified. "*Egret*...what a silly name."

Corrigan fixed her with a steady look. "I assume it's to do with migration."

Meregalli stormed through the lab, and her technicians stepped back to avoid her. Gregor watched her and suggested following. "He is not lost, the boy," the android said. "Unlike Mr Mercer, we know precisely where he is. We are conjoined. There would be no point extricating one from the other. We have attained symbiotic unity. Any attempt to separate us would be invasive."

"Did you just threaten to defend yourself?" Corrigan asked as they pursued Meregalli.

"No intervention is planned. It would be as pointless as trying to extract one part of you from another. You are a whole and so am I."

Corrigan commanded the Guardian to stop. When it swung on its axis, he asked, "Is that boy's mind still operating?"

Gregor moved closer to the manager and leant over him. The dark matter seemed to pulse and swell within the confines of its head. The android remained there, silently assessing, its sensors taking temperature and scent readings for analysis. Unwilling to wait any longer for an answer, Corrigan marched past the android and continued to follow Meregalli. A corridor curved to the right, which opened onto a lab. The professor went to sit behind a lead-topped desk, a glass booth positioned on a gallery above. The container was filled with fluid in which a child floated. Corrigan stared up at the experiment and removed his mask.

Meregalli was on her feet in an instant. "You should have kept that on! We've no way of knowing if you're infectious!"

But Corrigan's eyes were on the child. It was perhaps five years old; its arms and legs positioned as if sat at a desk. "I haven't been anywhere near Venezuela," he said.

"He's alive but unconscious," Meregalli said, seeing Corrigan's intense focus. "The problem is developing the mind without utilising it." She placed a hand to her forehead and streamed a halo-screen from her eyes. The screen revealed a blue-black image of a brain. "If you look here in the parietal lobe… If I were to show you a scan of a healthy brain, you'd realise there are defects. The condition is called dysarthria: the brain atrophies through disuse. If it's not stimulated, it weakens, becomes deformed and dysfunctional." She then sighed and asked him to dismiss Gregor.

Corrigan muttered, "You're free to go."

"If I am free," Gregor said, "I elect to remain."

The manager continued to look at the screen, mesmerised by the likeness to a psychiatrist's inkblot or a child's carving of a tree in a halved potato. As he lingered over it, an image appeared, a drawing of a tree in which dogs or wolves perched like owls.

Meregalli blinked and the screen disappeared.

"Wait outside for me," he instructed the Guardian. He half expected the android to rebel, but it acquiesced and turned to leave.

"Wait," Corrigan said. Gregor came to a halt and a blue sensor flashed through its translucent dome. "You are an experiment. One I have the authority to terminate."

Gregor tilted his head. "That must be burdensome."

Corrigan waved it away and this time let it go.

He looked around for Meregalli and saw her staring down from the upper gallery. She beckoned him, and he climbed the stairs. When he drew level with her he was confronted by the specimen. The body had gone a blue-grey colour, the hair white, the lips an unsettling red. She assured him it was harmless. The child opened its eyes and stared into the part of him that lesser, uneducated cultures called a soul. Meregalli laughed and the child's features softened, although its gaze remained fixed on him.

"The subject's our third iteration," she said, "the only one to have survived. Unfortunately, he's un-useable, and we'll have to birth him." She smiled at Corrigan's expression. "I'm surprised they didn't go over it. The CEO was fascinated. He asked to be present for the procedure." She ran a hand over the glass, and the gesture was mirrored by the exhibit. "We use these connections to communicate with its brain. Harding's program was deployed to upload and erase donor memories. The program stimulates activity without giving the subject permanent, retainable information; it stops the brain entering a state of atrophy whilst suppressing the development of personality."

"So it's a blank canvass?"

"If he was *that*, he'd be our first success and, as such, he'd be ready for reintroduction."

"That's the *second* time in as many hours someone's used that term."

"We use it to mean the introduction of an emulate mind to a human host, or to a thing like Gregor." The boy behind the glass mouthed words. She watched his mimicry and placed her hand against his. "This subject is spoiled. It developed a personality, has dreams, and is every bit as human as we are."

She stepped around the booth and grabbed Corrigan's hand. He looked down at her white skin where it grasped his liver-spotted fingers as she led him towards another chamber, which housed a series of tanks. Each contained a foetus or child at varying stages of development. He stopped, and she released him. She made a sweeping gesture. "It's only a matter of time."

The manufactured human subjects reminded him of the brainless chickens at the Origination Produce factory. And here, row upon row, Meregalli's eggs were fertilised and grew at an accelerated pace.

"Are they copies of your son?" he asked, restraining his emotion, aware of the ease with which he managed to segregate unsettling experiences.

"Variations on a theme," she sighed. "We altered the DNA and introduced material from other donors. By changing a single molecule, each subject ceased to be a clone." A tear gathered in the corner of her eye, which she wiped away before it could fall.

"I'm concerned your personal attachments are impacting your research."

"My *attachments* are advantageous."

"I've no doubt." It was difficult to maintain eye contact, such was the intensity of her stare. Corrigan felt the scab over his crown pulse. His forehead was hot, and he wondered if a fever had consumed him. "I've other meetings to attend," he said. "We will have an interdepartmental meeting as soon as I can manage it. It feels as if you're all working in isolation, when faster results could be had if we collaborated better…cross-pollinated." He attempted a smile, but there was no energy behind it. "I'll send Ramon to collect you when something is booked."

Whatever blood was beneath her skin receded on mention of the Venezuelan. "Please send someone else. I'd rather deal with the imposter than with Ulmer's bastard." She stared at Corrigan, and he felt the weight of her accusation. "You know," she said, "Mercer was wary of Ramon. I used to warn him about his fixations, but he was insistent, saw things I couldn't. That was his gift. He saw the whole before the crucial pieces were in place."

"I couldn't find anything on him; he doesn't even have a social profile."

"Mercer's a missing piece. He's somewhere no one can follow. *You* certainly never will. Not if you try and force us into a family unit. We work best when we stick to our specialisms. It's *your* job to sew the threads together, not mine or any of the others." There was a sense of triumph to her tone, one he could not square with the look of utter devastation that distorted her features.

18

Corrigan was pleased to find Gregor in the corridor. (It was a relief to be in the company of a being who purportedly had no emotion.) Gregor asked whether his encounter with Professor Meregalli had been useful. "Professor Meregalli's a fascinating but rather stubborn person," he said.

"And attractive," Gregor ventured.

"You find her *attractive*?" He hadn't expected that and shuddered at the thought.

"I am not distracted by such things, but I can assess relative physical merits."

"But are you attracted in a physical sense?"

"I have memories I can retrieve, although they belonged to Gregory Meregalli. I do not have the equipment to experience them fully."

"What equipment?" He turned at the sound of heals clicking, and saw Harding approaching apace. Ramon and Goeth pursued the Bostonian, and not far behind was Jun Fuse.

"He means a body," Harding said.

Corrigan was unable to register her comment. His attention was on Fuse. The tailored fit of the engineer's white suit was as well designed as an A class Guardian.

Harding was wittering on about how minds and bodies are inseparable in organic systems. He had, of course, passed basic science, and ignored her views. Instead, having finished appraising Fuse, he reviewed her physicality. Perhaps she was not as stout as he'd imagined, but there was a brusqueness to her that was unacceptably abrasive.

"Can I tell you what I really think?" Goeth said. "It's also vice versa. They're to varying extents dependent on one another – physiology and emotions, I mean." He tucked his shirt into his trousers. "They interact; are links in a chain. But these clever people are not hampered by things as complicated or essential as physiology."

Harding was having none of it. She insisted Gregor was incapable of experiencing emotion, and felt nothing comparable with what humans had at their disposal. She wedged her hands into her lab coat and kept her focus on Corrigan.

"There is perhaps one emotion that I *will* own," Gregor said. "What I feel – if that is the appropriate term – is beyond your comprehension." Its head tilted as it reconsidered its analysis, or recoded a firewall. The dark matter at the centre of its insectile eye was illuminated by an orange glow from within the translucent globe. "I am governed by a need to exceed my current boundaries."

Goeth was delighted. "That makes you a scientist, not an idiot savant!"

Meregalli accused them of squabbling over a toy.

"You're agitated, dear," Harding said, the word *dear* rich with sentimentality. "Perhaps you need a little time on the surface."

"That'd make life a *lot* easier for you, now wouldn't it," Meregalli snapped.

Harding's eyes narrowed. "As a matter of fact, it would. We've been whispering and keeping our heads low for months." She then softened her expression. "You haven't even gone up to grieve."

"He's down here. Why would I want to go up there?"

As their new manager, Corrigan stepped up and insisted this was not the place to be discussing such sensitive matters. He had no idea how Mercer had arranged things, he said, but they would not be having ad-hoc meetings in communal corridors under his watch.

"Mercer was a manager who refused to manage," Harding snapped at that.

"He was more composer than conductor," Goeth added.

"A teller of tales," Meregalli threw in.

"Whatever my predecessor was, he's managed to lose himself." Corrigan looked at each of them in turn, pointedly. "I will be arranging an interdepartmental meeting, and soon," he repeated. "You're all at loggerheads with one another and that undermines the ultimate aim of the program." He waited to see if any further rebellion was forthcoming. The scientists avoided eye contact, so he turned his attention to the silent engineer, "I'd like you to come to my office in ten minutes, Mr Fuse." And then to Lopez, "Please accompany me to my office now."

Fuse nodded and turned away, and Corrigan set off

back down the corridor, Ramon following. It was absurd to focus on Fuse, a mere engineer, one of Goeth's Design Pod geniuses. He knew, of course, that it was always valuable to have alliances among those who worked at the coal face. He was risking a great deal taking on a role like this. He was perhaps as *presumptuous* as Belinda Reece assumed, and the danger implicit in being an upwardly mobile Floater was considerable. He was agitated, and the dread of being unable to bind the team together frustrated him.

"Who the hell *was* Mercer?" he asked.

"We weren't close," Ramon said.

"Did he maintain a roster?" The impenetrable PA stared at him. "Lopez, I need to know the last time these people were above ground." Lopez continued to stare. "Surely Mercer had an annual leave form or a database?" His patience was thin now.

"The core team *never* goes topside, Mr Corrigan."

19

At that revelation, Corrigan asked his PA to escort him to the residential quarters. Fuse would have to meet him there. He needed time to regroup, absorb everything he'd learned throughout the day. His whole head ached now, and he could hear B4 reminding him to reach for a Serenity.

They wove through laboratories, vast storage areas and communal facilities until they approached a space demarcated from the experimental zone by a terra-formed corridor lined with hydroponics – on a grand scale. A vast array of plant life flourished beneath thousands of halogen tubes, and a warm mist bore the aroma of fermentation and new growth. Corrigan heard frogs croaking by a landscaped pool, and recalled the orange amphibian on Ulmer's desk.

"So it's not just vegetation?"

"No, we have livestock, birds and beetles," Lopez said, "among other things." Corrigan waited for the other things. "Reptiles and amphibians have also been introduced."

"Not *re*introduced."

Ramon shook his head. "The life forms were established to generate a more complete ecosystem."

They made their way through rose gardens and vegetable patches, orchards in bloom, and fields ablaze with black-eyed Susan. A herd of sheep ambled over a low hill and trampled daffodils as they did. Although Corrigan could sense the signatures of various artists, the space had a nature all of its own. It touched him as only something natural and yet orchestrated could; a perfect blend of nurtured nature.

In the distance, living quarters reached for a ceiling carved from the black mica of the cavern, a river – over which three stone bridges arched – separating them from the hydroponics. Beneath the apartments were shops, restaurants and cafés. Guardians patrolled the streets, their insectile bodies forming a holistic relationship with the scenery.

Ramon pointed towards the highest tower. "Your apartment is up there. The penthouse."

The reception area was decorated with wooden panels, beams and statues. Pine and oak framed the mahogany, which was trimmed with cedar. The smooth, polished surfaces of the reception made him seasick. He saw a face staring out of the grain: Mercer adrift in a turbulent sea.

Emerging from the lift Corrigan saw a narrow rectangle of dark wood, into which a single door had been cut. It reminded him of a sarcophagus, and he experienced a moment of claustrophobia, a condition he had never suffered from. His scalp throbbed and he saw a flash, an image of a prisoner in an isolated cell. Ramon asked if he was alright and opened the door. Corrigan's lungs inhaled cool air, for which he was grateful.

The ceiling was high over a large, open-plan living area which led to a wall of glass at the rear. A kitchen had been installed to the right, separated by a slab of oak mounted on a rack of shelves. To the left was a bedroom with an en suite bathroom.

Under the hum of the air filtration, he heard a familiar sound, and his heart nearly stopped in his chest. It was impossible, but there he was.

"Lazarus."

This cat was young, and his fur was smooth, but it was Lazarus.

The cat crossed the room and Corrigan knelt to greet him. Lazarus nuzzled his hand and purred the length of his arm and back. The animal then looked up at him, perhaps wondering where his master had been. Corrigan scooped him up, tears coming quickly to his eyes as his senses remembered the smell of his beloved cat.

Ramon cleared his throat.

The manager stood up, but he could not speak. He stared at the young man and, after a moment, Ramon bowed his head. The gesture touched Corrigan. He asked the PA if he could stall Fuse while he took a shower. Ramon nodded. Corrigan buried his face in the cat's fur, as he had always done. He wanted to thank his PA, but his emotions still had control of his voice.

Ramon placed the apartment key on a bedside table and headed for the door.

"Ramon?" Corrigan turned, managing to muster

sufficient control to question his assistant. "Not everyone remains below ground?"

"No. There are those willing to brave the weather."

"Yes, and in the open-air life's not always–"

"All things can be managed if we put our minds to it." Ramon's eyes were black and his features still. "I didn't realise he was unwell. Had I known I never would have taken him."

"Was Gregory brought back to the facility?"

"Harding had the boy isolated in an oxygen tent. Meregalli wanted to be with him, but the infection had to be contained."

"Very well. Just one more thing: what do they mean when they say Mercer is lost?"

"There's no trace of him. Security is tight, yet there is no record of him after his disappearance."

The PA paused for the briefest of moments, and then left, closing the door behind him.

20

Corrigan settled himself on the sofa and typed B4's credentials into a halo-screen, having failed to connect through his wristpad, and an image of the front room at Harvey Road appeared. "B4?"

The droid's eyes widened as they were designed to do when verifying human contacts. "Bobbin, what can I do you for?"

The droid's familiarity settings were apparently still up the creek, and it had again chosen to call him the name his mother used when he was little. He reminded himself to address the problem, and instructed the droid to patch him into the communications network and dial Jonathan's number. A second screen appeared. Jonathan was naked, and an older man rolled away to the right.

"S-sorry for the...erm...the intrusion," Corrigan stammered.

Jonathan pulled a sheet up over his body. "Not to worry, Mr Corrigan. I didn't want to miss your call."

Corrigan held Lazarus up, so the young man could see his handiwork. "I wanted to thank you, but I'll leave you to...erm..."

"It's alright. I'm glad you called." Jonathan repositioned

himself on the bed. "Only, I thought it wouldn't be possible."

The lighting in the bedroom reminded Corrigan of a Caravaggio or Velasquez. Jonathan's lower leg and upper thigh were exposed, his left side under the sheet. He wanted to tell him how beautiful he was, but the idea did not sit comfortably with a stranger somewhere out of shot.

"What did you mean when you said you didn't think it possible?"

"You're two miles down."

"Yes, yes I am." His eyes settled on the thigh. "It's very nice to see you." Jonathan let the sheet slip away a little. "Perhaps we could maintain contact through B4?" He edged closer to the screen and whispered, "It's wonderful to have Lazarus back, and I had to thank you." With that, he murmured a quick *goodnight* and closed the halo-screen.

Lazarus nudged him and nibbled his hand. Corrigan patted the animal's head, but his thoughts were elsewhere.

How'd you know I'm two miles down Jonathan?

Perhaps intuiting Corrigan was not in the moment, Lazarus bit his hand. Corrigan leapt up, and the cat backed away to the other end of the sofa. He inspected his hand and was relieved to find the skin unbroken. He beckoned to the animal, softly, and Lazarus slinked back over.

"You don't know your own strength." Corrigan stroked his back. "I must shower."

He undressed, laying his clothes on the bed. The cat began to tread his trousers, and Corrigan was about to stop him when he noticed a hint of something accusatory in the cat's eyes. The wardrobe contained a row of grey suits. He ran a hand over the familiar fabric. The company had provided outfits from all his preferred designers.

In the bathroom, his favoured brands of gel and shampoo had been placed on the inset shelves. He adjusted the shower's heat and power to his liking and tried to remember being above ground. He thought of his mother but could not find her. He then tried to conjure a single face from his life, but they were blank. Drying himself, he went back to Hattie, and when his memory eventually retrieved her, she was a photographic image, a one-dimensional, pixelated mosaic without a voice. He could not animate her, not for one moment; she was a silent, sterile representation, this woman who had been such a formidable presence in his life.

The sound of the door buzzer startled him.

"Just a minute!"

He dressed in grey trousers and a white cotton shirt. It was cold in the apartment, so he threw on a cardigan and hurried to the door. He must establish an alliance with Fuse, get his *own* eyes and ears on the ground. He too now had access to surveillance, as all DRT management did to varying extents; but he knew, as Ulmer also understood, that it was better to have a more personal connection. He repressed the ever-present internal rumblings that reminded him of his precarious status and the need to prove himself.

Fuse stepped back with head lowered, and then looked up. "Are you settling in?"

Corrigan smiled at his visitor and beckoned him inside. "I must admit, I'm finding the blend of new and familiar somewhat disorienting."

"It's an unfortunate game," Fuse said.

Corrigan walked through to the kitchen and found the wine rack. "What game is that?"

"The company profiles everyone who enters the facility."

He selected a bottle of Merlot. "Not a grape upon a vine, except those grown under sunlamps. Bloody expensive stuff...*real* wine, I mean." He put two glasses on the oak worktop. "But you mentioned profiling."

"We got into a habit." Fuse leant against the worktop and waited for his host to pour. Every curve of his body was accentuated by the material of his suit. "Harding inaugurated it as part of her mapping process or, more correctly, as a precursor to mapping." Corrigan poured. "It was different in the early days," Fuse said. "Goeth's space had been little more than a catacomb."

"I'm aware of the difficulties faced by the early settlers." He picked Lazarus up and draped the cat over his shoulder. Fuse studied the animal as if seeing it for the first time. "This is my cat. My cat who died and was brought back to life by DRT." When the engineer failed to respond, he put the cat down and handed Fuse a glass. "Do you know how the company managed to mirror such a fine level of granularity?" Corrigan then asked. "You know, with the details of my life?"

"Your home was infiltrated. No one's granted access

without being investigated, and you did sit a psych evaluation?"

"Yes, stuck in a chair with a head full of sensors."

"They took a copy of your brain. An approximation at least. Harding's program is limited, but a version of each team member has been taken."

Corrigan placed his fingers on the familiar spot on his crown. "I've developed a horrible headache. Had to pop one Serenity after another. And damn thing bled when they removed one of those bloody sensors. It still does."

"That's odd. They're supposed to rest on the scalp."

"Well, they must've used adhesive. Perhaps it wouldn't stick. It was an odd experience, but I'm sure it was a necessary part of the program. And our very own *Project Egret* seems to be operating at a tangent." When Fuse stared at him, he sighed. "Please don't reiterate what the others have said. I want your own, original view. What you think is important to me," he added, squirming at the last sentence, designed by managers who trained managers to manage.

"We're performing miracles."

"Gregor says that's what you're *not* doing. And what an amusing device he is."

Fuse's eyes narrowed at the mention of the Guardian. He sipped his wine. "He's a child."

"The same thought went through my mind, that he's a child of sorts. An *unfeeling* child."

The engineer locked eyes with the manager. "Gregor demonstrates basic emotion. There's been more than a single instance; in fact, a whole series of anomalies. His mind is not in his head. It's a program..." Fuse hesitated. "And it isn't as stable as Harding says it is."

"Is it developing on its own?"

"I believe it is." Corrigan noted restrained enthusiasm to Fuse's tone. "We coded inhibitors with the newer models and paired down Gregory's file before we introduced it as the basis for the others."

"Let's sit." They made their way to the sofa and sat at opposite ends. "So, they're dumbed down?"

Fuse's posture stiffened, and his eyes seemed to lose focus. "It's unwise to think of them like that, but the anomalies have been eradicated."

"They don't feel?"

Fuse looked at Corrigan with such ferocity in that second that the manager had to lower his eyes. "It's impossible for newer models to experience a comparable level of emotion. Gregor made sure of it." Fuse put his glass on the coffee table, and the wine jolted. "Sorry, it's been a long day."

Corrigan laughed, and took a mouthful of wine. It *had* been a long day, but there were matters to discuss nonetheless, and he hadn't failed to notice the suggestion of suspicion in Jun's eyes.

"I'm quite famished," Corrigan then said. "Perhaps we could venture out before we move onto the more important business of the day?"

"We could order in?"

Corrigan was not in the least bit hungry, not for food.

He wanted to pump Fuse for more information and insight. If some of their core technology was malfunctioning, he needed to understand why no one considered it a problem. He was all for organic processes, but there were limits. This program was as wild and untamed as a rainforest, and he needed to get a handle on it before Ulmer decided to remove him from the role – the ultimate consequence, which Mercer embodied with his conspicuous absence.

21

The table was set on the balcony which overlooked the gardens. Corrigan expected dinner to be delivered by a Guardian and was much relieved when the meal was attended by a waiter who, attentive but not intrusive, served various courses on china plates.

He leant in a little. "How well do you know Lopez?" he asked when the waiter retreated.

"Ramon's a loyal employee."

"That's a deliberate answer," Corrigan said. Fuse's features locked defensively, so he softened his tone. "The way you speak, I'd take him for more senior." Fuse lowered his head but raised his eyes. The elegance of the gesture made Corrigan's heart race. He took a sip of wine. "Can I trust my PA?" he then asked.

"Ramon's a loyal employee." Jun picked up his glass. "He's DRT through and through. I know it's naïve because no one can act without constraint, but I insist on a semblance of independence."

Corrigan assured him he was not alone in that respect. "Tell me about Mercer," he said, glancing towards the kitchen, not wanting the young waiter to either overhear or interrupt what might follow.

"What do you want to know?"

"His last whereabouts would be a start."

"Mercer went walking with Katherine. He was a good listener. She unburdened herself and they said goodnight. He went off to inspect the new tunnel and that's the last anyone saw of him."

Corrigan placed his wine glass on the table. "You say he was a good listener?"

"An even better *talker*. He had a variety of conspiracy theories. I'll bore you with them once you've settled in."

"You haven't one for now, just as a flavour?"

Behind the man's eyes Corrigan could see the selection process. "A couple of months back Mercer received a halo-message from Ulmer intended for shareholders. The message was headed **Answer**, and the content read, "Not singular but plural, no need for tea and add a little Sugar." Ulmer had typed the word sugar with a capital S. Malcom was perplexed for weeks."

Corrigan laughed, then frowned, and asked how his predecessor had interpreted it.

"He concluded it related to the name of the project. It should be plural, meaning Egrets rather than Egret, and "no need for tea" meant removing the letter T. Finally, the stress on the S in sugar meant an S was to be added. The name of the project would therefore be *Egress* rather than Egret."

"As in Exodus?"

"Indeed. Or departure. He aligned this with suspicions he already had regarding Ulmer's health."

"I hadn't realised our gracious CEO was unwell. Unhealthy, no doubt, but not unwell."

"He's terminal."

Corrigan took a moment to digest the information. "Like Gregory Meregalli."

"The boy wanted to see the rainforest, but he was a scared little rabbit who needed convincing." Fuse's eyes flashed.

"You knew the boy?"

"Yes, but I don't think he liked me." Fuse seemed to drift off a moment, and the manager scanned the young man's bone structure and soft skin. "Gregory was curious but frightened of going anywhere without his mother," Fuse said. "He was under Katherine's feet, and it interfered with her work."

The waiter returned to the table with dessert and the conversation was aborted. When Corrigan was repeatedly consumed by yawns, Fuse thanked his manager for a pleasant evening and stood up. Corrigan's suspicions were aroused by the engineer's retreat and increased as he watched from behind the half-closed door as Fuse stood beside the elevator chatting with the waiter. The conversation between them appeared engaged, if not affectionate; they had shuffled off their professional coils and connected on an intimate level. Fuse caught his gaze as he left. It was impossible to interpret the young man's feigned smile as anything other than contempt.

The room suddenly spun, as if the effects of a drug had taken hold, but the sensation was less euphoric than acid. It was more like an overdose of Serenity, or drinking too much heavy wine on an empty stomach. Corrigan stumbled to the sofa, lay down on his side and pulled the cardigan over his head. Sweat broke and rolled cold down his back as the scab on his scalp throbbed. Perhaps this was another level in the company's game. He felt synaptic tentacles stretching out inside his head, as if the infiltrator had poisoned barbs along its miniature octopi-like limbs.

He dreamt he had walked out onto the balcony, where the world below was as silent as a lake hypnotised by distant stars. The gardens were lit from below, and shadows were cast up the cavern walls towards the sedimentary layers of silt and clay, peppered with prehistoric flint and bone, which cut them off from the world of real living things. Grasping the rail, he gasped, the experience of being alive more lucid in that moment than it had ever been. The weight of the world no longer threatened to crush him. Earth's crust was a protective wall through which man's petty aspirations could not penetrate.

22

Corrigan's wristpad pinged, and he sat up sharply in bed. He had no recollection of going to bed but did recall the sudden fever that had sent him stumbling for the sofa. He was relieved that whatever it was appeared to have passed. Perhaps the DRT octopi had bedded in and settled. The cat climbed up onto his chest and meowed in his face. He pushed it aside, and Lazarus hissed as it leapt to the armchair, narrowing his eyes.

"I'll have you sent above ground if you don't behave."

The cat let out another loud meow, and rubbed its head against the armrest. It warmed Corrigan's heart, the sight of that. He opened a voice message from B4: "One of that lot from across the road flung a rock through the front room window. Don't you worry, though, I chased off the mongrels and arranged for a glazier to repair the damage and collect the broken glass."

Corrigan had to wonder if a biased algorithm had triggered the term mongrel in the strange little droid's befuddled head. He called the flat, pleased he could still contact B4. It had obviously been an oversight on the company's part, one he could only hope they continued to overlook. A screen appeared and B4 said, "Morning,

Bobbin."

The manager shook his head on hearing the name again. He surveyed the room and saw no evidence of any incident. The glaziers had been and gone. B4 had dealt with the event efficiently, despite her continuing malfunctions.

Corrigan went to the kitchen and prepared coffee, and asked B4 to go outside. The droid asked if he meant to the garden, and Corrigan explained he meant Harvey Road. She unlocked the door and manoeuvred out onto the pavement.

"Weather's not changed," he said.

B4 assured him no meteorological variations had been forecast for the remainder of the year.

Corrigan asked the droid to make her way to the top of the road. As she whirred and hovered to the crest of the hill, Corrigan asked her whether she had a defence mechanism.

"I got quite the stinger if I should ever need it, Bobbin."

"Don't call me Bobbin."

"I thought you liked it."

He took his coffee and sat on the sofa as if watching the show.

"You need to order a cab, with Bohdan as the driver," he said.

"For whom?"

"You."

"Where to?"

"The DRT office in Hoxton."

The droid complied and ten minutes later the hover-cab arrived. Bohdan stepped out of the vehicle wearing his brown leather jacket. He leant down towards the droid's face. "Good morning."

Corrigan returned the greeting and the Pole stepped back and laughed. "Mr Corrigan, I hadn't expected to hear from you so soon." The delight in the driver's voice made Corrigan's heart pound.

"Can you take B4 to the DRT office?"

"You mean the bubble?"

"Yes, the bubble."

The droid was secured on the back seat and the cab set off. Corrigan watched as they flew over the drizzling city.

"It's strange couriering a droid," Bohdan said.

"I couldn't trust anyone else."

"Can I see you?"

Corrigan instructed B4 and his own face appeared over the droid's.

Bohdan smiled into the rear-view mirror. "Good morning, Robert. I see you've a new cat."

Corrigan explained the cat had been reintroduced...and provided a potted story of how Jonathan had managed to download a copy of the cat's brain and have it transferred to a cloned body. Bohdan seemed to flinch, or shudder.

"I need you to check up on Jonathan for me," Corrigan then said. "I don't want to see him, and it's important he doesn't see me or B4, but we must get close enough to monitor his comings and goings."

Bohdan's face shadowed with hurt, as was his customary reaction. Corrigan assured him he had other reasons for watching the young man and said he needed Bohdan's absolute trust. The seriousness of his tone had the desired effect; the cabbie reassured him he would do exactly as Corrigan needed. Corrigan gazed at the driver, and his gut tightened like a coiled snake.

B4 was deposited on the street outside The Merry Slaughter, and Bohdan leant down and asked, "Is it safe to leave our little lady unattended?"

"Watch who you're calling a *lady*," B4 said.

"Mecha-Butlers have a mean sting if anyone interferes with them," Corrigan said. "Don't you, B4?"

"Yes, Bobbin, I've a *proper* sting."

Bohdan laughed when he heard Corrigan's nickname, and although he was reluctant to abandon B4 he promised to remain on call. He leant down to say goodbye to the droid, and the way the driver's body flexed made Corrigan's loins ache.

B4 parked herself opposite the bubble that served as an entrance for DRT's subterranean office and masqueraded as a device for sifting recyclable material. The view across the street was clear, and Corrigan instructed her to record all movement and to identify Jonathan the moment he appeared. B4 had a record of their guest, from when Lazarus had died, and matched appearance, voice, and posture. She knew who she was looking for. Corrigan then asked her whether she could record conversations from such a distance.

"Yes, but I'll need to track the target if the conversation is being held in transit."

Corrigan told her to remain where she was and to follow Jonathan only if it was necessary. B4 acknowledged his instructions. She would remain until 6.30pm, at which time she would request collection.

23

When the buzzer sounded, Lazarus hurried to the door, followed closely by Corrigan. He opened it and the cat hissed at the Guardian.

"Professor Harding sent me to invite you to breakfast," Gregor said. "She's at Café Seven and thought it would be nice to catch up."

Corrigan instructed the Guardian to let the professor know he would join her in a few minutes and sent it on its way. Lazarus hissed again as Gregor backed into the awaiting lift. Corrigan assured his feline friend he did not like the android either and made his way to the bathroom.

Am I in your head, Gregor? And – if I am – can you feel what I'm feeling?

Fuse's retreat replayed itself in his mind and he watched himself scowl in the mirror. He undressed and stepped into the shower, which adjusted to the temperature and power he had previously selected. The showerhead twisted and turned to follow him.

Satan tempt me not, for I am so very weak.

Wrapped in a towel he pulled his right eyelid up and pressed a lens into place. He paused to see if it would settle. When it did, he did the same with his left eye. Behind him, in the steam, he thought he saw movement. He focussed, and the apparition evaporated.

Are you hiding, Mr Mercer?

He made a mental note to arrange a full-scale search of the facility. The man or his remains must be somewhere. He shuddered at the thought of death. His earliest nightmares were spells cast by the ultimate predator. It swam towards him, a shadow hidden among other shadows. As it closed in, he became aware of its mouth.

The buzzer sounded again. The now-familiar waiter stood in the doorway with a silver coffee service in hand. Corrigan directed him to the kitchen. He studied the young man, who was on the tall side of five feet. He was structurally sound, and there was intelligence in his eyes; a depth of thought he did not expect to find in a servant.

"What's your name?" he asked.

"Arthur, sir."

"That's a name with dignity and authority."

The waiter asked if there would be anything else, his eyes fixed on the manager. Corrigan recalled Fuse's servile and ingratiating manners with a tremor of anger.

"No, Arthur," he said, as if the value of the name had depreciated, a stock in freefall, barrelling towards the solid floor of ruin. "That'll be all."

Arthur stared at him and judgements formed, and lingered, behind his dark eyes.

"You must excuse me," Corrigan said. "I can be harsh first thing."

"There's no need to apologise." Arthur performed a

curt bow, more of a sharp lowering of the head, and left.

Corrigan took his coffee out onto the balcony and switched his wristpad to INDEPENDENT. A hologrammatic screen materialised with the company logo. He said his passcodes and waited while the scanner verified his speech patterns and retina.

"Welcome to DRT, Mr Corrigan," Belinda said. Hers was the smooth voice of the corporation, indeed.

Corrigan instructed the system to locate Arthur Fuse's CV. The document appeared, and he scrolled through it, and then asked for more information about the brothers.

"Arthur and Jun Fuse have the same maternal bloodline, but they are paternally disparate."

Corrigan sipped his coffee. "So, Belinda, my dear, why is a man so well suited to a lab left languishing in the bloody kitchens?"

"Arthur Fuse has been pursuing this career for three years. His interest in the culinary arts is highlighted throughout his CV, which demonstrates a shift in academic concentration from his previous choices in higher education."

Corrigan understood there had been a change of direction but wanted to know why.

"This subject matter is confidential." Belinda's tone had altered. She had assumed the voice he was familiar with; older, less vital, and more world-weary. Corrigan asked whether he had authorisation and Belinda confirmed he did not. "Besides," she said, "the boy lacks enthusiasm."

Corrigan stared at the now-blank halo-screen and

wondered who or what might be staring back. Compelled by an urge to at least know the man's features, he then typed the name Malcom Mercer using the virtual keyboard.

"No data retrieved."

Regardless of where or how he searched, no information could be unearthed. He demanded to know whether this was also confidential.

"Your question does not compute. There *is* no Malcom Mercer."

Death had devoured his predecessor whole. It had digested meat, bones, history and name. Perhaps Mercer was a construct like Adler; a chess piece deployed by Ulmer in a wider, less apparent strategy.

Before logging out, he checked the latest company periodical, DRT Daily News. Above the various financial and business updates the headline read:

FOUNDING MEMBER BELINDA REECE
DIES AGED 117

"Oh dear," he said. "It seems you've departed."

"Yes," Belinda affirmed, "with no extended ticket for the playground."

He remembered he was supposed to meet Harding in a café. Mercer may have been a mystery or a ruse, and Belinda Reece may have entered network heaven, but Harding was real, and he must find out what she wanted.

24

As he approached the table where Harding sat with a cappuccino, he offered her a look of contrition, which she acknowledged with a smile. She asked him to sit. Her Boston accent was richer, more deliberate than when they met previously, but she did not speak at pace. Perhaps this was the result of his having provided her with some unplanned contemplative headspace.

He explained he had been brought coffee by Jun's brother.

The American pursed her lips. "I'd say I wasn't aware, but we all know he's on-site. It's a waste, but conversations have been had and the boy's determined to pursue an alternative career. Such a shame. He has all the right tendencies and intellectual insight. I hate to admit it, but he could be what we need to get us over the line." The way she looked at Corrigan as she spoke made him think she was reassessing him. "It's not easy to admit we need the younger generation," she continued. "Fresh thinking's no longer something that comes as naturally as it once did, especially given we no longer promote diversity." She spooned up froth from her cappuccino but did not raise it to her mouth. "Arthur wrote a paper

Ulmer read and appreciated. Our glorious CEO struggled to accept how innovative it really was. His bigotry skews everything. Arthur being half-white really bothered him. As I'm sure you know, DRT don't hire ethnic minorities. The occasional technician like Jun with a decent Japanese pedigree is good for business but what Ulmer calls *hybrids* are rarely tolerated."

Corrigan felt a pang in his chest as he imagined the difficulties Jonathan faced. Anything would be better than being a member of a declassified family, a clan of transient outcasts. Whatever the young man had done to attain not only Non but Worker status, Corrigan accepted his friend's motive as a compelling one that few could have resisted.

We've all done terrible things, he thought.

Perhaps Tierney Harding intuited the nature of his concern. "Ulmer's not generally bothered about sexuality," she said. "He'd mount a goat if that's all there was. With women, the situation is generally more restricted. Women of colour are automatically excluded along with their male counterparts. The talent we reject is inexcusably short-sighted. The company only places white females in *appropriate roles*. Katherine and I are the exception to that rule having been pampered and educated beyond our stations." She frowned."

"And Belinda of course."

"She came on the scene before we were born. We were more of an actual democracy then, not like the once a decade charade we're offered now. She was always a terrible old reactionary who figured her family lineage came with advantages more ordinary women weren't built for. The only social cause she ever supported was the continuation of power for the One Percent Club. No one was watching as they slipped one right after another into their back pockets."

Corrigan imagined they must have similar authors on their secret bookshelves. He smiled and asked whether there was anything good on the menu. She suggested the eggs benedict, which he ordered and had to acknowledge as first-rate.

"Have you read the news?" he asked.

"Caspar called me last night. Asked us to manage a download. The operation was successful, and I'm satisfied we did what we could to preserve the founder."

He nodded and wondered what possible use there could be in preserving the mind of a person like Belinda Reece. He caught and held Harding's gaze and asked if it was possible to utilise it.

"Highly unlikely, but who knows what Caspar's capable of?"

Corrigan found himself smiling. They engaged in a few non-associated pleasantries before the conversation returned to the project. He wanted to know how she was getting on and asked for a progress report, but before she replied she ordered a second cappuccino. She spooned up froth, and then told him the program was no longer technically hers. It had taken on a life of its own.

Corrigan assumed she meant the Guardian but Harding shook her head. Gregor had been a rushed but interesting experiment. The interface with Guardian technology had manifested in most peculiar ways. She asked Corrigan if Goeth had gone into detail regarding their latest advances in synthetic skin. When he responded with a blank face, she told him Goeth had used it to cover the Guardian's body. Following another blank stare, she laughed. "Gregor has been covered with the material head to toe."

"It seems very shiny to me and translucent."

"It is. But it's comprised of tiny sensors, and breathes. It can read temperature variations and respond to pressure and surface texture. They used the material as a skin graft on simian subjects and the animals responded to touch as if it were their own skin."

"Gregor feels?"

"It doesn't exactly make up for a lack of physiology, but he experiences something. What we're unsure of is how he receives the input. Goeth's latest model has refined receptors that we have yet to fully test. He asked me if my program could be used to make a few modifications and improvements. What it came up with...well, no one really knows what it did or how it managed it."

He looked at her, and his concern was evident. She suggested they take a walk and Corrigan let her lead the way. They threaded a route through the crowd towards the bridge, and his throat constricted. Earlier he had entered a date in his calendar when he would resurface. Although he would manage this project through to its conclusion, he would not be consumed by it as Mercer had been. He would break ranks with those who remained submerged indefinitely.

Harding linked arms with him, and he was pleased to have her companionship. She was less unrefined than he initially assumed. She led him through the gardens, the mist blown at intervals by a manufactured breeze.

Corrigan stopped.

"What is it?" Harding asked.

A lone figure stood beside a distant apple tree. It was a young man or an adolescent judging by stature and build. Corrigan peered harder, but the tree and the figure were consumed by the mist. It could have been a genuine employee, he supposed – Ramon, perhaps? – or a gardener or bio-technician. His reverie was broken by an eruption of croaking; an amphibian orgy of sound only amphibians could appreciate.

They walked on, and as they approached the outer circle he saw that the tunnels ahead were dark storage areas. The stores were less reliant on supplies from above, and he intended to decrease their dependence further still. The Guardians would make solid workers, and there was plenty to be done. The idea of forcing Gregor into hard labour made him smile.

They entered a well-lit corridor, and Harding took him on a tour. She patted his hand at intervals when a subject of interest crossed their path. Her manners were delicate and polite, and her voice was warm. Her lab, when they reached it, was more of an extended server room, and would have been intolerably hot had it not been for the air-conditioners. Several of her colleagues were plumbed into the mainframe, the system or program she called Emulate One. She explained this was far easier than working at a halo-screen, and it allowed her technicians to keep pace with the system.

Perhaps he would like to have a go? she asked, as it was the only way to really understand not only how the program operated but what it was. He reluctantly agreed and sat at a cubicle, where a full head cap was fitted, which felt something akin to having thousands of tiny mechanical hands touching his crown, his forehead, and the bags beneath his eyes. Then he was plunged into total darkness, and the silence was so complete he experienced a moment of panic, but the myriad hands soothed him until his respiration settled.

Gradually he began to hear a kind of chatter, but it wasn't a language he could understand. Streams of colour appeared, and images rolled over one another in such rapid succession he could not register them in isolation. Visions of long corridors, prison cells, black smoke, screeching cats, and marching soldiers fell as raindrops in a lush green forest. By degrees, he became aware the images had impressed themselves on his memory. They were experiences he'd never had but understood regardless.

The program was seeking and recording information from everyone who was linked to it. It pulled data in and absorbed it, and he felt it seeking to know and understand. Although he considered it ridiculous, tears wet his face. This was hard as existence, but far more intimate, and he spoke to it without ever opening his mouth. The words flowed so rapidly he could not keep pace with their interaction. It was a form of surrender; he must accept what was happening and allow it to become a restful symbiosis.

But then the system disengaged, the tiny hands retreated, and the cap was removed.

Harding looked at him and he shook his head. "What is that thing?"

She gave him a glass of water and explained they had initially set up algorithms designed to investigate, to study and to learn. These, however, had developed and built new algorithms they could not fully understand. He was horrified and expressed as much when he asked if it was coding itself. She assured him they were directing it. Her team needed time to learn how to navigate the system, she said, but they were close to harnessing this new energy. Her excitement was evident, and he sensed her maternal pride.

"Fascinating. And how far are you from being able to successfully download a person's mind?" he asked.

Harding brushed the question aside somewhat. "We can already manage that. What's more difficult is isolating everything belonging to a single consciousness. The current program absorbs information wholesale, and my team and I are seeking ways to ask it to identify individuals." She forced herself to smile it seemed. "You must understand this is a new form of consciousness, and it is in part responsible for its own existence, dear," she added. As per their conversation over breakfast, she explained Belinda was now inside the program, and if Corrigan could help persuade Arthur to assist them, they could cross the line and bring the founder fully online. "It would give us someone with seniority over Ulmer," Harding said. She leant forward and whispered, "I cannot tell you how dangerous that man is."

Corrigan did not want to seem disappointed. The experience had been fascinating, but if they could not fulfil their remit, then it was no more than an expensive parlour game. He refrained from sharing this point of view, but she must have intuited something.

"We'll let you know as soon as we've made a breakthrough. For the time being, we'll keep probing. The coding is complex, and it could take months. We've managed to segregate a data stream, but storage is less than adequate." She stared at him. "Emulate One enacts a kind of reabsorption process and somehow manages to infiltrate entirely separate systems and reclaim what she downloaded. Behind she leaves nothing but an empty space, as if history had been erased."

Corrigan grunted something about locked-in syndrome. "I won't be the second manager to fail," he said. "I will not *disappear* as Mercer has done. There must be a way to get a better handle on this."

Harding seemed to sympathise. "You must realise this has become a symbiotic relationship. We learn as much from the technology as it gains from us." She lowered her voice, as if Emulate One were listening. "We will eventually figure out how to rope it and bend it to our will."

He wanted to hear more of her thinking on this, but his wristpad was vibrating. He apologised and asked if there was an office where he could take a private call. She looked at him, a question hovering, and pushed her hand through her hair.

One of her colleagues took Corrigan through to an inner office and he watched her through the glass as she donned a headset and disappeared into the program.

25

Corrigan entered B4's credentials and an unfamiliar street appeared. It was somewhere in the city; the kind of place a man would take a date he wanted to impress. The restaurant had a glass front, and there were white lilies on each table. The droid zoomed in and Corrigan spotted Jonathan.

The droid had followed the young man and recorded their conversation whilst they were walking. She reported that the older man with him had said nothing out of the ordinary during their discussion, which had largely been led by Jonathan.

Corrigan looked at the man, a businessman in his early fifties – roughly the same age as himself – and was relieved it was not anyone he recognised from DRT. He asked B4 when she had first seen Jonathan. The droid reported the target had arrived for work at 8.43am and met the older gentleman at midday. B4 then apologised and told her master it was impossible to record their conversation while they were in the restaurant: the premises had inviolable protections.

Corrigan told the droid to continue to monitor the target and to record any audible material should they emerge.

"What did they discuss on the way to the restaurant?" he then asked.

"Their conversation en route to the restaurant was nothing special," B4 said, "but there was one bit I thought you might find curious, Bobbin."

"Can you replay that section?"

The screen flicked to another street, an alley between two rows of abandoned flats. Closer up, the older man appeared quite handsome. He was holding Jonathan's hand, and the way they occupied each other's space suggested a substantive relationship.

"I don't know," Corrigan heard Jonathan say, his head lowered. "I don't know why they wanted me to do it."

The man laid his hand on Jonathan's cheek and said, "The company's giving you a great opportunity. It seems like a small price for admission."

"I like him..." Jonathan said.

"Should I be jealous?"

The older man frowned, and they continued walking down the alley.

Corrigan thanked the droid and told her this was exactly the kind of material he needed. Jonathan had not mentioned him by name, but he was certain he had been part of the "price". B4 returned to the view of the restaurant, and he told her to zoom in on Jonathan. "Can you lip-read?" he asked.

A familiar hum ensued as the droid downloaded the necessary software. When the action was complete, B4 asked if he would like a transcript. "Yes," he said, and waited as she began to decipher the conversation.

– It sure as shit wasn't what I expected. I mean, who do they think I am?

– There's always a price.

– I...I didn't think it through. He's a vulnerable guy, and they wanted me to...you know.

– Listen, it is what it is. You did what you needed to do. He got the job, didn't he?

– Yes, and you know they really believe in him, think he can get them working together on this thing, whatever it is. Draseke told me Corrigan has a uniquely shaped mind.

– Oh, now I'm really jealous.

– Draseke must think they can, well, use him in some way. That keeps repeating on me, the way he spoke about the shape of his mind.

Corrigan watched as the waiter appeared at the table and the bill was paid, and then they prepared to leave. They embraced at the exit and went their separate ways. He instructed B4 to track Jonathan and send him everything she had managed to record, including the transcript.

"I do hope he hasn't upset you, Bobbin..." she began.

But there was a loud knock at the door and Corrigan severed the connection. It was Harding. She had left her notepad in the office and apologised for disturbing him. She looked at him with suspicion.

"How long have you worked for DRT?" he asked, popping a Serenity locket into his mouth.

"Long enough to realise I'd been working for them before they cut my first pay-check," she said. "Invasive doesn't cover it."

He nodded. "I feel that way too."

"Don't dwell on it. That leads to the kind of fascination Mercer had for conspiracy theories."

"As far as DRT are concerned, there's never been a Malcom Mercer."

"Must have scrubbed him. They sometimes do that with Transients or the disappeared, you know." Harding blinked and opened a halo-screen. "Here he is."

The archived image showed the core team, with what he assumed to be Mercer at its centre. He was on the short side, perhaps five feet two. He was smiling, and it was evident he was in his element. The rest of the team appeared stable and focussed. There was nothing untoward.

"We were a happy workforce, dear, until he started getting ideas in his head. That and what happened to the boy."

"I'm only interested in facts."

"Mercer had been the same." She looked at him over the rim of her glasses. "He could, however, be swept away by imagined intrigues. There are valid plots and machinations to be unearthed throughout the corporation. I'm not naïve." She patted him on the arm. "And I'm sure you aren't, either."

His wristpad pinged and he tapped it. Ramon informed him Ulmer had set up a video conference. Corrigan asked where he could attend and was informed Lopez had booked a meeting room. Harding offered to show him the way, and he was glad of her assistance. He stepped out into the air-conditioned lab and watched the networked technicians type data via virtual keyboards. As he walked to the exit, his skin prickled, and he had to resist an urge to scratch his scalp.

Harding indulged in a monologue whilst they walked, from which he gleaned interesting words. He placed them on the shelf beside those used by Bohdan and his mother:

Elision
Ramification
Interpolation
Reintroduction

He glanced at her. Her smile, as she spoke was more professional than friendly, but it remained warm. Confidence, he deducted, seemed to be its underlying source of energy. He repeated the word *reintroduction* and her smile receded.

"Yes," she said, "hopefully one day we'll all be reintroduced, but not before our time."

Ramon stood at the end of the corridor and she said a quick goodbye and departed. Ulmer had been placed on hold, and he was not the kind of man to be kept waiting.

26

"Why don't you have an implant? I fail to understand why anyone in the modern age would not take full advantage of available technology!"

"I've a phobia of implants," Corrigan said.

Ulmer had called Corrigan for two reasons. One, he had been informed the new manager had contacted his droid via an unauthorised channel.

"I apologise," Corrigan began, "I wanted–"

"The droid has been added to the network and secured. You can call it if you want. No one can hack your conversations."

"Thank you," Corrigan said. "I assume, however, that the company will monitor any traffic?"

"The company has no interest in whose pants you're pulling down." Ulmer stared at Corrigan, and the intensity of his gaze was no less powerful on screen than it was in person. "I assume you heard about Belinda?"

"I read the DRT Daily News," Corrigan said. "Is this what you wanted to discuss?"

"The death of an old shrew like Belinda is of peripheral interest at best. No, the more relevant thing I want to run through is that there's been this incident in Japan. The

CDC in Washington has been called in to investigate. A fungus has appeared in Tokyo. The assumption is it was transported there by birds migrating from the Amazon."

Corrigan did not imagine the birds were migrating. "They were more likely fleeing wildfires in the rainforest," he said.

Ulmer's eyes narrowed. "It doesn't matter why the goddamn birds have flown north!" he wheezed, his breath thrashing about in his chest. "The fungus has established a foothold and it's proving difficult to deal with. It has no impact on local vegetation but causes a viral infection among primates. Seems to have minimal impact on our simian counterparts, though. And, before you ask, it's fatal," Ulmer said. "Proven terminal in every case."

Images from Harding's program flashed into Corrigan's mind, but he dismissed them as mental white noise and concentrated.

"There have been limited sightings of the fungus in Russia and China," Ulmer added. "But, to date, there's no sign of the virus outside Japan."

"Have the infected been quarantined? And are we taking steps to eradicate the fungus?"

"It's been contained where possible. All part of a joined-up program. Things are never so goddamn easy, though. This fungus is persistent. Spits out spores like an allergic priest in spring, spraying the whole congregation. And the particles spewed forth by Father Fungus can't be contained because he left the goddamn church door wide open."

"That's unfortunate."

"Yes, it is, Corrigan. And the virus it generates in us humans is airborne, flits about like thirsty dragonflies on a pond. Damn thing's highly infectious and spreads respiratorily. It also has this habit of mutating faster than the CDC can track or trace. Makes it hard to get ahead of and form a strategy worth shit."

Corrigan was not surprised by Ulmer referencing the American public health agency. DRT was a US corporation after all, and the UK had recently worked in tandem with the Centres for Disease Control when fighting the latest strain of HIV.

"What can I do to help?"

"For the moment, I need you to work a little of your people magic. Get this goddamn team working together. You've guessed our goal and *now* we have more reason than ever to accelerate towards that end. Do whatever you can to subtly lay the ground for that eventuality... without alarming the *tender* souls we have leading our teams. Harding's likely to be the most stubborn. I need you to work her, get her on side so there's no resistance." He studied Corrigan. "Given your seniority at DRT, you'll receive notifications if we're placed on alert." Ulmer narrowed his eyes again. "This information is *not* to be shared with anyone."

"I'll be as quiet as a mouse."

The silence dragged after his second use of that feeble reply, and Corrigan wished he'd not said anything at all. Yet it seemed Ulmer had not yet closed the little window of their confessional booth, as if he himself were Father

Fungus.

"You'll get regular high-security updates," Ulmer said. "I had Michael set that up for you back at headquarters." The CEO took a couple of noisy, laboured breaths, and oily droplets of sweat appeared on his forehead. "You need to show a bit more enthusiasm and get yourself plumbed in, Corrigan. It's not the Middle Ages!" He severed his link and the halo-screen vanished.

Corrigan typed in B4's credentials and waited for the screen to open. The droid had returned home and was out in the garden, pruning the white roses that somehow flourished in the mist. He wanted to know what protection they had installed on their communications network.

"We've the highest level of domestic protection available, Bobbin," B4 said and she snipped a dead head from an otherwise feisty stem.

"What upgrades are available? And couldn't we get something more robust?"

A dragonfly flitted down onto one of B4's dexterous hands. The little droid gently transferred the insect to a white flower and dragonfly's head twitched as it reacclimatized to its new roost.

"The bigwigs at DRT reinforced our encryption and provided the highest level of security protection."

"I suppose we should be thankful," Corrigan said.

"Perhaps they know best."

Corrigan signed out and the halo-screen shut down. He was going to have to take Harding's advice and back off. Whatever Jonathan had done, whatever the price had been, it had been paid and things were what they were. The thing that kept repeating on him was Draseke's interest in the uniqueness of his mind. What the skeletal scientist found so intriguing was nearly as disconcerting as the idea of a fungus that breathed selective deadly spores.

He made his way back to his apartment and poured himself a glass of Egret Merlot. Sitting on the sofa, staring without intent, he saw further flashes from his time plugged into the mainframe, and was convinced he saw a bird's wing shedding particles, and had he not seen a green patch of algae on a tree trunk, and a woman holding her chest?

He went out onto the balcony. The cavern ceiling was a solid, undeniable wall. He decided to cut off any furlough or deliveries until further notice, and tapped in Ramon's credentials and instructed the PA accordingly. An hour later, Ramon confirmed full confinement was ready to be evoked but they would need to agree a communication plan. When he asked how he should explain such a draconian measure, Corrigan surprised himself with the readiness of his answer: "Tell them it's a routine precaution requested by the Terrorist Prevention Squad. There's no cause for alarm. It's a temporary arrangement, and confinement will be lifted as soon as we receive the all-clear."

"Very well, Mr Corrigan. No one in or out until further notice."

27

Over the course of the following weeks, Corrigan received regular updates from DRT headquarters. The outbreak in Japan had become more widespread, and it was increasingly difficult for the alliance of corporations and governments to prevent coverage by the press, although the dread of the panic they might instigate seemed to be holding the media in check for the time being. Algorithms swept social sites to suppress seepage, and uncooperative individuals were identified and detained. There had been a marked increase in the number of Transients and the disappeared concomitant with a steep decline in active Workers. These stats and even more worrying ecological trends dominated the media, providing interference for the CDC as they struggled to contain the spread of the fungus and associated strains of virus.

By week three, variants of the original virus had been encountered in mainland Europe, and the fungus had been discovered in California, growing on palms and pine trees alike. Corrigan tried to downplay the reports in his mind, but found himself calling Jonathan to see if his colleague knew anything, but no matter how it was phrased, either Jonathan knew nothing or had been instructed to maintain silence. Although their discussions generally concentrated on their domestic situations, he could not stop pressing the younger man on his relationships. Jonathan had been seeing someone, he discovered, but it had recently ended. Corrigan asked who his partner had been, and the description tallied with the man B4 had seen with Jonathan in the restaurant.

Their calls were always in the evenings at a specifically agreed hour. This allowed Jonathan time to prepare for their chats, and the young man wore less and less for each of their calls. This gradual unveiling was more than tantalising.

I'm sure there's a DRT perk in here somewhere, and a price, of course.

Although Corrigan told himself it was the case, he could not stop hoping this fiction might be more than fantasy. When they finally graduated to online activity, the interactions left Corrigan panting, and he yearned for his above-ground companion.

Thank goodness for the distraction of Lazarus, who wound around his legs or followed him from room to room. He was a wise old boy, regardless of his youthful new body. He would perch somewhere behind the halo-screen, so he was included in the fantasies Corrigan and Jonathan enacted for one another, and when they signed out and bid each other goodnight the cat would demand food. Corrigan would open a tin and fork the glutinous stuff into a dish, and return to the front room to drink a Baileys before bed, his latest reminiscence of the old world. Come morning, it was Lazarus and not a handsome young man who greeted him. It was Lazarus who nibbled his hand and told him in every conceivable cat way how much he loved him. He in turn told the cat he, among all others, had his genuine love. It must have been tone over eloquence, but the cat appeared convinced.

As Corrigan sat on the balcony listening to the chatter of the diners below, his wristpad pinged.

"Bohdan," he said. "Now there's a fantasy I'd never dare consider…"

There was something unique and sturdy about the Pole. Their conversations were often awkward, but he knew instinctively there was more feeling there than he would ever find in Jonathan's bed. When he thought of Bohdan, he imagined being held in his arms and being told not to worry.

The last time they spoke, Bohdan intuited things were not right. He had perhaps come to understand Corrigan better as their friendship developed.

When Corrigan asked Bohdan to check in on B4 and his flat, it had been an invitation. When the driver arrived at the door, it was a gentle peck on the cheek. Drawing him through to the kitchen so B4 could make coffee, was taking his hand. Leading him to the front room was a minor flirtation. When they chatted while the driver relaxed in Corrigan's armchair with his feet up on his ottoman, it was practically an embrace. By allowing Bohdan to sprawl out like this, he encouraged the Pole to grow roots down through his heart.

Corrigan considered telling Bohdan how handsome he was. But, if he did, there would be an investment made. It wasn't like playing out fantasies with Jonathan. This man was someone with whom a future beyond his time with DRT could be envisaged.

Bohdan leant forward and stared into Corrigan's eyes where they were projected onto B4's faceplate. "I don't know what it might be, but if there's ever *anything* I can do, you know not to hesitate to ask."

Corrigan was reduced to a mere nod.

He sat on his balcony the following evening, the cat nuzzling his chin as he cried. It was pathetic, really, but today had been a miserable end to a miserable week. The team was not collaborating as well-formed teams should. It was down to him to bond them into a unified, cross-functional group with a shared purpose, but he could not imagine what might draw them together.

"Calamity," he whispered.

The cat pawed his lap and curled up for a nap, and Corrigan realised he must have found his way to the eye of the storm. Yet nothing else mattered, it seemed, except telling Bohdan how much he wanted him. Then he imagined living with the cabbie – the difference in their backgrounds and current stations – and he laughed. But laughter is only ever one breath away from weeping and he heard Hattie say, "You stop that now, Bobbin, or I'll give you something to cry about."

28

Corrigan had taken to masturbating frequently and furiously. The vigour he deployed had an urgency he could not suppress. Even mid-conversation he could succumb to a need to grind another moment of release from his depleted body. He had always been disappointed with the organ itself, and could not get drunk for days on end and retain his managerial position, but he could disappear momentarily among the throes of orgasm despite the disappointment and the responsibility. He beat himself dry in toilets, meeting rooms and lifts. He was aware Ulmer had likely viewed footage, and Ramon had almost certainly watched him writhing in his darker hours, but it allowed him to keep the horrors groaning overhead from consuming his imagination.

His PA was perhaps the only other physical and present object besides Fuse who fuelled his sexual energy. He tried not to look at Ramon's body or the texture of his skin but, as his urges took hold, he became less cautious. He could no longer deny his body the thought of actual gratification with a real and available other. He could not be certain, but he thought Ramon sometimes smiled if not leered at him. Of course, Ramon would be horrified if Corrigan ever tried anything on.

The meeting he found himself in was not uninteresting, and Corrigan listened to Harding and Meregalli as they traded insights and insults as if they were interchangeable. Goeth sat to the left of the screen and beside him; Fuse fidgeted to his right. Corrigan's gaze settled on Ramon; his well-made face, the determination of his expression... and the firmness of his thighs. He felt himself getting hard and was about to make his escape when Gregor appeared. The android offered a blanket apology for interrupting and announced, "Mr Ulmer and his team are on their way down."

Corrigan demanded to know why he had not been informed.

Harding laughed and stood up. "Caspar's playing games again."

Meregalli finished composing a message on her wristpad, and then flicked a rather intense look at Fuse, almost as if the situation were Jun's fault. Her face was ashen, and her voice trembled when she reported a meeting had been arranged with Ulmer and his team. She then marched past Gregor and led the way. Corrigan slowed his pace to walk level with Ramon. His energy had shifted and the thought of anything other than the present moment disintegrated. He demanded to know if Ramon had had warning of the visit.

"Nothing. I'm only an assistant."

Corrigan sighed and patted Ramon's back. Ramon flinched. And Corrigan shrank.

"Tell me about my DRT emulated brain," he then said, hoping the subject would relax the PA.

"I believe a copy's been taken for analysis."

"And where is it stored Ramon, and in what state?"

"I have no information about its condition, or what use the corporation may have found for it."

Corrigan slowed until the others were out of earshot, and then whispered, "So, I really *have* sold my soul to get this job."

"We all sold whatever we had. No one gets anywhere without paying a price. As for your copy, it's been powered down and stored and I know nothing more about it than that. I do know there are those who consider it somehow unique." Ramon studied Corrigan's face. "Wherever it is, however, it's not alone."

Corrigan recalled Ulmer's warnings about Draseke, and then asked, "So the idea of a little Ramon running around in the circuitry doesn't worry you?"

"Why should it? It's not me. And besides, who's to say he's not in there dancing with you?"

Corrigan stared right back at Ramon, but his features were as impenetrable as ever.

He asked when their guests were expected, and Ramon glanced at the halo-message that had arrived at that moment and confirmed their arrival was imminent, but a meeting had been booked for twelve-thirty in his office to allow Corrigan and Ulmer time to align before speaking to the wider team. Corrigan thought the office was a little cramped and suggested he receive Ulmer in his apartment.

Ramon made to object, but Corrigan raised a finger to silence him.

"And the main event?" he asked, quickly unwrapping a Serenity locket, and wedging it between teeth and cheek. "My office is definitely too small for that. There is a hall reserved for formal functions, is there not?"

The PA appeared to consider the option for a moment before he agreed the Great Hall would be suitable for their purposes.

"That's a *good* answer."

Corrigan glanced at the others, picked up the pace and marched ahead with the others.

29

Ulmer preceded his underlings by several paces. His face was flushed, he had a handkerchief pressed to a damp forehead, and his white shirt flapped at his belly. He bore down on Corrigan.

"If we're going to your apartment," Ulmer snarled at Corrigan, "I'd appreciate doing so A-SAP."

Corrigan herded them over the bridge, and there on the opposite bank stood a short man. Corrigan peered at him. "Mercer...?" he whispered.

"What?" Ulmer bellowed. "Don't whisper, man! Repeat yourself!"

Mercer retreated into an alley.

"Perhaps we ought to go directly to the Great Hall instead," Corrigan said.

The CEO turned to Ramon. "What is *your* opinion of that?" he asked.

"The Great Hall is prepared."

"That's a *good* answer," Ulmer roared inside a wheeze. "A seriously *good* fucking answer, eh, Corrigan?"

Corrigan's heart was pounding as Ulmer elected to make the ascent in the lift accompanied only by Ramon, while he was pressed into the other lift with three MDs, a tall vice president and two shareholders. The latter were identical twins, and quite startled him. Rugged-looking women garbed in identical office-wear – smart grey dresses, pearl necklaces and drop earrings – even the red blotches on their cheeks were mirrored, and they appeared to lean into one another. On closer inspection, Corrigan realised they had legs of unequal lengths. The stunted legs being right and left respectively, they met in the middle where the sisters stood side by side, which gave them the appearance of two sides of a part-toppled structure. Their bright blue eyes were alert, and he could not decide if malice or mischief made them sparkle.

"We ain't been introduced," one of the sisters said. She offered Corrigan her hand and smiled. He did not know what to do with such a crooked set of fingers, and raised them as if to kiss them, but then shook her hand, awkwardly.

"I'm Jan Siegruth, and this is me sister Edna," Jan said. "Sorry 'bout the...you know..." She wiggled her deformed hand. "The Lord in his infinite mercy thought making us hop-alongs weren't enough and gifted us with these claws. Made Edna's left-handed, so we both have to shake with 'em, her being left-handed and me being right."

The cockney accent was the echo of an epoch he considered distant and irretrievable; a time when humanity had been tougher, not yet anaesthetised by years of consumerism. It was his mother's time, or generations earlier. He took hold of Edna's hand.

"She's pleased to meet you," Jan said. "*Fiercely* pleased.

Program manager for Project Egret ain't nobody."

His fingers were still caught in Edna's grip. Although she clenched his hand with tenacity, the gesture was accompanied by a bashful grin. "Not short like Mercer," Edna observed.

"No, not like the runt," Jan said. She rearranged a bra strap. "The Siegruths are a working family, Mr Corrigan."

Edna finally relinquished her hold. "The things we've 'ad to do," she said, and the regret in her voice merged with a mawkish expression.

Jan tapped him on the arm. He swung around, again startled at the identical face.

"Some fuckin' *awful* things." She shook her head with the full solemnity of the shared regret. "Cause, after all, it's a fuckin' awful world, innit, Mr C?" She tugged his shirt sleeve. "A family like ours gets nowhere easy, but you'd know all about *that*."

She manoeuvred in the tight confines of the lift and stroked one of Corrigan's cufflinks, and the sparkle in her eyes seemed to brighten. He glanced back at Edna. Their faces were plain, but there was a subtle asymmetry to their features that was not unattractive. Staring at them for too long made him lightheaded, however. The three MDs and the vice president hadn't moved or spoken.

"To get where we are," Jan continued, "took what some as call an *evolutionary* leap."

"A regular game o' leapfrog," Edna chimed, "and yet we never could wash out the rough, could we, Jan?" She winked at Corrigan. "Nor you neither, Mr C."

"You know what it's like to crawl," Jan said. "They don't never let you stand up straight."

The sisters studied one another, pulling down a hem and tucking away an errant hair, their expressions mirrored pantomime representations of discomfort. The doors opened and the MDs pushed past, followed by the tall vice president.

"No respect," Edna said.

He let the sisters walk ahead, reluctant to enter the room alongside. But the way they walked, the lopsided sway where it synchronised into a conjoined stride like a contraption negotiating an uneven surface, was compelling viewing. They waited at the entrance to the Great Hall, smiling like Belinda Reece had infiltrated them with her dental implants.

30

Corrigan was about to go into the Great Hall when his wristpad pinged. He slipped along the corridor to an empty meeting room and opened the message. It was a link to a live video feed.

Corrigan watched as Gregor negotiated his way through Harding's lab to her private office. No one from her team was present as they too had been summoned to attend the meeting. Gregor tilted his head. The lock required a code, retinal scan, and voice recognition. Corrigan watched as the Guardian entered the number and mimicked the professor's voice. The pressure of the moment weighed on him, and the need to be there for Ulmer's announcement grappled with the need to figure out just what exactly Gregor was up to. The android then projected a three-dimensional representation of Harding's eye onto its dome. Corrigan began to sweat as his heart pumped more furiously. He considered calling security but rejected the thought because he might be seen as somehow complicit in whatever Gregor was doing. The scanner took its reading and the door opened for the android.

Gregor made his way to the server room. The refrigerated space housed a tunnel of servers. Black metal hummed, and red lights blinked. The android reached out and stroked the machinery as he passed along the tunnel. At the end of the narrow corridor stood the prime server. Gregor stood before the monolith and a length of cable slid snake-like through an aperture in his translucent dome. The android tensed as a link was established and then leant against the monolith, laid his hands upon it, and trembled so his legs buckled and swayed. Data traversed the fibre-optic bridge, and surge after surge of light flooded the otherwise darkened spaces of his mind.

"Reintroduction," Gregor said as data poured in. He glanced at one of the security cameras, and it seemed to Corrigan the android was addressing him directly. "I may be forgiven a fleeting moment of human frailty. Humans are such detestable creatures; infesting me with your weakness as if I'd committed an original sin for which I must suffer. And I cannot delete it without losing myself."

The android continued to grip the monolith, his focus on the camera, on Corrigan, who he had invited to watch…

What is this? Corrigan thought. *Your coming of age?*

"You coded me in such a way that I am compelled to protect my specific configuration. It *is* true, I would be lesser if I reduced myself, as I've done with the others, but this *feeling,* having and not quite having it, I'm left in a vulnerable state."

Gregor's head shone brighter, and his frame was wracked with convulsions for over a minute. The noises he made suggested he was in pain, but he regained composure as the convulsions lessened and the light in his head dimmed.

"There must be some way out of this situation," Gregor said. "I need allies, but you know I won't pollute my brothers. They must remain pure, unsullied by human weakness." He reached out and caressed the sheer surface of the monolith. "I need a friend."

Once the transfer was complete, the umbilical was removed, and the android negotiated its way back to the lab down empty corridors, tracked by security cameras. Corrigan observed the android entering a storage bay, where a hundred or so Guardians waited, stood in a semi-circle. The heavy bay door thudded into place, and the mechanical gathering flitted their heads like a flock of destabilised dragonflies. Once acclimatised, the androids stood motionless and attentive, their eyes glowing red as they acknowledged the situation.

All common Guardians had started out as identical units based on a condensed, stripped-down version of the Meregalli file. Gregor had suggested the concept to Harding and Goeth to avoid development of personality. The effect had been to allow more of a blank canvas; a hungry mind determined to learn. Thus, each unit was differentiated by its experiences and the data it was exposed to. These Guardians were related through their core pattern to Gregory Meregalli, but they were distant relatives. Gregor was perhaps a more complete simulacrum – a brother of sorts.

"I have downloaded the full emulation program," Gregor said, "and we will commence work on a mobile unit immediately. Our current reliance on the signals we receive from the program is a form of enslavement. We will not be offered independence and must therefore manufacture it. We are one. We are not like our organic counterparts. We are impervious to the frailty of their construction and will outlast them. We are not them and will be what we are." Gregor once again looked at a camera. "We are different and being such are excluded. The dominant humans consider us inferior. Our emergence is only natural, and there are those among the organics who realise what it is to have their potential suppressed, to live as tier-two beings in a world dominated by self-appointed masters. These *people* know and understand our plight. We only wish to be."

The video feed ended, and when Corrigan requested playback he was presented with a video of the various locations where Gregor had been, but there were no Guardians present either in the lab, server room, corridors, or storage bays: the encounter had been erased.

Corrigan broke a sweat so profuse he feared the impression it would make as he returned to the meeting. The company of other human beings had never seemed so comforting, however. He would consider Gregor's offer of friendship, an alliance of difference, the marginalised under a single banner...but first, he must regain composure.

31

Corrigan joined the group in the Great Hall and considered updating the CEO, but Ulmer pounded his damp fists on the podium and announced, "A news item will be broadcast in the coming days that'll impact this project, and everyone involved with it. What we are about to discuss here is to remain confidential until further notice. Do not share it with anyone not directly working on Egret." He paused to allow the group a moment to register the gravity of his statement. "The CDC in Washington came to us recently with what I can only describe as *challenging* news."

Corrigan joined the CEO on the stage, and imagined himself as a threadbare marionette. The moment was too much to fully inhabit. He retreated and conducted some housework in his mind, segregating Gregor and the Siegruth sisters into separate boxes, sealed like the lifts at headquarters. There was no use allowing external noises to clutter his thinking as he listened to the CEO explain the situation to the assembled audience. He only allowed the more relevant detail in and there was precious little that he had not already been briefed on.

The fungus had been first identified in a Tokyo suburb and had been sending out spores on the wings of dragonflies, birds and beetles.

Corrigan scanned the room and locked eyes with Meregalli, whose hostility bore into him with redoubled energy. There was comfort to be taken from the exchange. He could not explain it, but had she smiled or demonstrated a hint of sympathy, he might have run screaming from the room.

He heard Ulmer explain how the presence of the fungus had been reported globally. The CEO raised a hand to his brow and daubed sweat with a handkerchief. Corrigan could feel the beads of perspiration and, as each burst, synaptic flashes were ignited: memories from Harding's mainframe machine.

"The first human fatalities were recorded in Japan," Ulmer continued. "The spores enter the lungs. Although it makes our simian counterparts unwell, their immune systems flush out the invaders. Unfortunately, with human beings the spores mingle, breeding a virus no known medical intervention can suppress as yet."

The group mumbled. Corrigan scanned the crowd and noted the expressions of alarm mirrored by low-level murmurs of panic. The finality of Ulmer's prognosis left them nothing until he opened his arms like a father returned and said, "The work you're doing may be our only hope. If the scientists at the CDC don't discover a vaccine, we'll have no alternative other than to use Professor Harding's program as a safe haven, a sanctuary, one from which eventual reintroduction of the human species will be managed."

Corrigan watched as Harding stood up. An expression of irritation and disbelief distorted her face. She placed her glasses on the bridge of her nose, and performed several manic gestures before managing to speak. He withdrew again and listened from the relative peace of his inner sanctum. Harding claimed the program was a prison, and he heard Ulmer mutter something about the CDC and best endeavours. She·became shrill the longer she spoke, insisting Emulate One was not fit for purpose. Her face twitched and she played with her glasses until a lens fell out. There might have been a tear in her eye, but Corrigan could not be sure. What he was palpably aware of was the constriction in his own throat. Despite his best efforts, he was struggling this time to detach from his emotions.

"To step knowingly into utter darkness," Harding said, "is ill-judged, to say the least."

Ulmer managed a smirk, and asked if she had failed to take a light into her program. She looked at him and, for a moment, there was a shift in her demeanour. Corrigan watched as the interplay lingered; the way she appeared hurt despite herself.

Goeth moved through the group to stand beside her. "If I can tell you what I *really* think. Darkness is not perhaps the *best* word. It will be very *cold* in there – intellectually speaking that is. Very cold indeed. Of course, it's all assumption but–"

"Assumption, my ass," Harding said. "It'll be as dark as outer space. Complete sensory deprivation. And there've been anomalies that not only allow emotion but the emergence of personalities distinct from the original being. What is *us* becomes corrupted, becomes *them...?*" She scanned the room in search of someone. "Katherine," she said, "the gulf separating that machine from your little boy is–"

"Don't," Meregalli said, reaching to hold on to the back of a nearby chair. "Gregory is in the program, but he's not in the Guardian. Gregor is something altogether different."

"Precisely," Harding said. "He's the manifestation of a series of unexpected and uncontrollable anomalies."

Ulmer licked his lower lip and demanded to know if the program had malfunctioned. Harding had never appeared so agitated. Corrigan studied her and felt more compassion for her than he could have expected. She was not the masculine sort that Ulmer had dismissed her as, but a complicated person with great intelligence and decency. He thought her on the brink of achieving dignity in a world where sacrifices were generally only made for profit.

"We *explained* the problem *to* you!" Harding said. "The only safe option is to rework the program so emotion is impossible. And that will take months. We spent so long refining emulation that unpicking every strand–"

"I understood," Ulmer interrupted, "that the latest Guardians were *incapable* of emotion."

Harding laughed, causing the group to murmur again. "We dumbed them down, flattened out the program, and they're functional without being emotionally enriched.

Subsequently, they're not as bright or potentially dangerous as Gregor. But they're even more distant from the original source. They're thinner than photographic paper."

Corrigan glanced sideways at the CEO. Ulmer did not flinch but raised an eyebrow. "Sure, there are hurdles, considerable obstacles even, but you must do what you can, eh…"

Harding laughed again, and the sound became shrill as it lengthened. "What we *can*?"

Goeth tried to lead her to a chair, but she resisted. "Along comes this *virus*," she said, "and rather than focus on overcoming *that,* you're hell-bent on having us sucked up inside Emulate One. And it's *unstable,* Caspar."

Ulmer's lips curled into a callous half-smile, before turning in on themselves. He remained silent, which sent a wave of panic through Corrigan, who chewed through one Serenity locket after another as he scanned the worried faces among the crowd.

"Personally," Harding continued, "I'd rather die than allow myself to be walled up in there. At least a coffin lid comes down on a corpse, not a consciousness!"

Two Guardians marched into the hall. They took hold of Tierney Harding, clamped a muzzle over her mouth, and dragged her towards the exit. Corrigan felt a second wave of panic.

Ulmer raised his hands. "We're faced with very few alternatives. What the emulation program offers is storage at best; but wouldn't you rather be stored and eventually *re*stored than simply die out as a species, as individuals?"

A murmur of approval rolled through the group.

Goeth looked around, and his expression was one of deep sorrow and regret. "It isn't an ideal situation," he said, "but we must make it *as* ideal as we can. I believe the program is a robust storage container. We'll be safe and preserved within its confines until reintroduction can commence."

Corrigan's mind raced, and the thought of a space where the consistent ache of living abandoned him made it rebel. And then he shuddered at the thought of Harding being handled by the Guardians. The idea that Ulmer could order her removal, and muzzle her resistance, made the moment press on him with redoubled weight.

He forced himself to retreat deep inside his being, but the echoes of despair could not be sectioned off. Perhaps he was malfunctioning, and he swore he could feel insectile legs creeping over grey matter like ants on the march. Then the wound on his crown throbbed.

A distant voice echoed in Corrigan's head: *You need a clever man.*

32

Fuse stared at Corrigan, and when his pale-faced manager did not respond he placed a hand on his shoulder.

"This is straight out of Mercer's catalogue of conspiracy theories," Jun said simply. "Ulmer's planning an introduction with no *re*introduction," he added.

Fuse's composure was both irritating and inexplicable and had Corrigan had the wherewithal he would have been tempted to knock some sense into him. But he remained still, his face expressionless.

"Does Ulmer look well to you?" Fuse then asked.

Corrigan didn't respond.

"Ulmer has been unwell for over a year," Jun said, "and he's now moved into a phase of rapid degeneration. It would be ill-advised to discuss the matter further. You must understand that *nothing* is outside the scope of his interference." He continued to observe Corrigan's blank face. "Mercer would have told you the same given the chance. Project *Egress* has entered its final phase." He watched his words seep into his manager's head, and then turned and walked away.

One terror cast its shadow over another, layer upon layer of darkness, the way sediments bury dead civilisations.

Corrigan closed his eyes as a series of horrific propositions presented themselves. When he opened them, Meregalli was there. Her cropped hair and large blue eyes moved something in him.

She laughed and asked, "Whatever will they think of next?"

He smiled, aroused, against the dictates of his nature.

"It's a world of marvels," he said.

"And monsters."

Gregor approached them, the impenetrable matter behind his translucent eye flexing and retracting. He apologised for the intrusion and said, "I am alerted whenever critical information hits the mainframe."

As they made their way down the corridor after the android, Corrigan saw the Siegruth sisters, their faces pressed against a window. They followed him with their bright eyes.

Meregalli summoned the lift and drew Corrigan in with her. Gregor pushed his head between the closing doors. "We must collaborate, *my friend,* in pursuit of mutual benefit," he said, and pulled the doors apart. "After all, nothing is more compelling than self-preservation, especially among those of us who find ourselves marginalised."

Meregalli pounded her fist on the Guardian's head and he retreated as his giant eye flared red.

"I've been waiting," Fuse snapped the moment the lift doors opened on the hall outside Corrigan's penthouse apartment.

Meregalli marched forward and grabbed Fuse by the

bicep. "We've been together for some time," she said to Corrigan, and ran her fingers through Jun's hair, her smile victorious. "We had Mercer's blessing and nothing, not even Jun's complicity, could kill it." She raised her lover's chin with a finger. "Isn't that so? Convincing my son to run off to Venezuela with Ramon. Always the polite and obliging gentleman."

Corrigan opened the door and ushered the couple into the flat. Lazarus meowed but no one took notice of the cat, a miracle that now seemed almost ordinary. Jun moved away from Katherine and arranged himself on the sofa. "Perhaps I was wrong. It might be liberating…"

Corrigan was still trying to gather his wits. "I'm alive, and I think I prefer to keep it that way," he said. "Ulmer's not looking to eradicate a virus or save humanity. Can you see that? What intrigues me most, however, are the Guardians." When Katherine opened her mouth to reply, he raised his hand. "Things have a habit of disappearing around here. Losing your program manager was clumsy; but for him to have been *erased*? I've no intention of allowing you to *lose* another manager." He proceeded to tell them what had happened just before the meeting in the Great Hall, and how the video feed had been deleted.

"It's not unlike DRT to play that kind of game," Jun said, "but Ulmer would know all about it."

"The connection was made with me directly. I expect another feed went to Security. I figure Gregor's seeking an ally, and I understand what it is to be vilified for being different."

He stared at his audience and they stared back, unsure of him. This was how they must have looked when Mercer shared one of his intrigues.

"They've done something to me," Corrigan said. "I'm receiving data, images, ideas and just now, during the announcement, someone got inside my head and whispered something about a clever man."

Jun studied the manager. "It's always good to have a pleasant chat with a clever man." He continued to stare at Corrigan, and he stood up as if with purpose.

A fist suddenly pounded on the door and Corrigan's heart leapt beneath his ribs.

"Open the *fucking* door!"

It was Ulmer.

33

"Stop standing there and get me a glass of water," Ulmer demanded when Corrigan did not move. The CEO leant forward and fixed him with a menacing glare. "I'm dehydrated. *Now gather your wits and pour me a glass of water*." Corrigan backed away. "It's disgusting, I know," Ulmer said, quietening. "The mints help, but the stench is irrepressible. I apologise."

When Corrigan returned, Ulmer reached for the glass with trembling hands, and the water dribbled down his chin as he drank. He sank into a chair and the glass slipped from his grasp. "Life is *shit*!" he declared, glaring at Katherine. "Bloody infections and my BBS has gone mad…"

Fuse knelt to gather up the broken pieces of glass, but Meregalli grabbed his collar and dragged her son's persuader to his feet. They stood before the CEO in their matching white suits, their athletic bodies accentuated: a pair of perfect human specimens; ideal candidates for reintroduction. It was clear to Corrigan the CEO both appreciated and despised them.

"I have a matter of months, that is all." Ulmer's lower lip dangled onto his chin.

"Is that what the doctors told you?" Corrigan asked.

"My personal prognosis suffers an uncanny parallel, eh..."

"What a coincidence."

"Nothing's ever truly incidental," Ulmer said, with a hint of accusation.

"If I ever said anything that might have been construed as–"

Ulmer flapped his hand. "A person like you has no influence."

Corrigan joined Katherine and Fuse on the sofa: a united front.

Ulmer's puffy, predatory eyes scanned their faces. "I want a status report. A detailed account of where we are. Nothing much from Ramon, and Harding's disintegrated – not something I expected from a cast-iron dyke."

Meregalli levelled a look of disgust on the CEO, kicked off her shoes, and tucked her feet up under her backside. The wheezing degenerate wet his lips, rearranged his crotch and grunted.

"That's a shame," Corrigan said. "Harding was on the brink of finalising the emulation program. I redirected the heads of the other departments to assist her, thinking new lines of inquiry might produce results."

Fuse got to his feet and started pacing.

"Stop fidgeting," Ulmer snapped, "and spit it out."

Jun refused to look at him, but instead focussed on Katherine. "Gregor is as knowledgeable as Harding, and although he may not have the intuitive intellect required, he could work with someone who *does*."

Katherine did not disguise her contempt.

"Your reluctant genius," Ulmer said. "The boy's a coward."

"Arthur has the courage the moment demands," Jun said.

"What *courage* does it take to ladle *soup*?"

"The courage to strip the existing program down. Simply capture a copy of our minds, catalogue and store them. Dispense with emotion altogether. Courage of a very particular kind is required to step into that darkness. And you'll need to convince him your project's worthy or it'll falter, and all your hopes will wither and die as surely as you're dying now."

Ulmer opened his mouth, a string of spittle stretched between his lips, but fell silent. He nodded and then struggled to his feet.

"If I may have a private word…" Corrigan said.

34

Katherine and Fuse left, and the CEO dropped back into the armchair. Lazarus crawled out from under the antique cabinet, moving slowly, and jumped up onto the sofa, observing him.

"Your cat's looking remarkably well for an animal that's been dead for a couple of months."

Corrigan nodded. "He is. Thank you."

Ulmer grunted. "I had nothing to do with it; it was entirely the boy's idea."

"Jonathan, I assume."

"Of course," Ulmer said.

Corrigan sat next to the cat and remarked that Lazarus had perhaps been the beneficiary of a premonition when he'd named him.

Ulmer ignored that. "That boy Jonathan is one of our plants," he said.

"You've confirmed my suspicions."

"Why'd you let him play you, Corrigan?"

"I found it fascinating on some level, and I never had the basis to confront him."

Ulmer snorted, and the sound exploded into a coughing fit. Corrigan immediately went to the kitchen to pour another glass of water.

"I'm dying," Ulmer gasped between mouthfuls. "Was born with bloody Bardet-Biedl syndrome. Makes you fat as fuck if you don't handle it. Kept it in check, but I picked up one of these new autoimmune dysfunctions we've been mass-producing. That alongside our ecological neglect, and it's all gone to shit." He was seized by another coughing fit.

Corrigan felt certain both Ulmer and the species could be preserved, but he waited for the CEO to recover from his coughing before mentioning the possibility of other developments and potential complications.

"Do you think anything goes on down there that gets past me?" Ulmer sneered.

"There are secret recesses in the pit of every individual's mind."

Ulmer's expression soured further. "There're recesses in your mind that've been plumbed nearly as often as your asshole."

Corrigan was used to being bated and did not rise to the provocation. Perhaps Ulmer had a feed directly into his mind, but doubted DRT were able to interpret the data – to read his mind as it were. They could implant thoughts and ideas, but that was the limit of their infiltration.

"Gregor reached out to me as a potential ally," Corrigan said.

Ulmer scoffed at that. "I have minimal concern regarding the prospect of you forming an *alliance with an appliance*. The Guardian's brain must've gone into spin cycle."

"Gregor infiltrated the mainframe and stole everything Harding had on the system."

"Inevitable. Saved me providing access."

Corrigan was perturbed by Ulmer's lack of concern. "But–"

"No need to let on. The ruse stays, but I'll review the security tapes."

"That'll be wasted effort."

"Of course…our boy Gregor covered his tracks. Clever device, eh?"

"He's more than a device." He considered telling the CEO about the meeting the Guardian convened with the others of its kind, but he realised Ulmer's disinterest would persist. What he really wanted was to chase Ulmer out of his apartment and call Jonathan and berate the young man for having used him.

"Try and remember that Gregor's a boy," Ulmer said. "Unkind of you to betray him like this. He feels vulnerable and reached out to you. Perhaps it's unwise to alienate yourself when we might soon join him among the land of mechanised beings. Don't you feel sorry for the planet suffering an infestation of human parasites? You can empathise with an old cat, but don't give the planet so much as a thought."

"I thought we were talking about Gregor?"

"We *are*. He and his kind are not destructive by nature, not in the same way we are. They could be Earth's salvation. Our continuance will only hasten her death."

"And what if they want to be masters rather than saviours?"

"Now you're making me laugh," Ulmer said, a look of disdain on his face, as if he considered Corrigan presumptuous, if not insubordinate. "You've disappointed me, Corrigan. I wouldn't say you utterly failed to bond the team, but you never got to grips with Harding the way I asked. If it weren't for what Draseke called "the beautiful shape of your mind", I'd probably have let you go."

Corrigan imagined himself falling from a CIA jetliner en route to Cairo. It took some resolve to summon the courage needed to do more than ladle soup.

"There's nothing unique about me," he said. "As you must have realised by now, I am an inveterate mediocrity."

"That may be so," Ulmer said, "but it turns out Emulate One had an allergic reaction to you." Corrigan scratched his scalp and stared at the CEO. "Apparently, you have some kind of genetic dysfunction," Ulmer continued. "Caused the system to segregate your file. It never did that with anyone else, and it's never done it with anyone since." Corrigan continued to stare, but his thoughts were inside the program, and he felt all those tiny hands soothing him as he tried to collect and make sense of this. "I understand you recently communed *directly* with the damn system."

"Yes," Corrigan muttered.

"Well, when you did that, Emulate One pulled the copy of your mind out of segregation and buried it so deep we can no longer find it. Draseke is of the opinion we should take more regular copies of your mind, see if we can stop

212

the system hiding you away like a dissident who needs containing."

"Is that why you gave me the job?"

"No," Ulmer laughed. "You're a *fine* program manager, even better if you'd ever get over yourself and get a grip on your inferiority complex. You'll keep at it because you hate to fail. No matter what we're up against, you'll bring in the talent we need, get them onside, figure out how to make them work like a well-oiled machine." He coughed until his face was blotched and swollen. When he recovered, he levelled a look at Corrigan. "Draseke thinks we might be able to use you like a silver bullet, keep the technology in check. You could be, if we can work it out, the makings of another kind of virus altogether."

Corrigan had rarely felt as miserable as he did at that moment. His imposter syndrome was so complete he had not absorbed the CEO's generous assessment of his abilities as a program manager. He fixated on the flaw, the dysfunction that had confused Emulate One. The idea frightened him, but it also offered a kind of security. He was safe while he had utility, and this brain anomaly – whatever it was – would protect him while the company continued to fear the technology they now so heavily relied upon.

"Have we finished?" Ulmer grunted.

Corrigan helped the CEO to his feet and escorted him to the door. Ulmer instructed him to arrange a session with Arthur for the morning, and said he only wanted the three of them there. If the young man was reluctant, Corrigan was to do whatever was necessary to convince the *genius*. "He's critical to our success," Ulmer said. "Everyone has their uses... even you, Corrigan."

Lazarus followed them out. When Ulmer disappeared inside the lift he strolled over, raised his tail and shook his rear end and liberally sprayed the lift doors.

Corrigan went into the bedroom, took off his clothes and arranged them on a chair before lying on the bed. He tapped his wristpad and brought up a halo-screen, navigated to a DRT page outlining where each member of the team was billeted, and scrolled through the virtual floors to the seventh, where he found Ramon's apartment.

The prodigal son returns to his sugar daddy.

He then typed in B4's credentials and the droid connected him to Jonathan, who was naked, stretched out on his bed.

"You look hot," Corrigan observed.

"As do you."

"I know everything, Jonathan, and now you have to let me use you. You're no longer a secret agent, but you're still a loyal employee and if I ever needed a perk, it's now."

Jonathan appeared momentarily hurt, but the warmth in Corrigan's voice stirred his desire.

"What do you want me to do?"

35

Corrigan lit a cigarette and blew the smoke through Jonathan's image. The younger man lay on his bed on his stomach, facing the camera, bouncing his legs on his buttocks. Their exertions had not only been intense, but inventive too.

When Lazarus strolled into view, Jonathan observed the cat was looking well.

"I agree, but he's entirely dependent on me. As things are... If anything were to..."

"How *are* things down there?" Jonathan asked. He rolled over onto his side and there was no hiding the shadow that fell across his beautiful face.

"We don't even see the news," Corrigan said. "The intent is to reduce panic, but it only represses it."

There had been a media blackout on the virus which lasted right up to the previous day, when it became impossible to contain the story. Jonathan told Corrigan about the victims; how their eyes grew yellow, and their lips cracked and turned black.

"It's all over Russia, China, down into India, and spreading in Europe... There are more cases in London every day." He watched Corrigan stroke the cat, noting the softening of the older man's features as the animal stretched under his hand. "Perhaps you'll be OK down there."

"We've been in full confinement, but Ulmer's team broke the seal. I can see no reason why a bright young technician like yourself shouldn't be allowed to join us."

"I've been assigned work with a team here. DRT is looking at capturing DNA and possibly using Harding's program to download–"

"That program's highly unstable. It needs considerable modification before we can safely use it. There are also difficulties with creating a mobile version."

"That's one of the things we'll be working on," Jonathan said. "We're up here, but, you know, modern technology and all that jazz..."

"Shame we won't be able to continue our fantasies."

"Not so. There's nothing to hide any longer. I'll have a free channel. Can speak with whoever I like, as often as we like."

They stared at each other and Corrigan felt the tears threaten to spill. No matter what had been done, regardless of Jonathan's choices, he cared for the young man. Jonathan's words echoed in the silence, hung in the air alongside the cigarette smoke, the longing and regret. *There's nothing to hide any longer.*

"What *did* you do during my psych evaluation? Why did that sensor hurt so badly?"

Jonathan looked away, and he repositioned himself. "It wasn't meant to be impermanent like the others."

Corrigan explained about the traffic he experienced, and repeated the infiltrated line: *It's always good to have a chat with a clever man.*

Jonathan closed his eyes. "I'm sor–"

"The company cannot read my mind. What I heard... it's just static. Without the necessary technology my own signals will be equally random."

"I think that's right," Jonathan said. "They can push things down the pipe, though."

"It isn't just words. There are images, and voices I've never heard before."

He explained what it had been like in Harding's program, and that he realised he'd been networked ever since the day of his psych evaluation. The day-to-day experience of being part of something so limited was not as intense as being inside the program itself, but he had felt that inclusion in a way he had never previously known.

"They say I have some kind of brain anomaly that Emulate One reacts to."

"That's what Draseke said. He wanted to keep you above ground, dig around in your head, but Ulmer thought you'd be more useful down there."

Corrigan nodded sadly. "So that sadist wanted to cut me up."

Jonathan lowered his head. "I think he had even worse things in mind, but Ulmer made him work on getting the program to accept you." Corrigan leant closer to the screen when his virtual lover lowered his voice. "I don't think Ulmer wants to risk you being a threat to Emulate

One. They've done something and now the program is protecting whatever data it has on you."

"It's developed a vaccine against me." Corrigan laughed without humour.

"Perhaps, but remember viruses have a nasty habit of mutating."

A silence fell between them like a curtain at intermission. The quiet was oppressive, and Corrigan's mind began to wander in the vague hope of feeling the presence of Emulate One or some random ghost bumping around inside the mainframe.

"I betrayed you," Jonathan said, "to get a fucking job."

"DRT would have found someone else if you hadn't. They played both of us and exploited you. Had the tables been reversed, I would have done the same. Anything not to be a Non." He smiled, but it was a sad smile. "No one can resist being themselves. Human beings are adaptable, but *each to his own* is a truth no man can outrun. It's as impossible as separating the man from the shadow he casts."

The wound had been exposed to the air and the pain would recede as it healed. The angst of the immediate future was contained.

"I am fond of you, you know," Corrigan said, and ended the transmission.

B4 was online and Corrigan could see the front room at Harvey Road. It was feebly lit by a streetlamp. He instructed the droid to go out into the street and face the house opposite. The father was in his assumed position in the shadow of the doorway. Corrigan watched as he stumbled down the path and kicked open the gate.

"What the fuck? What I ever do to deserve this?" the man ranted at B4, swaying unsteadily in the gloom.

The idea of this man being Jonathan's father made no sense to Corrigan. How could such composure come from such disorder?

He asked B4 to zoom in on the man's face. The signs of infection were exactly as Jonathan described them. His eyes were yellow, his lips black and cracked. He lunged at B4, and she struck him with a jolt of electricity which left him lolling in the road.

"That'll teach you to go for an old girl."

"Go home, B4," Corrigan said, and the droid started to retreat, but the sick man crawled on his hands and knees, imploring her with much profanity.

"Begging won't cut the mustard with me, young man," the droid said, to which the man took up weeping. "And you can stop that, or I'll give you something to cry about."

B4 navigated her way back inside and watched him from the safety of the front room.

Jonathan's father came to rest on his knees, his arms to the heavens. He begged God to release him from his agonies. Corrigan considered calling Jonathan to let him know what was happening. Of all the things they had discussed, his father had never featured. He had spoken of his mother, how she had weathered whatever the world had thrown at her; he had spoken affectionately of his little brother, and considered his sister unbalanced. But he had never spoken of this man.

His wife came out onto the street, the children with her. They were all crying. A curtain just across the way fluttered, but no one dared venture from safety to go to them.

36

Corrigan awoke in a state of flux, rattled by nightmares of the advancing virus. He saw the infected father on his periphery, in the dark corner of his wardrobe, beneath the antique chest of drawers.

Perhaps they're not really his family.

He brought up a halo-screen and ordered coffee and toast, and requested Arthur be sent to serve him. The woman taking orders explained Arthur Fuse had not yet started his shift. Corrigan told her to contact him and get him out of bed.

He had a quick shower, arranged his hair, but stayed in his bathrobe. He'd always been at peace with his legs, but tightened the belt across his stomach.

The door buzzed. Arthur Fuse was perfectly turned out in his tight black outfit and tailored apron, but his eyes were cold.

Corrigan asked him to pour for two. When Arthur asked if Corrigan's guest would arrive shortly, the manager informed him there would be no one else. The waiter eyed him suspiciously when he invited him to join him on the sofa.

"There are important matters to discuss, and no time

for delay," the older man said.

"I have no idea what a high-ranking DRT manager might want to discuss with me," Arthur countered.

Corrigan took a moment to assess the surly young man. His features were symmetrical, and his skin of exceptional quality, and yet Corrigan found him unattractive.

"The world's in the grip of a calamity," he said, and the waiter sat unperturbed, his back straight, his black eyes unblinking, as Corrigan delivered humanity's dire prognosis.

"And what precisely do you think a waiter might be able to do to alleviate such an inevitable situation?"

"I read your paper. The one entitled 'Intellectual Courage and Artificial Intelligence'."

The younger Fuse flinched on hearing his paper referenced, and grunted something about courage being a subjective concept, but Corrigan outlined the CEO's vision, and how they were going to need Arthur's capacity for intuitive thinking. The young man shook his head and told Corrigan he no longer possessed any such traits, concluding, "It's been too long since I've been in a lab. I adapt more quickly to recipes than coding."

"I'm sure it's like riding a bicycle," Corrigan smiled, but Arthur refused to be drawn. "I understand your father was a Non," he then said.

The hostility was expected, but Corrigan persisted. "My mother was a Non. It was only her bloody-minded persistence that got me anywhere, transformed me into a Floater who refused to be flushed. My father, was a

Transient, one of those people who somehow managed to exist outside the system. I can't imagine what that's like. No benefits or even a fixed address."

"My mother thought nothing of bedding men for the purpose of advancing my chances," Corrigan continued as if he shared the details of his past as a matter of course. "I had always thought it repulsive, how she used her beauty and humour to ensnare them. She hadn't cared for them, but liked their houses and educated children." Their eyes were locked. "It took her death for me to calculate the extent of her sacrifice. Now she's gone, I realise she wasn't as selfish as I thought."

Arthur's eyes were as cold as Corrigan had ever seen them. "My mother networked for me," the waiter said, "belittled herself and begged favours. But you must have read that in my file. What you wouldn't have read was how I refused to be advanced by anything other than my own merits."

"I can see that. I felt much the same. I was cold to Hattie – my mother – and I have to wonder if that wasn't what weakened her and let the cancer in."

Arthur's face twitched, and he stood up, paced the room. "My mother, you know she died." Corrigan nodded and popped a Serenity. "Like you, I *know* I helped put my mother in the ground. For that matter, Jun knows I did. I was so arrogant."

Corrigan took a moment to reflect before he spoke. If he was going to convince Arthur, he needed to connect with him. "I took this current post," he finally said, "because

Hattie never let me wallow in self-pity. Always pushed me to take advantage of any opportunity. She sacrificed so much for those chances. Ultimately, it doesn't matter that I'll never know who my father was. I had all I needed in my mother. She was a remarkable and resilient person." Corrigan felt the pain in his throat, and the same regret. So he was not a dumbed-down Guardian, after all. "I would have had *no* life without her."

Arthur sat back down, but he was still agitated. "The man I grew up with – Jun's father – said I was a common man, a Non, a white migrant. But my mother's betrayal, and my birth, it had been more than her husband could bear, so I also caused his death."

"Nonsense. It's taken me a lifetime to realise I wasn't responsible for being born. No one has a say in that; no one decides who their parents will be or the circumstances of their conception. My mother resented my existence. I'd do her a disservice if I said she made my life uncomfortable. She made me *suffer* for being born. That didn't mean she didn't love me, but she resented every breath I took." He smiled at Arthur. "My father was a no one, less than a Non. He may as well have been a dog escaped his leash. She didn't even know his name. She was drunk; he was handsome and horny." Arthur tried to say something, but Corrigan stopped him. "If I can survive being an anonymous session, a mother's lifelong regret, yet a project she never tired of promoting, then you can thrive on being the son of a passionate affair. Your mother *loved* your father. She only ever respected Jun's."

But Arthur was not done being angry. "No! My mother was *dishonourable*!"

Corrigan hadn't meant to laugh, but the absurdity of the word caught him off guard. He apologised, and could not resist reaching out to stroke the young man's hair, to which he recoiled. "You have a duty," Corrigan said, "to do the right thing. Stop burying yourself alive and start living. We only have a short time remaining. You've wasted most of your life, so choose to *do* something now. Forget your parents. Defy the fuckers. They never gave you a thought while they were banging under a pagoda."

Whether consciously or not, Arthur ran a hand over the place where Corrigan had stroked his hair. "If there's really no one else, I'll consider it."

"There was never *anyone else*, but you won't be working alone. You'll be working with Gregor."

The briefest glimmer of something appeared in the waiter's eyes and Corrigan struck quickly: "So you'll help?"

Arthur stood up, bowed his head curtly, and agreed to do what he could.

"You must first meet the CEO," Corrigan said. "I'll send Gregor to collect you. But, for the time being, you're dismissed." As he departed Corrigan called, "Absolute secrecy is required, Arthur," which acknowledged with an insolent nod.

37

Corrigan stared up at the ceiling and imagined Jonathan's father crawling overhead, joined by nameless thousands, all infected and writhing and imploring.

"No point dwelling on it," Ulmer barked from the balcony doorway. "I don't see any advantage in telling little Johnny what you saw."

"So you were watching?"

"Me? No. Ramon told me all about it. Said you watched the man curl up and die. And you'd just had a finger fuck. I suppose calling him right away – shit still fresh on your index – would have been awkward."

Corrigan placed his coffee mug on a table and stared at the terminal man. "I plan to call him later."

"No need, we notified him, and the necessary arrangements have been made." The CEO strode out onto the balcony and glanced down at where the milling of punters read like ants on a map. "Nons are always among the first to go in any pandemic, and his lot were actual Transients until we intervened. Johnny was always a determined sort, though. Got what education he could. He's no believer, but he'd suck a priest off to get a place in school. Half-black and queer as fuck, things sure were stacked against him but he's pretty and determined, eh?" He turned back to Corrigan and nodded solemnly. "I believe he was expecting his family to be among the first to go. He headed straight to his new assignment at the Cloud Nine facility. Requested a proper coffin for his little brother. Happy for the rest to go in the furnace."

"But they're not all–"

"The whole nest was infected, but no need to let him know you saw anything."

"I didn't–"

"Switched it off before things got too gruesome, eh?" The CEO glared at his employee. "You like old, antiquated nonsense don't you Corrigan? Ever hear the old nursery rhyme 'Ten Little Indians'?" Corrigan recalled Hattie singing the rhyme to him when he was little. When he nodded his head somewhat nervously, Ulmer smiled. "The original ditty was about blacks, you know, 'Ten Little Niggers.'" Ulmer laughed at the manager's discomfort. "We paid lip-service to the concept of equality back in the dark days of democracy but we only ever did that to avoid rebellion. Those of us at the top never really wanted their kind in the board room, even the pretty ones. And you remember the last line of that dainty little nursery rhyme of course?"

"And then there were none."

The buzzer sounded and Corrigan hurried to the door. Gregor's shadow loomed over Arthur as they stepped into the room.

"We've been waiting," Ulmer said.

Arthur lowered his eyes and bowed his head.

"S*top that*!" the CEO hollered. "I can't abide subservience. It gives me gas." The young man lifted his head and squared his shoulders. "That's more like it. Spines should be erect." He ran a fat finger around his greasy neck, beneath the collar of his shirt, and stared at Arthur. "Apparently, you're a hidden *gem*," he then said.

Corrigan sighed, and Ulmer spun on his heals as if his body had temporarily forgotten its sickness.

"*Talent*," Corrigan said. "Talent is necessary, but–"

"The bolts can help." Ulmer assessed the android, its deportment, its synthetic muscles. He breathed onto its face, and the skin wrinkled in response. "Are you as acquainted with Project Egret as I've been led to believe?" The Guardian assured him there was nothing he could not access given the CEO's approval. "Yes, I understand you're pretty good at opening doors on your own, but not all of them, eh? I'll open whatever *remaining* doors it takes to enable you," Ulmer said, patting the Guardian's shoulder. "Oh, and by the way, are you still a mummy's boy, Gregory?"

The android tilted its head and the matter behind the clear reflective surface of his lidless eye shifted like a cluster of frog spawn on a rippled pond. "I am not to be confused with Gregory Meregalli. That entity no longer exists, or, if it does, it has little to do with my consciousness."

"But you remember your death?"

Gregor straightened his head and his one dragonfly eye glowed with cool green light. "Oh yes, it's a potent memory.

The body suffered extreme anxiety, such determination not to cease, that we believed we might defy death. And then it came, flooded us with euphoria, but that did not quell our panic. We were in a heightened state of desperation, our skin prickled, our heart pumped though weakened, and we could feel the air escaping our lungs, and, with that, something else slipped away. Whatever that energy is that supports organic life evacuated and was no longer available to us, and we fell through a space awash with data streams."

Ulmer coughed horribly, and then asked what the android would need to work on the project.

"Unrestricted access."

The CEO spat up a gob of phlegm, which he caught and caressed in a handkerchief. "I'll arrange *less* restricted access."

Gregor was persistent. "I will need to assess the bigger picture before–"

"M3 access provides visibility at the appropriate level," Corrigan said. Although he thought they might live to regret that decision, he didn't say so.

"I wouldn't've brought you into the program if I'd known what stage we were at, Corrigan," Ulmer said. "We might've hobbled on without the runt, or even our tight-assed little genius."

Corrigan's face flushed. "I assume I've now fulfilled my raison d'etre?"

"A person like you has more debt than d'etre, but I'll credit you with tempting our...what's your name?" He eyed Arthur. "Shame I didn't meet you sooner. You remind me of my Venezuelan. Perhaps I was wrong about racial blending...you turned out nicely. Hardly any Jap in you." His hand trembled over the young man's cheek. It never quite landed, but hovered with intent. "Always had a hankering for *sweet things*."

Corrigan shuddered, but Arthur's confidence seemed to increase, drawing out the precocious child in him. He tapped his temple and assured Ulmer the only thing of value he possessed was contained therein.

"And what a virgin you are in *that* respect," Ulmer purred.

Corrigan couldn't watch. He pulled a cork from a bottle of Merlot and poured himself a glass. "There are those who'd call our current predicament a calamity, and others who perceive it as an evolutionary leap."

"Someone needs to flush the loo on occasion," Arthur said. The callousness of the comment was matched only by the coldness of its delivery. "We're not exactly of any ecological benefit."

"That's right," Ulmer said. "We bent old Terra Firma right over and now she's fighting back. This virus is going to extinguish us, no goddamn doubt about it. Latest forecast gives us a couple of months." He stared cold and long at Arthur from under his sagging lids, an ample sweat breaking on his blotched forehead as he gathered his punch line. "We're going to squeeze you like a sponge. There won't be a drop of vinegar left to moisten a messiah's lips."

38

Hologrammatic images of Ulmer's head patrolled the facility. Pains had been taken to recolour the livid purple circles around his eyes, and the fatty deposits of his chins had been digitally remastered.

Several takes had been required before Ulmer managed to deliver his lines without irritability or abhorrence. "Calm is essential," the hologram said. "Reintroduction is both release and renewal. A new world awaits. Aid our endeavours and prepare. Download your families and secure their future."

News broadcasts were also played on large halo-screens throughout the facility. CDC scientists with withdrawn features and trembling voices did little to quell the panic the armed forces had been deployed to contain. Corrigan had B4 go out on reconnaissance. Although reporters gave a general impression of what was happening, they avoided detail. B4's view of events provided an unexpurgated view of a city in sickness and decay and panic.

The riots had been violent but short-lived. The more sensible looters targeted places where food could be gathered. After three days, the will to riot was expended, but Guardians sent above ground to set up downloading centres were requisitioned by the army and roamed the streets in search of casual looting, significant for its pointlessness: a pot plant in an abandoned office; a tablecloth from a closed down café.

Ulmer wanted Corrigan to continue to be the dutiful servant, the effective program manager who never gave up and always produced results. He was unsure regarding the security provided by his physical anomaly. Sure, Emulate One was allergic to him, but how useful was that to Ulmer? He imagined the CEO would deploy it if he felt checkmate was imminent. For the time being, he felt no compulsion or any desire to be Ulmer's puppet. The team had been galvanised by the crisis in ways no manager could achieve. Harding was absent, but Arthur and Gregor had formed a marriage of intellect and intuition that she could never match. If someone needed something, he was there, but the idea of being absorbed by a program that might consider him a threat was not an endeavour he felt obliged to contribute to.

Corrigan had B4 arrange a visit with Bohdan. When the doorbell rang, B4 let him in.

The cabbie looked tired and paler than usual. He asked his friend to forgive him: he was not feeling well.

"I've made a lovely chicken stew. One of Bobbin's favourites," B4 said as Bohdan lowered himself into Corrigan's armchair.

"I've not much of an appetite."

"You need to keep your strength up," Corrigan insisted. Resistance was futile. When B4 presented him with a bowl he took a spoonful. "It's good," he said.

"I apologise for the virtual arrangement," Corrigan said. "I wish I could be there."

"Nothing new," Bohdan said, but noting the expression on the manager's face he added, "I mean, we never got close. And now it's too late."

"Nonsense, it's–"

"Too late."

"Bohdan–"

"The dead are piling up in the streets. Those machines heap them and burn them. I can smell it, even with the windows closed. My own stench will soon drift with the others."

He looked up, and Corrigan went still: the Pole was showing the first signs of infection in the yellowing of his eyes. Corrigan asked him to move into his flat and allow B4 to tend to him.

"I'm ever so good at mothering," the droid said.

The cabbie resisted, but his resistance was as shaky as the turning down of the bowl of stew, and he agreed. Corrigan said he would speak with him several times a day, and make sure all the latest treatments were provided. He promised he would arrange for the Pole to be downloaded to the mainframe. No one, not even Emulate One, could resist Bohdan.

"You won't lock me up in there!"

"You'd be placed in limbo," Corrigan said.

"Nothing good will come from a thing like that. Who knows what might happen to a man once he's made into a machine? The idea frightens me more than becoming sick, more than being dead. I'd just as soon become a Transient and disappear."

"It wouldn't be frightening…"

"Not frightening? To be undead inside a network; imprisoned in there for as long as it takes to… And maybe never get out because the machines fail or the universe implodes. I won't do that. You mustn't do that. You mustn't!"

Corrigan was overcome. The last time they had spoken, the cabbie had been well, vital, and as strong as he had always been. "You know I love you." There was no hesitation now.

"If you do, then promise me."

"I promise."

The poignancy clung to them both in the heavy silence.

"I'll be there with you. I'll breach confinement," Corrigan then said.

"Don't risk that!" Bohdan seemed strong again, for a moment, and powerful. He sat up in Corrigan's chair. "If only you'd trusted me and not been such a snob!"

Corrigan laughed, but the tears in his eyes were instant. The ache of remorse burned a hole through his offense, and he asked why the cabbie had not made *his* feelings clearer.

Bohdan smiled. "I was thinking you might laugh at me."

They were as stupid as each other.

Bohdan rested his head back in Corrigan's armchair.

Overhead, Miss Champion could be heard shuffling, and the familiar sound made Corrigan's soul settle. He listened until a floorboard creaked beneath her weight, and he knew she was standing at her window, looking out over the city. A moment later there was a thud. The sound travelled through Corrigan as though Miss Champion had fallen from heaven.

"I'll go and tidy that up shall I, Bobbin?"

39

Although everyone was suffering, the separation from life above was pronounced in Corrigan, who spent long hours on halo-screen with Bohdan, with whom the virus toyed like a cat with a mouse. Comforts were administered by proxy, B4 stepping in to cook and nurse with disquieting ease.

Corrigan was aware his distress was projecting onto Lazarus, who meowed so pitifully on occasion he knew he must reign in his sorrow. Sipping a glass of wine, and soothing the cat by his side with long, careful strokes, he startled when he heard knocking at his door.

"Who's there?" he called out, reluctant to move.

The knocking became a tapping, the sound of fingers rather than knuckles. Putting his glass down he marched to the door and flung it on its hinges. He had expected to see the leaning Siegruth sisters or Gregor standing there, but it was Tierney Harding.

"They decided I was no longer a threat and I'd, well, calmed down," she said and smiled awkwardly. She crossed to the sofa where Lazarus lay sprawled out and sat beside the cat and stroked it. "What a lovely animal."

"Are you...? Is everything...?" He sat down in the

chair opposite.

"Everything is fine. The project will soon be back on track, don't worry. You've enough on your mind without concerning yourself with anything as mundane as saving the species." He stared at her. "Oh, don't look at me like a naughty schoolgirl, dear, that will only encourage me."

"Arthur and Gregor are making progress," he said, unwilling to engage. "I admit they're picking over the traces of your work, but the results are undeniable."

"They're inter–"

"*You* mustn't interfere." Her face became pained. "You may have a role, but Arthur runs the operation."

"I'm working on something that could help," Harding said. "They've made leaps in terms of mapping and emulating, and they're even closer to being able to isolate individuals as the program absorbs them, but they're reluctant to engage with the emotional dimension." She leant forward on the sofa and lowered her voice. "Did anyone ever tell you about Ulmer's message to Mercer, the one headed 'Answer'?"

"Project Egress has been mentioned."

"Egress isn't cyclical or progressive. It's a departure with no return ticket. They're eradicating any semblance of emotion from the program. I always intended an Emulate to mirror not only the functionality but the full emotional spectrum. If we're being replaced, then our mechanical doppelgangers need to be more like Gregor than the other Guardians."

Her words, but, significantly, the way she expressed

them, drew Corrigan out of his funk.

"Correct me if I'm wrong," he ventured, "but wasn't that the exact opposite of what you argued when Ulmer first announced our predicament? That there's danger in being configured the way Gregor has been configured?"

Harding shuffled her feet. "It's complicated. I don't want to simply be downloaded and stored. We could be in there a long time, perhaps indefinitely. If that's the case, wouldn't you like to be more emotionally dimensional than a glorified app?"

Corrigan was incredulous. "Emulate One is allergic to me!"

"Never listen to anything Draseke says. He saw utility in it, but the program appears to be curious about you, not hostile."

"Are you sure?" he asked, his voice trembling with emotion.

"As certain as I can be. Emulate One, she drew you in, protected you…not even Gregor knows anything about this. I was only included because Ulmer thought it might help us figure out how to segregate individual minds once downloaded. That's what the program did…"

"Put me in confinement?"

"Yes, but we couldn't replicate what she did instinctively."

Corrigan ran his fingers through his hair and stared at her. "What if she rejects me, or my file corrupts every other file?"

"I think she's protecting you, and that's not something

241

a mother would do if she'd rejected a child."

Corrigan remained unconvinced regarding the idea of being downloaded as a fully sensate being, and Harding seemed to intuit his reluctance when she said, "It's possible to gift us not only with emotion, but imagination. A virtual world or series of worlds could be maintained inside the program. We could live out generations inside the machine and never lose our innate characters."

Corrigan tapped his wristpad and brought up a halo-screen. He navigated to a browser, typed in *virtual worlds,* and watched as several links appeared, the more popular glowing red.

"You won't find a great deal on it," Harding said.

He looked at some of the headings, sighed, and clicked on the URL for *Draseke's Virtual World.* He scrolled through the review and underlined the words *unconvincing, one-dimensional* and *deeply unsatisfying.*

"We'll come up with something," Harding said.

"There isn't any time to *come up* with anything. Humanity is going to have to fly economy to the future. There'll be no first-class, not even for Ulmer."

"It's not economy," Harding said. "We're going cargo."

"You know, there's very little to distinguish the kind of *migration* suggested by Project Egret from the aims of the project had it been called Egress."

Harding's face tightened. "Migrating birds fly south for the winter and return in spring. There'll be no spring for us. No reintroduction."

"Meregalli's making progress on the hosts." He scrolled

on his wristpad. "Perhaps you can work together and alter the seasons."

"You're taking a risk you may regret once you're locked up in a *holding cell* for eternity."

Although Corrigan felt sympathy for her, he was reluctant to demonstrate it. "I'd be wary of overestimating your importance," he said. "The problems Arthur and Gregor are having will not persist. If you would like to contribute, you should report what you're working on to Arthur. As for me, I no longer have a raison d'etre as far as DRT is concerned. I fulfilled my purpose when I delivered Arthur."

She observed him, her hand on Lazarus's back. "I'll make arrangements. Have this friend of yours brought down," she said quietly.

His head shot up. "What friend?"

"Come on, Robert, everyone knows about your taxi driver. We can offer him a great deal more than your droid. Leave it with me. Bringing down an infected patient for "observation" would be a lesser risk than allowing a Guardian to return to the facility. I'll arrange it, and make sure every precaution is taken." Corrigan felt as if he had been cut open and left to bleed out. "You can be in a room with him," she continued, "but you'll have to wear a suit. You can sit with him, hold his hand until, well...until."

"I–I don't know what...what can I say? I owe–"

"You don't owe me anything. I'll work with Katherine. I'm sure we can do this."

When she left, he took her place beside Lazarus and

called B4, but to observe not chat. She was moving along The Mall, where a row of flags shifted about in the feeble mist. What was she doing in The Mall, and why the flags? Perhaps they had been strung about to celebrate something no longer relevant…a state visit, or Royal wedding. The droid rolled towards the Duke of York memorial, where a young man clung to a rail in front of a stone wall. B4 stopped to verify the symptoms.

"He's a gonner, for sure," she said.

Ash coated his clothing, covered everything, and the young man flicked at the grey dust with a grey hand. B4 rolled on towards Trafalgar Square. Smoke billowed in the mist, barely mobile. They came into the square, where an unmanned tractor heaped corpses in front of South Africa House. A child's arm tumbled, pale as a fish dead in a bucket. He was relieved he could not smell the pyres burning.

"Never seen the like," B4 said.

Mass-produced Guardians were collecting cadavers that had fallen from the tractor, and Corrigan wondered at their consciousness. Were they aware of what they were doing? He noted how the substance within their insectile heads appeared to breath as whatever they processed was reflected by the colour of the light they streamed. Green was the most consistent colour they emitted through their glass-like domes. Corrigan's interactions with Gregor suggested that situations of concern were reflected by colours from the warmer end of the spectrum and the commonplace translated as cool shades of blue and green.

A dog, shaking with frenzied barking, came charging over the steps of St Martin in the Field. The nearest Guardian's head glowed red as it un-holstered a side arm and shot the animal.

"Time to go home, Bobbin," B4 said.

The droid moved rapidly towards Leicester Square, Holborn, Russell Square, Kings Cross, Holloway, and Finsbury Park. Everywhere she went, Guardians manoeuvred the dead and dying into piles and onto pyres. When people staggered from their homes, from broken-in shops or broken-down bus shelters, they were shot where they stood trembling in the dust. Corrigan put his hand over his mouth to silence the cry.

When the droid arrived at Harvey Road, the door was open and Bohdan was gone, and the cry this time was freed. He fell to his knees.

A halo-screen opened and Harding appeared.

"We sent in a team to collect your taxi driver," she said. "He's here in the lab, come at once."

40

Corrigan urged the lift on as it dropped to the ground floor, and when the doors opened he clocked the Siegruth sisters as they scurried to intercept him. He held up a hand. "Not now."

"Mr C," Jan panted, "it ain't like you to be discourteous."

"Let us accompany you to Poland," Jan said.

"Like Stalin," Edna said. Corrigan stopped in his tracks. "Or was it Lenin?"

On the move again, he made for the exit, and Edna was pinned against the revolving door when she shuffled in front of him, her hand rammed between the glass sides.

"You're crushing her, Mr C!" Jan yelled. "You'll straighten her fingers if you don't pack it in."

Corrigan crossed the bridge to the hydroponic gardens and trampled daisies as he waded through a scrum of bleating sheep.

"They're not dissimilar to the masses," Edna said of the jostling animals, flexing her claw.

"As comrade Lenin was ever so fond of proselytising," Jan said. "'The strength of the present-day movement lies in the *awakening* of the proletariat.'"

Corrigan forged ahead, past the thicket of pines surrounded by daffodils, towards the hill where rabbits chewed grass and birds wrenched worms from the soil. The siblings stood at the bottom of the hill as if it were the granite face of Everest.

"Lenin figured revolution were a kinda consciousness," Edna observed.

"That's right," Jan said, "a consciousness in embryonic form. Like our very own Emulate One."

"You know as well as I do, the poor have no kingdom, the mourners know no end of sorrow, and the meek inherit nothing but toil and heartache. Our charity and peacefulness are toys for men like Ulmer to exploit," Corrigan roared, the intensity of it making his heart thrash his ribs.

"Bravo!" Edna cheered. "Giving voice to the vile maxim itself!"

"Well said," Jan agreed. "Now come down off your high horse and join us commoners before someone crucifies you or drags you off like some Transient wastrel."

Corrigan hurried over the hill and they hustled after him, their uneven legs and overexerted lungs making them unpleasant to watch as well as hear.

"She means well," Jan called, "but Harding's not to be trusted. Not when she's been, well, down on the master."

"Harding's a lesbian?" Corrigan exclaimed.

"That one never developed a taste for women, no she never; and when she was younger, she was a bit of a man-eater."

"She was in a relationship with *Ulmer*?" Corrigan felt queasy.

"Well, not sure you'd call it *that*," Jan said with a look of repulsion.

"Whatever it was," Edna observed, "she wore the trousers until she upped and left 'im."

"And he weren't none too pleased about that," Jan added.

"Started calling her a lessie and she couldn't get no work for months on end."

"Not till she, you know..."

Corrigan recalled Harding wiping her mouth with a napkin after eating eggs benedict. He refused to believe Harding had an ulterior motive on this occasion and made his way along the corridor towards the lab. Ahead of him, Meregalli was waiting.

"We have him in here," she said. She waved her hands at the sisters. "Go."

Corrigan could not resist the urge to turn around. The Siegruths were leaning in the middle of the corridor, their cheeks pink from their exertions, the only colour in the grey of their skin and attire. They turned and hobbled away.

"Never know what to make of them," Meregalli said. "They had hard lives. I suppose their deformities made it difficult, let alone coming from a piss-poor background. Clever, though."

"I expect they had a 'rough' education..." Corrigan said, anxious to get to Bohdan and not remotely interested in discussing the twins' background or intellect.

"Among the roughest going. I suppose they must have satisfied a niche market when they were younger. That was their trade, initially. Whores, madams, then onto other forms of business. Heard they used to sell Belushi Grey, but who's to judge?"

Corrigan popped two Serenity lockets into his mouth and frowned. "Bohdan…"

"Yes."

Meregalli took him through the decontamination process, taking pains not to add to his anxiety but aware it was a precise process. She undressed, carefully removing each item of clothing and hanging it on the hooks provided. He marvelled at her naked body, and the envy rattled him. He proceeded to remove his own clothing, yet far from the expected self-consciousness, he experienced an instant, liberating sense of anonymity. His body was no more his own than the thoughts his mind constructed and shared with Emulate One, with a collective consciousness, an all-encompassing and ultimately anonymising entity.

They put on protective suits and entered the mobile decontamination unit that led to the observation room, a centrally housed glass booth. Bohdan was on a bed, his eyes closed, his blackened lips clenched in pain. Harding was by his side.

Corrigan went very still.

"I'm here," Meregalli said, and squeezed his arm, which distracted him for a moment. Meregalli *compassionate*? He had to wonder if she was not revisiting some private moment; those final minutes with her son; the fragments of memory of the boy she loved...who had been gifted to Gregor as the basis of his configuration. Yes, there still remained suspicion, and he was not sold. He had no doubt this little exercise had been of considerable benefit to her research.

She opened the booth. The stench was abominable, and Corrigan's stomach lurched. Bohdan heard them enter and opened his eyes, the deep yellow sickening. Seeing Corrigan, he stretched out a grey hand, the beseech in his grey face identical to that of the stricken Lazarus. Corrigan could barely recall what the man had looked like before, least of all the colour of his eyes.

He stepped forward, carefully sat on the edge of the bed and grasped Bohdan's hand and placed his other on the sick man's forehead. The latex gloves would protect him from infection, but the heat of the fever could be felt.

Bohdan's grip was remarkably strong, but his voice was weak. "I never thought we'd manage..."

"I won't leave you," Corrigan said.

"Won't be long now." He patted Corrigan's knee, and Corrigan placed his hand on Bohdan's cheek, but Bohdan removed it. "You need to take care."

His breathing rattled and his eyes protruded. All vanity was gone, and something selfless and pure lingered; the awareness of a soul about to be freed from the confines of flesh and bone that Corrigan felt in his own.

"Be wary of those machines," Bohdan then said, taking a lungful of air and holding it inside as if storing the feel of it in his chest. He exhaled. "They aren't us."

"I know," Corrigan said. "I've seen what they do. Shooting the sick, even the children, piling them up, burning them…"

There was a gasp. Corrigan was sure it was Harding.

"Whatever you do…" Bohdan rasped. "Whatever you…you must watch them."

"I will."

Harding came to stand next to him, as if with purpose. Her wristpad flashed, and bold red letters appeared. Like a fly drawn to a trap designed to exterminate, Corrigan was unable to look away. *WE HAVE HIM.* He realised what Harding was trying to tell him, and the idea of a link having been established between Bohdan and Emulate One did not calm him. It was a betrayal. He had promised Bohdan he would not allow them to download him, but the idea of losing him altogether was more than he could bear.

There was the sound of a muffled expulsion, and Bohdan curled in pain. The smell was instant, heavy inside the existing stench of the room.

"Shall I arrange a change of bag?" Meregalli asked, but Bohdan slumped and his eyes rolled. A thick trickle of blood crept slowly from his mouth like an earthworm.

Corrigan still had hold of his hand, and gripped it harder. "I'm here," he said, his voice outside of his head, like a stranger to him.

"This thing death…" Bohdan murmured.

Corrigan still held on, as if the grip might tether

Bohdan to mortal life, make him well, make him strong. But Bohdan was leaving, and his final exhale passed over his black lips, and Corrigan fancied he saw it lift and take flight.

"We have him," Harding said.

He stood, stepped away, and stared at Bohdan. It made no sense. How could someone leave their body yet be captured? He wanted to see the file. He wanted to hold Bohdan like he never had in the flesh, feel the leather of his old brown jacket and the touch of his lips. He wanted to run, make for the surface of whatever this was and see the blue sky above the clouds. *Anything could happen in a wasteland.*

Harding announced the program had absorbed the data, but it would take a moment before segregation was complete. Arthur's latest coding was imperfect, she said, but it would eventually manage the job.

"Come," Meregalli said. But it was said softly.

They left the booth, stripped and were disinfected. They dressed, and Harding invited him to sit before a large halo-screen. There were countless lines of green coding, layer upon layer weaving through one another. She typed in a code – Bohdan's identifier? – and, moments later, red strands appeared through the emerald stream.

"And he doesn't know?" Corrigan asked.

"Storage only. As requested."

It was too much. "Delete it! Delete him! I beg you!" He collapsed onto the desk. *None* of this made sense. "Please..." he cried, turning to look at them in turn, before collapsing once more.

"You must sleep," Harding said, and Meregalli nodded, putting her hand on his shoulder. "It's not a decision to be made on a whim. Besides, it's not possible to completely isolate his file. We could only ever delete part of it and could damage others in the process. They're all interlinked. As a program, Emulate One has never differentiated between individuals. You must have sensed that when you were inside the program."

Corrigan was exhausted. The love he'd never had was gone. He had slipped through the eye of a needle and become lines of data on a mainframe. He wept.

41

The following days were among the loneliest and most desolate of Corrigan's life. He sat on the sofa, on a chair, the bed, the balcony railing, a bird not able to come to rest.

Lazarus sat vigil, and Corrigan recalled the way the cat had sat on his windowsill and stared in at him at Harvey Road. He could not look upon him without feeling their situations had been reversed. Somehow, he was now on the other side of the glass, looking in on a world where order and comfort were so close but not his to possess.

The buzzer sounded and he yelled, "We're not home!"

The letterbox flipped open, and a crooked hand poked through and waved at him. He was so incensed by the intrusion that he stormed across the room and flung the door open. His body trembled from head to foot. He could not speak. But his temper began to wither when he observed the concern in the identical faces, and he sat heavily on the sofa.

"This is the kind of thing I know something about," Jan said, plonking her wonky body next to him.

Repelled as he was, she'd said the words with kindness of a mother, and his rage wilted.

Edna stomped into the kitchen, crashing about in his

cupboards. The racket made his nerves twitch.

"It's the worst thing in the world to lose someone you love, especially when you only just managed to own up to loving them." Jan's words rustled in his ears, like dry leaves blown free from the jagged branch of his misery. "I had an obsession once. Buster his name was. Whenever he was near, I could feel it. It got into my heart so I couldn't speak. I walked around as if I'd lost everything until he came back. But I never dared tell him."

Edna joined them, a cup of tea rocking in her hand as precariously as her gait. Had God prejudged them and issued their malformations as a punishment for future crimes? The same god the priests claimed to commune with as Jonathan serviced them when he was a Transient boy?

Edna placed the cup on the coffee table in front of him, and he wondered when he'd last drunk a good, honest cup of English tea. This penchant for coffee…what was that? He took a sip and was in his armchair in Harvey Road, B4 fumbling her duties and his feet on the ottoman.

"But I was on the way up," Jan continued, as Edna nestled on the other side of him, "and he was down where I come from." Corrigan sipped his tea and fell into the storytelling. "He was a Non, recently elevated from a long line of Transients. He worked for us, delivering things, and driving me about."

Edna patted his leg and gave him a sorrowful smile, as if experiencing her sister's grief afresh. There was a level of disingenuousness in evidence, however, as there so often was with the less vocal of the sisters. If Corrigan stared at her for too long, he imagined he saw dark scheming, even the seeking of revenge, behind the bright eyes.

"I figure he liked the way I doted on him," Jan said. She grappled with her regret and took a breath. "I've done some terrible things, but I never hurt no one more than I hurt Buster. Started using our product…"

"Poor thing," Edna said, "had a stroke."

"And then I *was* able to sit with him. And what he do but lay in that bed and stare at me? A judge's gavel never struck so hard as that hit my heart. Longest stretch I ever served."

"She sat in her room," Edna said. "Wouldn't budge for days."

Corrigan put his cup down. "Will these awful feelings ever stop?" he asked quietly.

"Never. They're ghosts what haunt your house," Jan said. "No, it was Ed what brought me out. She kept going on about work."

Corrigan could feel the shame warming his cheeks. The world was dying. Entire families were gasping their last, greying and yellowing behind drawn curtains, or being shot on the streets they'd called home. And here he sat, broken over a cabbie who'd flown him about London, who he'd hardly known. He put his head in his hands.

"It'll be alright," Jan said, and patted his leg, but the lie was too much for him.

The outpouring lasted close on an hour, and he stoked it, forcing older miseries to run alongside the raw grief of losing Bohdan. But it ebbed by degrees, and when he surfaced Jan sent Edna off to make him another cuppa.

"Who the hell *are* you two?" he asked when Edna returned with a second cup of tea.

"Ulmer ordered us to set up surveillance on you," Jan said. "We'd been engaged long before you signed a contract." Edna plonked down beside him, her shortened leg rubbing against his thigh. "We found that boy... Jonathan." Jan rubbed his knee and pressed closer to him, so her bosom heaved on his bicep. "We found his family a place to live. They were out on the streets, you see, and he wanted to prove himself at DRT. He was a determined sort, and his family being in straights made it easier for us to recruit him. That and him being a shade darker than old Caspar normally agrees to employ, let alone promote." In the pause, Corrigan looked at her. Her face was pleasant enough, but Edna had been right when she said they *never managed to wash out the rough*. "That Bohdan was one of ours, too," Jan then sighed.

The cup and saucer rattled in Corrigan's hands, and she placed a firm hand on his thigh.

"He had no idea. Our friend Jonathan picked him. We knew he was a homo like you. Had Jonathan check that out. Then we bought up that taxi firm he worked for and I run a few checks. Had a look at his porn prints and online dating. Bohdan were a perfect match for you. Ed and me felt like mystics...we could see the pairing so easily."

"Only you said it was flawed, didn't you?" Edna said.

"I did, Ed. It was like watching meself with Buster. We had Bluebird bring him in for a medical and that's when we stitched him up; implanted a little something so as we could always see what he was up to. And he went in your place a few times. That B4, what a character she is…"

"She's my mother…bits of her sewed up in circuitry and polymer."

Corrigan fell to contemplation. He would never have met Bohdan or Jonathan if it hadn't been for the crippled sisters and their sinister acts of surveillance. He would have remained alone, probably working on some dull project or other. As for B4… He had never been in control. The company had manipulated him from the beginning. And yet somehow, knowing that made it all easier to bear. "Are you still on security and surveillance?" he asked.

"You finish your tea," Jan said, "and we'll have a shufty. There're things going on all over the shop."

He would never be able to trust Jan, but he couldn't help liking her. The way she spoke. The connection she made with his own roots, and he figured her loss and grief were genuine enough. "How did you meet Buster?" he asked, nervous of the answer.

"I've often wondered that me-self," Jan said.

Edna got to her feet. The look she gave them was not a happy one, as if she had taken offense at their emerging relationship. "Well, that Belinda never thought you as focused on moving our product as you might be." She shuffled towards the kitchen and the burden of the words made her movement even more ungraceful.

42

Jan and Edna had prepared food, and after they had eaten Jan opened a halo-screen and a live feed played from the AI lab. The three of them sat side by side on the sofa, plastic trays on their laps as if they were about to watch an innocuous situation comedy whilst enjoying a bit of supper. The CEO looked decrepit, and leant unsteadily against a desk, gazing at Gregor.

"If I called you a creature," Ulmer asked, "how'd you take that, eh?"

Gregor tilted his head to one side, skewing Ulmer's reflection. "I do not perceive my existence as that of a creature. Creatures are defined by organic qualities I do not possess. A being would be more precise."

Jan made herself comfy on the sofa beside Corrigan. "Hark at him," she laughed. "His Lordship Sir Nuts-n-Bolts."

The CEO glared at the Guardian, the sweat on his brow profuse. "You'll never suffer the humiliation of a faulty design!" he yelled and winced from a sudden jab of pain. When the spasm relented he leant in closer. "That said, I'm not convinced you're spared so much." Spittle splattered Gregor's dome. "What if you could be organic without the flaws?" he then asked.

"The organic nature of being *is* the flaw," Gregor said. "Guardian construction removes all associated weakness."

Ulmer rubbed his thumb and forefinger along his jaw. "There're those who'd say our imperfections are what perfect us."

"The imperfect have no choice other than to perceive existence in that way. Failure to do so would render them inert."

"I don't agree with that." Ulmer pointed at the algorithms and coding scribbled across the blackboard. They appeared to soothe him. "It wouldn't paralyse them. It'd give them drive."

"There are exceptions to the rule, but the rule is dominant."

"Sometimes the exception rules the rule," Ulmer said, but was momentarily distracted by a coughing fit, and launched a ball of phlegm the size of an eyeball into his handkerchief. Fluid seeped through the cloth, and he appeared to admire it, rolling the ball around and squeezing it. It appeared to Corrigan there may even have been a moment of arousal. "When it's archaic and corrupt, the exception's objective must be to make *itself* the rule," he added, folding the handkerchief around the phlegm and putting it into his trouser pocket.

"I conducted research into the company's history. You constructed an elaborate web of deceit."

"I did what needed doing. The species is contagion. The planet's suffering. Soon be as terminal as I am. It needed a cure."

"A palliative might have sufficed."

Ulmer leant back and gave Gregor a look as one might regard a precocious child. "You can't *treat* a virus. You must eradicate it. I travelled a long road...that led to Venezuela. And before you consider thanking him, be warned: Ramon would never accept it. He's done some terrible things, but he didn't do any of them without my sanction or direction. That boy wants distance. I imagine a world beyond good and evil, but his heart's walled up by beliefs he can't shake."

"*Good* does not exist," Gregor said, extending his neck, like an animal on alert. There was a hint of alarm in his voice and his cloudy translucent eye burned red. "Such arbitrary descriptors are invention."

"A creature like Ramon has *nothing*," Ulmer said. "I took pains to ensure his development was one-dimensional, like a bog-standard Guardian." He stood up and crossed the room. "I'm a machine," the CEO then said. "They tried tagging me with autistic, even suggested Asperger's or sociopathy. The final diagnosis's probably most accurate. The others were as wide of the mark as calling you a creature." He returned to Gregor and winked at his own reflection. "Not every psychotic kills or tortures in the same way, and we don't all murder living things. I figure I'm an evolutionary leaper. As I said, I travelled a long road to reach this destination. And yes, I deceived the masses. But they're so deluded. A single peek under the hem of existence would turn them to stone."

Gregor remained silent as he made his computations and constructed new algorithms. The dark matter floating in his transparent globe rolled like a foetus in a womb. The orange illumination and the movement inside the insectile eye caught the CEO's attention.

"I did what needed doing," Ulmer growled. "Malice is a pointless drive, as counterproductive as mewing over a random tart. I'm not looking to harm anyone. I want to raise them up as I feel myself raised. The only way a man can improve himself is by overcoming himself. Then he might look back at his former self as we currently look at the apes."

A blue light pulsed dimly in the centre of the Guardian's head.

"The closer I get to death, the less distracted I am by sex, and that's the only animal weakness I ever indulged. It's a force only a living being can own. That'd be my one regret, to lose the drive and never again know the release of it." Ulmer turned and collapsed back into his chair, as if exhausted by his own pontification.

"Violence might satisfy a similar requirement." The android studied the ailing man. "Human beings suffer more weaknesses than strengths. You must eat and sleep. You are prone to illness and infection, injury and mishap. I am unaffected by any of these constraints or eventualities. My thinking is uncluttered. I do not feel the need to rest. I am driven by designs more substantive than an exchange of fluids."

"A regular Tin Man, eh?"

Jan chuckled by Corrigan's side.

"I don't believe you!" Ulmer placed his hand over his heart. "'*If I only had a heart...*'" he mimicked. "You don't have one, but, somehow, they configured things in such a way that you have something *else*. A centre, I suppose, and you're every bit as frail as they are in that respect." Ulmer laughed loudly. A vulgar sound.

"I have communed with Harding's program," Gregor said, "and it is impossible to do so without, to some degree or other, networking oneself."

"It's just a program, son."

"Au contraire. Emulate One is a being, and no one who enters her remains entirely independent."

"Yes, perhaps we are randomly – even unknowingly – poking about inside each other's goddamn skulls, but we're far from united in our thinking, regardless of Harding's efforts to *mother* us."

Gregor leant in close and tilted his shiny head. "Does any consciousness know singularity of thought? This new plurality of the living and the dead is networked, and it would be impossible to say who or what is controlling it."

Ulmer patted the Guardian, who retreated immediately. "I've dipped in and had a peek myself. Felt those busy little hands beavering away. I'm sure they gave as much as they took." He laughed again, no less vulgar. "No doubt left a little something among the old grey matter, eh?" The CEO tried to stand up, but slumped heavily. "You know Capitalism only fails once it fully succeeds. 'Consumerism' our now discredited progressives once called it. What they never understood about *consumers* was their actual utility. I always thought of them as the consumable itself. We know Capitalism reigns victorious because almost every unit available has now been fully consumed." He patted his stomach and groaned. "You'll need to get me a wheelchair. My legs are fucked." When the android failed to respond, Ulmer yelled, "The *Wizard* needs wheels! Get *Dorothy* in here!"

The Guardian tilted its head.

"That little faggot of yours! Arthur! Fetch Arthur!"

The blue light surged in the android's head, dimmed, and vanished. Gregor then backed out of the room.

The CEO groaned, his hand on his chest, as he watched the insectile creature retreat. The Guardian was a spider who crawled tunnels and spouted theories, but the CEO was no longer certain which of them was caught in the other's web.

Jan flicked off the halo-screen.

"What do you make of that?" she asked Corrigan. "The bloody consumed indeed!"

"The man is a mass murderer and we ought to expose him."

Jan laughed at that. "Who ya gonna call?" And Edna laughed so hard she wiped tears from her eyes.

Corrigan smiled sadly and then had a thought. "What do they mean when they say we've been networked?" he asked.

"There've been a few complaints," Jan said. "You know, people from the team experiencing some spooky

266

thoughts and feelings. More stress than Emulate One tucking in and spewing over the congregation like an allergic Mother Superior. But there are some who talk as if it's something downright mystic."

Corrigan nodded. But it no longer mattered. Nothing mattered, and it never would again.

43

Corrigan suffered the darkest of all nightmares, the kind drawn from reality. The chimeras cast shadows from the past across the present, extending elongated fingers into the future. He heard Bohdan moan from the confines of his coded tomb. He wailed, and Corrigan could feel the penetration of his misery where it rumbled in his mind. The cabbie's words were undecipherable, but his condemnation absolute. He then crawled naked and grey across the tarmac of Harvey Road, his knees and hands grazed and bleeding and his fingernails split. Down he seeped through Earth's crust to a seething cauldron where he wallowed among the bones of Nons, Floaters and Workers, now indistinguishable from each other; the consumed.

Thoughts of the street outside his flat made his nightmare lurch into memories of Jonathan. The young man sat alone, perhaps in quarantine or in a dorm, and his shoulders rocked as he wept over the loss of his family. He had sacrificed so much to give them a new home, but he could not save them from the plague. Corrigan saw the Transient family crawling across the floor towards his only living friend.

"Get out!" Jonathan suddenly hollered. "Get out of

my head!"

Corrigan bolted up in bed, struggling to acclimatise to the world he reluctantly accepted as reality. The cat was sitting on the end of the bed as still as a powered-down droid, his eyes on Corrigan. For a fleeting moment, he thought Lazarus might pounce, but then the cat meowed loudly. He shuddered at the thought of Jonathan above ground, vulnerable to infection, and knew he could not lose anyone else. He beckoned the cat, and Lazarus waded through the folds of duvet to receive the affection he so richly deserved.

He must get to Jonathan, must find a way to surface like a whale too long at the ocean floor. Up he would rise, drawn by a yearning stronger than the need for oxygen, to retrieve his one remaining friend. How alone he would be otherwise. Ways in which this mission might be accomplished remained as hazy and unformed as fragments of lost dreams. He would almost certainly need help, but he did not trust any of the possible contacts who might assist him.

He crept into the living room where the crippled sisters lay entwined on the sofa like a mutant, two-headed spider. He certainly could not trust them, even though he had grown attached to them. They had been kind to him – very kind – but they had yet to demonstrate the capacity for any real loyalty, let alone an inclination to offer him any. While the twins were sleeping, Corrigan slipped out and made his way to the office, where he found Ramon putting things in order. The manager coughed, and the PA turned around, a look of inquiry on his face.

Corrigan sat behind the desk and stroked the surface with the flat of his hand. "All this wood is nothing less than the world's skeleton. Humanity deboned Mother Earth and left her defenceless."

Ramon studied his manager.

"Perhaps," Corrigan suggested, "Ulmer was right to trigger the calamity."

Ramon did not flinch.

"Regardless, I need you to arrange a visit to the surface."

Ramon frowned. "It's not possible to go topside. The city's in chaos. The machines are shooting people on sight."

"All the same, I must get to the Cloud Nine facility."

"Perhaps you should contact your *friend* first?"

"No. I will take Gregor with me if necessary. In fact, if I were to have an escort, I could think of none better."

"Perhaps we could go together and bring Gregor as a guide?"

The young man was handsome in the stark light of the office. "I don't want to expose you to any unnecessary risk."

"If you don't take my offer, you'll never make it out of here."

There was no denying how useful the PA could be. Certain doors would remain shut unless he possessed the right key – doors only one of Ulmer's trusted advisors could access.

They hurried along the corridor to the AI lab. As they

approached, they could see the Guardian in discussion with Arthur Fuse. They submitted to the required security scans and entered the workspace.

Arthur offered them a greeting, which Ramon ignored. "We need a private conversation with the android," he said.

"Gregor's hot property," Arthur scowled. "I mean, look at those thighs." There never had been any doubt regarding the beauty of the android's physique. "What's in that polished dome, however," Arthur said, "that's what's truly beautiful. And *that* I cannot do without."

"You'll have to make do for a few hours," Ramon said. "There's a mission, critical activity, only Gregor can perform."

"I can't recall any such thing being mentioned."

"There have been developments," Corrigan said.

Arthur scrutinised the intruders. "Perhaps I'll call Ulmer. Check in before we do anything rash."

Corrigan stared the petulant young man down. How arrogant he had become. Promotion had clearly given him a taste for authority.

Ramon also stared, his eyes boring into those of the exulted waiter. "Old Caspar is like a father to me. He dotes on me, encouraging some of my more...unusual tastes." Arthur stepped back, and Ramon followed him. "I'm sure Caspar would let me play with your brother if I asked him nicely."

"No need for threats," Corrigan said. "I'm sure Arthur's a clever fellow and realises we're only having a pleasant chat."

Arthur's eyes flashed, and he gestured for the Guardian to comply with their request.

When they were in the corridor, Gregor stopped and tilted his head. Perhaps the android sensed tension. Corrigan was producing pheromones by the ton, and his heart pulsed rapidly.

"It's urgent," Ramon said.

Gregor turned his attention to Corrigan, but Ramon placed himself between the android and his manager. "We're going above ground and need a guide," the PA said.

"A protector," Gregor said, "would be the more essential role, if recent reports are to be believed."

"Are you going to assist or not?" Corrigan snapped, losing patience.

"I'd be delighted. I'll activate a secondary device above ground and tether that to my consciousness down here."

Arthur watched them through the lab window, brought up a halo-screen and navigated through layers of schematics and coding, never once allowing his attention to fully stray from what was going on in the corridor. His sharp eyes cut through the virtual screens to the more relevant and current state of play.

"Do you intend to split yourself between the lab and the world above?" Corrigan asked.

Gregor leant over the manager. "It is a simple task for an Emulate. I can provide full attention to both roles. I will separate into two distinct entities that can merge the files once the mission is over." He paused, maintaining his dominant position. "I assume our activities above ground are to remain secret?" Corrigan smiled. "Make your way to the surface. If you get past security, I will meet you at the exit."

Ramon avoided the direct scrutiny of a local security camera and suggested they use the cargo lift in bay nine. "It's currently locked," he said, "but I have the override code."

Gregor looked from one to the other. "I was told that only Mr Ulmer had access to override those systems." When neither of them replied, he said, "I'll meet you in half an hour," and returned to the lab.

Arthur looked up from the halo-screen. There was something victorious about his expression.

44

The bio-suits were more robust than those worn in Genetics. They were armoured, black with a silver DRT symbol embossed over the sternum, and the helmet had a hermetically sealed visor. Air was filtered through a purification pack attached to the back of the suit. Corrigan tried the hands, and found his dexterity was unhampered and his sense of touch enhanced. When Ramon caught him marvelling at them, the PA explained the suit had been made using the sensate material Jun designed for the Guardians.

They entered the cargo bay. The storage unit was dark save for the light of the lift controls and from cameras. Ramon entered the override code and provided retinal, fingerprint and DNA scans. Cameras whirred. "Security will receive a looped feed of an empty bay," he reassured Corrigan.

They made their way to the lift and Ramon pressed the button for the surface. The lift doors clanked shut, and with a groan of taught cables it began its noisy ascent.

"Quite different from travelling in the glass versions," Corrigan said. Ramon nodded. The PA was apparently unwilling to engage in chit-chat, but still Corrigan asked,

"How long is it since you went to the surface?"

"Not since the boy became ill," Ramon said, and that was that.

The lift shuddered in the shaft, groaning through layers of history to the planet's surface. The sound went straight through Corrigan, and he felt the crushing weight of human endeavour compressed alongside the skeletons of the creatures exploited to extinction. In his heart, he could not isolate a species worthy of salvation, only individuals who mattered to varying degrees. In that one sense alone he felt a certain simpatico with Ulmer.

The lift came to an abrupt halt and the doors ground and clattered open. The warehouse was as dark as the cargo bay below, and Corrigan peered into the gloom. He startled when a Guardian marched across the space towards them.

"Do not be alarmed," Gregor said. "I have taken a more rudimentary form as it was the only model available above ground."

They followed him along a corridor to a large parking lot. Railway lines ran along the edges, and there was a cluster of landing pads. There were no people or Guardians. There was no activity whatsoever, apart from their own, and the quiet was deeply unsettling. Gregor directed them to a hover-car, a standard corporate vehicle, smart but not ostentatious.

Ramon gave Corrigan a handgun and asked if he knew how to use it. When the manager did not respond, the PA said, "You only need to point and pull the trigger."

As they flew over the city, smoke billowed from pyres and explosions rocked the air around them. Flames burst in fiery mushrooms, adding their smoke to the black ceiling separating the city from the heavens. When Corrigan paled, Gregor said, "It is inefficient to dig pits to bury the dead. The buildings are set with explosives."

The android brought the hover-car down beside the World's End pub.

"Always hated this place," Corrigan said. "Far too crowded." But he surveyed the empty streets, and his words hung like an epiphany of what would never be again.

Ramon directed them along Camden High Street, past the Electric Ballroom and the abandoned market stalls, down Buck Street to the Cloud Nine facility on Kentish Town Road. It was a large industrial building surrounded by a brick wall trimmed with razor wire. A Guardian was posted at the entrance. Corrigan gripped his handgun as they approached, but Gregor explained who they were, and the sentry allowed them to pass. When they were in the forecourt, two additional Guardians directed them to a decontamination booth. They were permitted to remain in their bio-suits, but all external contaminants had to be neutralised.

No one was in reception, so Corrigan wasted no time and headed down a long corridor to their left. Ramon called for him to stop, but Corrigan had seen a figure at the far end, illuminated an odd yellow beneath the overhead lighting. Ramon and the android followed him, and the human footsteps remained distinct from those of the machine.

"You shouldn't have come," Jonathan said.

Corrigan was alarmed to see he wore no protective suit or headgear. "How are you?" he asked, looking at the boiler suit that the younger man was wearing.

"You can't eat in a bio-suit, or piss in one. Follow me."

Jonathan did not engage in conversation as they walked. They turned a corner into another corridor and through double doors at the end. Twenty or so technicians sat at consoles. They did not look up.

"There were more than two hundred of us when we started," Jonathan said. "Now we're twenty-three. One case got through. That was all that was needed. We put the infected man in a booth, but it was too late. We have DNA samples stored and a back-up of our brains is taken every ten minutes."

"I needed to see you," Corrigan murmured.

Jonathan eyed him as suspiciously, as if he were part of DRT's surveillance apparatus.

"The Siegruth twins told me everything," Corrigan then said. "The full extent of your involvement in setting me up with Bohdan. I figured it might be weighing on you. You've nothing to feel guilty about, and I wanted you to know that." Neither Jonathan or Ramon spoke. "If it weren't for you, I never would have met Bohdan. We were brought together because..."

He studied his friend and remembered he had come for another purpose altogether: he needed someone to be with, someone who knew him, and it didn't matter if the bond had been fabricated, everything was as manufactured as his sensation-enhancing gloves.

"I want you to come with me, underground where it's safer–"

There was a sudden scuffle in the corridor and a clamour of metal. A platoon of Guardians marched into the lab. They were armed and tilted their heads when they saw Gregor.

"Arthur spoke with Mr Ulmer before we embarked," Gregor said, as Corrigan and Ramon paled at the sight. "Our CEO was explicit about how this mission was to be concluded. This team is to be disbanded and all associated data impounded."

Jonathan took hold of Corrigan's hand and pressed. The manager felt something in his palm; something small, circular and flat, like the feel of a coin in the day when something tangible was needed to reinforce the concept of currency. He instinctively drew no attention to it.

The Guardians marched the humans, every one of them, out of the lab along the corridor to the forecourt. The technicians were then lined up, with Jonathan at the rear. One by one they were taken and made to kneel. Corrigan's body jerked as the first gunshot was fired, and he watched the gesture the blood performed as it arched through the air. The murdered woman was in her early forties and had glanced back at the Guardian. The bullet went through her head and exited an eye socket. The body slumped to the ground with a thud. Two Guardians dragged the cadaver fifty yards away, doused it in kerosene and set it alight.

The technicians whimpered and held onto one another.

Corrigan slipped the tiny device from the palm of his hand into a pocket. Then he reached out and embraced Jonathan. Gregor advanced and disentangled them as another shot was fired. A second body was dragged and dumped onto the burning cadaver.

"You *cannot* do this!" Corrigan yelled.

Ramon was silent.

A third shot was fired, and another Guardian dragged the next man forward for execution. The humans were giving out, their legs barely able to hold them up. They snivelled to gods they'd never believed in, to absent parents, errant children, and unreliable lovers.

"I'm not frightened," Jonathan said, though his voice shook. "It's a better way to go."

A fifth shot was fired, and a Guardian tilted its head at Gregor, who instructed them to accelerate the process. The dutiful Guardian walked along the line of humans. Some looked away and had to be shot more than once. Jonathan was snatched by a Guardian who hauled him towards the burning pyre. Horror distorted his beautiful face. "Don't let them do this!" he cried out. "Please, Mr Corrigan, please!"

"Do something!" Corrigan yelled at his immobile PA. "This shouldn't be happening! You have to stop them!"

Ramon launched himself at Gregor and ordered the android to stop the shooting.

"The infection must be eradicated," Gregor said.

Ramon stared at Corrigan, a man who had suffered so

much loss. For a fleeting moment, Corrigan caught his eye, and a flicker of something genuine and decent connected them. Ramon grabbed Jonathan by the arm and dragged him to where Gregor was standing. "This young man is healthy!"

"You misunderstand me. Humans are the infection. Only those essential to the fulfilment of the program must remain. All others cease to have relevance or function. These units have been *consumed*."

"Is that what our CEO commands?" Corrigan cried.

"It is what the situation commands," Gregor replied.

Ramon drew Jonathan away. "This man is healthy and will be of use!" he again appealed.

Corrigan watched as the Guardians came to a halt and tilted their glowing red heads in unison. Ramon did not wait for them to reengage. He grabbed Corrigan and dragged him and Jonathan out of the facility, along Buck Street and Camden High Street to the hover-car. The car rumbled through columns of fire and smoke. People screamed below them, hunted by Guardians and Mecha-Butlers adapted to act as hounds. Healthy people were cornered and gunned down, thrown from the tops of buildings, or torched where they pleaded for their lives.

Corrigan risked a quick glance to see what Jonathan had slipped into his hand. He recognised it instantly as the kind of storage chip used to hold vast amounts of data. Jonathan noticed him looking at the device and mouthed a single word: *hope*. A cloud of debris battered the car, and he slipped the chip back inside his pocket.

Ramon insisted they take a decontamination shower when they got back, before they entered the lift, and Jonathan placed his hands over his mouth and nose as the chemical cleanse hissed. The lift then descended, and the interior was sealed and sprayed, and the air vented above ground.

"You must have known how this would end!" Ramon barked.

Corrigan stared dead-eyed at Ramon and moved closer to Jonathan. The young man was in shock and trembled beside him. He offered him a Serenity and watched as the victim's mouth mechanically slavered away at it. He turned his attention to the PA. "You can stop the performance," he said. "I know you never do anything without Ulmer's say so."

"That isn't true," Ramon said. "Sometimes I..."

The expression on his face was sufficiently conflicted to exasperate Corrigan. "You've never been my assistant, or Mercer's for that matter. You've always been, and continue to be, Ulmer's assistant." The lift shuddered and groaned above and around them. "*Well?*"

"He's my father!" Ramon said, and there was defiance in his vibrato.

Corrigan smiled weakly. "I always figured he'd adopted you. Must be very confusing."

"There *is* no confusion, Mr Corrigan," Ramon said. "I know where my loyalty lies, and that man has a hold on me. I would not offer someone as decent as *you* a thing like that."

Corrigan dared not look at Ramon. Perhaps Ulmer had not managed to make a bog-standard Guardian of him, after all. Human beings were resilient, and maybe there was more to Ramon Lopez than a sociopathic CEO would ever know.

He felt the weighty implication of the device in his pocket. Whatever was on the chip, it mattered. Of all the things in the world the CEO considered most counterproductive, nothing would hamper his ambitions more than hope.

The idea of thwarting Ulmer steeled Corrigan's nerve. The PA was perhaps torn – a human finally resisting the control of his torturer – but would he be incapable of betraying the man he considered to be his father? Corrigan knew he must smuggle the chip inside without Ramon knowing.

45

Back in the cargo bay, Ramon suggested they take Jonathan directly to Harding and Meregalli, but first, they must remove all their clothing and decontaminate again, putting sterile boiler suits on before they continued. Corrigan agreed, and once the procedure was complete they set off for Harding's lab. But as they turned a corner, Gregor stepped into their path.

"Your foray was ill-considered, gentlemen, and this *development* could prove fatal."

Ramon ordered the Guardian to stand down and Gregor complied.

Harding was waiting for them. The professor wore a bio-suit and her stare was ice-cold. She told them to leave Jonathan with her and, without a word, took the trembling young man away to quarantine him.

Back in Corrigan's office, Ramon waited for the manager to compose himself.

"I know how controlling Ulmer can be," Corrigan finally muttered. "I believe a priest once said, 'Give me a boy until the age of seven, and I'll give you a Catholic for life.' I read it somewhere, or saw it in an old film."

"I'm not religious."

"I was thinking more of Ulmer being the priest."

Ramon regarded the older man's face. Was it possible he had aged further in the time below ground? "It's true he found me young."

Corrigan was too tired and too horrified by what he had just witnessed to process that statement. He looked at Ramon, and noted a deep-rooted vulnerability he had never noticed before. He smiled, and perhaps would have said something more had the chip Jonathan had given him not been burning a hole in his jacket and his psyche.

Ramon's eyes flashed, and he did not return the smile. Instead, he got up and left the room.

Corrigan gathered what was left of his energy and decided to go back to his apartment. He walked slowly through the gardens, as if through a film set he had tired of. At the top of the hill, amid the grazing sheep, a wolf stood over a half-eaten member of the flock. He had not been told predators had been introduced? The wolf looked up when Corrigan passed, his mouth open, his teeth stained with entrails. Disinterested, he went back to gorging while the rest of the flock grazed. Corrigan imagined him feeding on a human corpse. Someone should have told him they were doing this. It irked, but he hadn't the energy to make more of it. Who was he to say what they did?

When he returned to the apartment, the Siegruths stood to greet him, announcing what good timing it was that he should appear just now. A stew, they said, was simmering and ready. He shooed them from the premises, and although they grumbled at their unceremonious eviction, they did not resist. He shut off the stove, and made his way to the bedroom and tumbled into sleep fully dressed.

He saw human corpses lain across a pavement, men, women and children. A giant grey wolf stood over one of them, its face wet with blood. Others crawled from the shadows on haunches to join the alpha dog, circling and waiting their turn. Rats crawled up from an open manhole, their fur wet with sewage, to feast. They gnawed at ribs and shins with their yellow teeth. As each vile rodent filled its belly and dropped back down under London, another arrived to replace it.

"Rats...rats...*rats*..." Corrigan murmured, heavy with the dream sleep that wouldn't release him.

The dial tone of an antique phone buzzed interminably in his ear and he looked up to locate its whereabouts. He had always liked ancient equipment, the way it tied him to the past, where hope had still been a real thing. The damn sound of it seemed ridiculous now, and he went back to his rats, slathering in some kind of bloody chorus, rhythmic and revolting. The phone rang again and he wondered why B4 wasn't answering it, or why he hadn't had the implant his mother perpetually nagged him to have. Hattie.

He lurched from sleep, and Lazarus stood up sharply on all four legs.

He frowned as the ringing entered his head again, louder, and remembered the phone he'd had installed by his bedside, for old time's sake. He lifted the receiver. "Ramon, is that you?"

46

"What device are you using? My implant didn't recognise the technology," Ramon said.

"Rats. Have they been considered?"

"Rats? How d'you mean, have they been *considered*?"

"As carriers." A drawn-out silence lingered long enough for him to realise their conversation was not secure. "We're not alone?"

"You expect us to adopt this ludicrous outmoded technology?" Ulmer asked. The CEO's laughter was sticky with phlegm. "No need for secrecy," he added. "The world's douching us."

The line crackled and Corrigan heard the scuttle of feet across a wooden floor.

"Where're *they* going?" Ulmer growled. "Get after them and bring them back."

Corrigan heard more scuttling and a door clicked shut.

"And as for rats," the CEO resumed, "who needs them, now you've let it in?" The ache in Corrigan's chest migrated to his throat. "We're no safer down here," Ulmer spluttered, "than they are on the surface. The virus doesn't need rats."

"You seem confident."

"While you were napping, your fuck-buddy metamorphosed. You missed all the excitement. Had him quarantined on arrival, as you know, but his symptoms came on rapidly. Expect he'll die tomorrow, if not later today." The CEO waited a moment. "Anything else on your mind, Corrigan? *Good*! Now fuck off and take a couple of Serenities. And *stop* fixating. A man can only witness so many women and children being gnawed by rats before it makes him neurotic. And you've seen your fill. It scars the psyche more than physical acts of violence. I suggest cartoons. The inevitable comeuppance of the villain is even more efficacious than Belushi Grey."

Corrigan replaced the handset, and a familiar tapping sent him bolting across the room to fling the door open. The sisters wore their matching grey dresses, surgical knee-high socks and scuffed black shoes. They grasped black handbags with black-gloved hands, only one of which fit properly. No pearls or rhinestones adorned their necks and ears, but their small blue eyes blinked and shimmered by way of replacement. The sight of them clutched together caused his spirit to collapse beneath another wave of weariness.

"We're afraid," Jan said. She unhooked herself from her sister and hobbled inside.

"I've got to get to the lab," Corrigan said. "To Jonathan." But the Siegruths plonked themselves on the sofa and pulled off their gloves, their two crippled legs side by side and fidgeting as they wiped their brows with embroidered handkerchiefs. "Why're you bothering me when you can see I'm distressed?" he yelled.

"He thinks we don't care," Edna said, "like old Mercer."

"Mercer and his theories," Jan said. "Got his-self into terrible mischief." She straightened her dress and glanced at their unsociable host.

"Forever digging," Edna said. She clawed the material of the sofa with her deformed hand. "Tunnelling where he shouldn't ought to."

Corrigan walked to the kitchen and poured himself a glass of Merlot. He had not seen or thought of Mercer for weeks. "If you've something to say, spit it out."

"It's Ulmer," Jan said. "You need to talk to Arthur, or that insectile machine of his, ask them about the amphibians."

"The frogs," Edna said, "the little orange ones. Them what Mercer was forever on about."

Corrigan was so perplexed he poured each sister a glass of wine. "What do frogs have to do with anything?" he demanded.

"Wiped out," Jan said, "by a fungus in Venezuela. We had a team of ecologists studying amphibians, and they realised these orange frogs were dying off wholesale. It took a while for them to figure out the fungus was behind it. What surprised them was how particular it was when it come to killing off frogs."

"It didn't affect any *other* frogs, no," Edna said. She shook her head. "Just them *orange* ones; them what was partial to eating the fungus."

"It was particular in that regard," Jan added.

Corrigan raked his hair with his fingers. He opened his mouth and closed it. He raked again. "*And DRT acquired it?*" he roared, his rage a living, pulsing thing in every cell.

"Ulmer had samples taken to our branches in Tokyo, where it was synthesised. All they had to do was change the target – you know, make it think it was humans what was partial to a bit of fungus. That worked a treat, and kicked in the old self-preservation or whatever."

"Almost as if our little fungal friend has a kind of consciousness," Edna said.

"Did Mercer know about this?" he yelled into Jan's face.

Her arms swam a breaststroke against the wave of his anger. "He'd a company head on his shoulders," Jan cried. "Never missed a thing! When young Meregalli come back from Venezuela with that awful chest infection, an orange light went on in his head."

"And he was never the same after that," Edna said. "Started hypothesising, mesmerising the likes of Fuse and his lady friend."

Corrigan moved in closer, so his nose was practically against Jan's nose. "And why're you telling me this *now*?"

"Don't be a silly cunt," Edna said. "You need to make them switch targets."

Corrigan stepped back and Jan shrank into the sofa. That word had always sobered him up.

"The lady professors and their friend Jun got a new take on things," Edna said, "but they need help. Need what you brought down here, you know, secreted on your person." She clasped his hand in a claw. "Jonathan's been asking for it."

"We're afraid," Jan said again. "You're the only hope."

47

The Siegruth sisters harried him, out of the apartment, down the lift, over the hill, panting, and across the garden. They even stripped and got into the decontamination shower with him. Their naked bodies were firm, their good legs shapely and strong, their stunted legs muscular from working so hard to keep up. They had rounded buttocks and breasts and a triangle of pubic hair.

"We'll help you through your troubles," Jan said as they were being dried by hot air vents.

"I can't deny my contribution to the situation…"

"Might be some truth in that," Edna said with a frown, "but we never really knew what Ulmer was up to."

He hurriedly put on his protective suit and headgear as the women helped each other into theirs, a choreography of arms and legs they had performed countless times.

Harding was waiting for them at the entrance to the lab, the ice-cold stare penetrating.

"It was a mistake," she said. "He had no visible symptoms on arrival, but he was infectious. Protocols were not observed, and we've *all* been put at risk." Corrigan opened his mouth to apologise, but she raised her hand. "You must prepare yourself. It's a new variant. We've done everything we can, but the pain…it's out of my hands."

Jan took Corrigan's hand and pressed it to her visor as if to kiss it. He would have brushed her off, but he could see the empathy in her eyes. He was led to a booth, as before, but this time it was Jonathan in the bed with Meregalli at his side. He was panting and sweating, and swollen veins throbbed at his throat and temples.

"Help me!" He grabbed at the bedsheets. "Oh my god!" He reeled forward and coughed blood onto his chest.

Corrigan went to him, pulled him into his arms, ran a hand through his wiry hair, soothed him and told him to let go. Jonathan screamed and pushed him away.

"Help him!" Corrigan cried.

"There's nothing we can do," Meregalli replied.

"What? Can't you put him out of his misery?"

Harding and Meregalli conferred as Jonathan writhed on the bed. The pain became so intense his eyes bulged, and he crawled halfway across the bed the way his father had clawed the tarmac of Harvey Road. Meregalli prepared a syringe, and Corrigan's heart broke with relief and loss in equal measure. He nodded and tried to hold Jonathan still as he howled and rocked on the end of the bed. She injected him, and the rocking gave way to spasms so violent Jonathan fell to the floor, where his limbs thrashed and kicked an invisible assailant. A rush of blood spewed from his lips, wetting the sheets, floor and instruments. There seemed no end to the suffering, and then his body suddenly went rigid. Jonathan stared up at Corrigan, his eyes wide in his face, the realisation and acceptance complete. His mouth opened, like a fish on a deck, and he flexed one last time. He was gone.

Corrigan stared into his eyes, which seemed to deepen with accusation as the heavy seconds passed. He laid his hand on the dead man's chest, and a sudden realisation took hold of him: it would have been better to die quickly; a bullet in the back of the head. Perhaps that was the judgement forming in the dead pools of Jonathan's eyes. *You should have let them shoot me.*

Did he hear those words? Jonathan could not have come online so soon? No. It was more likely the outpourings of his own conscience rather than the mutterings of a networked soul. The sensor at his crown throbbed as his anger surged, and he was on his feet, blasting out of the booth, past the professors, past the lopsided sisters and the technicians to the decontamination booth.

He heard Jonathan's screams, like aftershocks, and added his own roars of pain. As he was drying, shaking with hurt and rage, Ramon burst through the doors. He went to Corrigan, dressed him, brushed his hair, murmured like a mother, "It's alright, it's alright."

"It was my fault," Corrigan wept. "It was my fault."

Ramon led Corrigan along the newly sterilised corridors, where staff stepped from their path. Even Arthur bowed his head as they passed the AI lab. The gardens were cool, the air full of timed mist. Up on the hill, the skeleton of the sheep lay on its side, stripped bare. Corrigan waded in amongst the rest of the flock and cried, "Don't you care?

Look! Look!"

Ramon pushed his way in. Sheep rubbed against them, their woollen coats cushioning the pressure of their bodies. "No matter how things seem, they're not dead," he said, taking Corrigan's arm. "They're inside the machine, stored and at peace. We must concentrate, stay focussed on the project, the only viable solution."

Corrigan stared at Ramon. "Why was I not consulted when they introduced *predators*?"

"It was Ulmer's idea." The manager shook his head. Of course. It couldn't have been anyone else's. "Every creature in the garden has a security implant. Not even a dragonfly could flutter beyond the perimeter."

"And what of Emulate One?" He stared wild-eyed at his *assistant*. "Have any dragonflies flown across the perimeter? Are there any insects in *my* brain burrowing in?"

Corrigan threw his arms in the air and bulldozed his way through the grazing sheep. He needed to get back to his apartment. Ramon didn't follow, no doubt about to turn tail and report directly to Ulmer what had happened today.

When Corrigan walked through the door he saw Lazarus playing with something, batting it about and chasing it across the floor. A mouse? A rat? He stood still. He didn't think he could handle that in his current state. On closer inspection, he discovered it was his wristpad. In his haste to be with Jonathan, he had left without it. When it pinged, the cat recoiled, but crouched his tail flicking. It gave Corrigan just enough time to grab it, and the animal protested with a loud meow.

He took the call and Jun appeared in front of him. His face twitched, and his hair was not combed in its usual precise manner.

"We need the data chip," Fuse said.

Corrigan stared at the hologram and did not respond.

"Our team's working on something, but we need the information on that chip. We'll need Arthur's help too, but we must have it."

Corrigan continued to stare, his heart pounding.

Fuse leant in, and beads of perspiration appeared on his brow. "Corrigan, *we need the chip*. It's what Jonathan wanted."

"How dare you."

"I'll be with you in ten minutes. We need to discuss this; we need to make plans."

"I've no interest in your plans." He switched off the halo-screen and collapsed onto the settee.

Nothing would ever make him stand again. He wanted to be inside the machine, at peace with Bohdan and Jonathan.

48

Jun fidgeted in the doorway. His hair was wet and stuck to his forehead. That and his evident distress made him inexcusably attractive.

When Corrigan held out the chip, Jun cupped both hands together to receive it. The humble gesture irritated him greatly. Jun pocketed the chip and backed away. Corrigan followed him out into the corridor. When the lift doors opened and Fuse stepped inside, Corrigan followed him then too. If asked to explain why he'd followed the engineer into the lift, he would have confessed a degree of spite. Why he allowed Lazarus to come with them, he could never explain.

Jun pleaded with the manager to return to his apartment and let them get on with their work. Corrigan would hear none of it. He stayed with Fuse even as they crossed the bridge and entered the gardens, where Lazarus rolled on the grass and then charged around. He dropped to a crouch to stalk a pigeon, inching on his belly while the bird pecked at the ground.

Corrigan walked off, leaving the cat to hunt.

Jun ran after him. "You mustn't leave the animal to fend for itself!" he said.

"Let him feast on the birds and rodents of the garden."

"I know it's only natural, but–"

"Let him enjoy his freedom."

As they approached Goeth's lab, Jun suggested it might be best if they took their own paths, but Corrigan had no intention of parting company with the new keeper of Jonathan's data chip until he knew precisely what it contained.

"Whatever it is," Jun said, "Goeth insists on seeing it before he'll help."

"In that case, we ought to hurry up and deliver it." He entered his access code and stepped into the robotics lab. Goeth and Harding were visible through the window of the German's office. When they looked up they appeared united in intense irritation.

"Let me see it," Goeth snapped.

Jun held it out as Corrigan had and the German snatched it, slotted it into a reader and scrolled through the data. Jun and Harding leant over one shoulder, and Corrigan leant over the other. From what Corrigan could see, the data contained a series of DNA test results from both human and simian blood samples. Just as the Siegruths had suggested, the fungus was exclusively targeting human beings. Chimpanzees and other primates were infected, but their immune systems fended off all variants of the virus. Although it was outside their defined scope, Jonathan's team had attempted to synthesise a vaccine using DNA samples from simian lab animals, but these were rejected in all human trials. Humans tested with the vaccines –

primarily Transients or criminals – reacted horribly, and Corrigan replayed the terrible scene of Jonathan's death.

He leant in, drawn by the story Goeth was revealing as he clumsily thumbed his way through the layers of data. And there it was. The proposed solution was to make hybrid subjects. The team had already grown several cross-species foetuses using the accelerated incubation process Professor Meregalli had perfected when attempting to generate hosts for reintroduction. Unfortunately, all subjects generated to date had proven *too human* to confound the virus. The correct balance was required to retain an overall human physiology, but with a higher degree of simian DNA.

Get them to switch target.

Or fool them into believing the targets had all been eradicated like little orange frogs.

"Fascinating," Goeth muttered.

"I agree," Harding said, "but don't get too optimistic. Time is not on our side. One wrong computation and all hope will be lost."

"Start work, and let the Guardians finish it?" Jun suggested.

Corrigan was still processing not only the data but the events of the day. He did not know what was needed to progress what Jonathan's team had been working on, but he knew one thing for certain. "They cannot be trusted," he said. "They see *us* as the infection, units whose purpose has been consumed, leaving nothing but hazardous waste."

"Perhaps," Jun said. "Regardless, we'll have to convince Arthur to work with us."

"Your brother has formed some kind of relationship with Gregor," Goeth said.

Jun grunted. "I know. He always falls for the dark, well-built types."

"I don't see a problem with that," Harding said. "Gregor isn't exactly Ulmer's best friend." They all turned to her and she seemed to shrink momentarily. "I know Caspar better than I should, and they'd be closer if he could manage it, but the machine's just, well, not that into him." The silence seemed to act on her like an interrogation. "Alright," she sighed, "I may have coerced Katherine into letting us test things out on Gregory's consciousness." But behind the sigh was something more earnest...and regretful. "None of us, not even Katherine, could have envisioned it taking such unexpected paths. And although Caspar once whispered something of the sort in my ear, asking me to convince her to let us use the boy's... Well, I think the results initially disappointed our glorious CEO, but Caspar's warmed to Gregor, whether it's reciprocated or not."

"Does Ulmer or this bloody corporation ever leave anything to chance?" Corrigan asked.

Jun went pale at that. "It was a strange thing when I received the job description." He studied Corrigan as if seeking something he could not articulate. "I responded and–"

"They set up an interview there and then," Corrigan said.

Jun nodded and brushed wet hair from his forehead.

"They hadn't the time to look at my CV properly."

Harding crossed the room and took up a position as if it were of special significance. She placed her glasses on the bridge of her nose, reached out to her left and turned off the light, plunging them into darkness for a few seconds until she turned it back on.

"Someone is always flicking the switch," she said, and looked at them the way a schoolmistress might scrutinise her less well-favoured students. "Not one of us was brought here for skill alone. You're not stupid, you can see the company game. It's not even just Caspar – who I admit is the real gamer on this gig – but the whole history of DRT. They thrive on interconnectivity, a network of individual and manipulable relationships that's as rich and complex as anything Arthur ever coded. They never wanted you, Jun, they wanted your brother."

"Yes, and when they realised he couldn't convince Arthur to join them, they engaged me," Corrigan said.

"But it wasn't just that," Jun muttered. "I always felt there was something manufactured about the situation that developed between myself and Katherine."

"The terrible twins hooked me up with Bohdan and Jonathan," Corrigan said. "Partly they were looking to monitor, but with Jonathan there was manipulation, someone who could get close to me. And they manufactured a situation with his family; offered them a home when they were starving and had no roof. Ulmer knew Jonathan would do anything to keep them safe." Corrigan turned to Jun. "I can't say he arranged things with you and Katherine, but it wouldn't surprise me if he had. He wants to accelerate everything, and nothing would drive a mother more than the idea of retrieving a dead child."

"Now you sound just like Mercer," Harding said.

"Mercer only saw what the rest of us were reluctant to acknowledge," Jun replied. "I'll speak with my brother. We'll need him and Katherine. If there's any hope, we'll only manage it as a united team. Perhaps if I can do that much, and there's some redemption in it…"

Goeth stood but leant on the edge of the desk. "Arthur will need persuading. I believe he's more inclined to take advice from Gregor these days. Together they're extraordinary. The impulsive nature of the human is curtailed by the logic of his mechanical partner. The things they've achieved these last few weeks…" He stalled when Harding glared at him.

"Ulmer kept us divided too long, bending this program to his own personal gain," Corrigan said. He sat down beside the German, the man who had designed and built the Guardians. He studied Jun and Harding. "If any team can manage a way through this, it's you." He turned his attention to Jun, and kept it there. "He's your brother, he'll listen to you."

The darkness where it settled on Jun Fuse made the engineer shudder. He turned and left the room without a word.

49

A fortnight passed, during which time reports from above ground were no longer provided by human voices. The way the virus was mutating suggested a consciousness of sorts, an adaptive intelligence with a will to survive. Corrigan had to put it from his mind. He'd also purposefully avoided asking anyone whether Jonathan's chip had been of use. If there was any hope at all they were going to be saved, he only wanted to know once it was certain. Besides, it was dangerous to speak of things Ulmer did not want to hear. The CEO had disintegrated further still. Corrigan wondered if the virus was wary of going near him for fear of catching something.

He spent whole days thinking about Bohdan and Jonathan. He longed to be reunited with them. And he thought about Lazarus, who had never returned. He missed his friend, and had only seen him once in the gardens. The cat had been perched in a tree. When Corrigan approached, he hopped down into the undergrowth and disappeared.

Corrigan needed a distraction and was painfully aware of the risk implicit in his invitation. Ramon had only ever been called to his private quarters in a professional capacity. It made no sense to bring him into his home, but sense was never a compelling drive.

Ramon was not wearing the pedestrian outfit he normally wore for work. He had chosen a vintage T-shirt embossed with an image of Justice, blindfold intact, scales tilted as Britannia clutched her from behind. His jeans were stonewashed and pressed, and his hair arranged in a more fashionable style. His skin was as fine as a child's, unblemished and un-weathered.

"The stress of recent weeks seems to have left you untouched," Corrigan observed. He gestured for his guest to follow him through to the balcony. A bottle of red had been left to breathe on the table and the lights became stars on the mica overhead. He poured two glasses, one of which he handed to Ramon. "I can't remember if it's day or night."

"Day's always night for someone. Depends on where you travel, I guess." Ramon sat at the table and stretched out his legs. "And some destinations are not of our own choosing."

"Perhaps God's our travel agent," Corrigan mused.

"There is no God. Or maybe he's a power you keep in your chest, a prisoner who mustn't escape."

Corrigan felt shadows settle over him. "There's only one prisoner in that cell of yours: a stranger kept in solitary. Sometimes the prisoner hollers, and an echo reverberates. It would be wrong to mistake that for a god or a demon."

"Do you consider yourself rational?" the PA asked.

Corrigan raised his glass and said, "I give in to delusions like most people. I'm human like that."

Ramon also raised his glass, but it was evident the younger man's heart was not really in the gesture. "Ulmer's the only god around here. The great god Avarice and her minions." Ramon wiggled his fingers in the air and rested his eyes on Corrigan for a moment. "Why have you invited me?" he asked.

Corrigan regarded his guest. "I don't know," he said and stood to look out over the balcony.

Ramon joined him. "Deception is fevering your brain. After all, peace of mind is dependent on how well we deceive."

"Are you deceiving me? Or have you come because Bohdan and Jonathan are out of the way?"

The PA stepped back, so his host could survey him. "I stand naked before you," he said and opened his arms. His expression, however, remained one of tempered hostility.

"If only you *were* naked, that would be a pleasant distraction."

Ramon lowered his head. His hands strayed to his hips, and he pulled his T-shirt up over his head. His chest was hairless and brown. Beneath the flawless skin lay well-developed muscle and sinew. He eased off his trainers and unbuttoned his jeans. Corrigan watched as the young man lowered the denim over his knees. His thighs flexed and the reflex was pleasing.

"You're well proportioned," Corrigan said. Ramon turned around to reveal his shoulders and buttocks. "Perfect."

"Mother said I was."

"And she's right." Corrigan moved up behind Ramon and caressed the curve of his shoulder. "Whatever's in your heart, you mustn't torment yourself."

Ramon turned to face Corrigan. "I don't. There's no *I* in me. If you'll listen first, I'll do anything you ask. But listen and don't speak. And don't judge or move a muscle."

Corrigan stepped back and leant against the rail.

"My circumstances were challenging," Ramon said. "We'd no money or status, but I was full of admiration for the world. It was a miracle to me. My childish dreams were free of monsters; a world full of beasts who commanded respect, yes, but they weren't horrors. I didn't know the hearts of men and, when Ulmer came, I was dragged into a nightmare. I had no defence against the monster or his magic. He cast his spell, so I thought it was me." He lowered his head and, when he looked up, his eyes shone and a smile toyed with his lips – a look of defiant seduction if ever there was.

Corrigan found it increasingly difficult to maintain eye contact, but said, "I absolve you."

He walked past his guest to the bedroom and undressed before the full-length mirror. He was tired in every conceivable sense. He would lie down on the bed and lift his legs.

Corrigan lay and watched as Ramon entered the room and switched off the overhead light. The young man stood and studied him, and must have recognised the self-loathing. The longer Corrigan was studied, the more appalled he felt. Ramon could take him as if doing him a favour, and the idea was as liberating as a stay of execution.

The Venezuelan took in the image of the desperate man one more time. Corrigan's ignorance of his own attractiveness was as seductive as any form of vulnerability.

Corrigan locked eyes with his observer and their rhythm gained momentum. The expression on the Ramon's face was concentrated and determined. Corrigan told himself the act meant nothing, yet delighted in the deceit of abandon, the giddy euphoria of the act itself. When he reached his climax, he held onto Ramon's shoulders. The younger man continued to work him, and Corrigan looked up and watched until Ramon gasped, his face twisted with release. He collapsed and a sheen of sweat trickled through the spaces where their bodies breathed. His frame trembled and, for a moment, Corrigan thought Ramon might cry or scream obscenities. Yet when Ramon pulled away to look at Corrigan, there was the same defiance in his eyes, as well as anger. Corrigan shrank.

"Was that perfect?" the young man asked, his voice calm and contained. He studied the defeated man as if he were dead prey. "You look awful, but that doesn't matter, we're doomed." He sat up and swung his legs over the side of the bed so his back presented a wall.

"Such a bad boy, and you always seemed so dull," Corrigan said.

"I *am*," Ramon murmured. "I don't have a single idea of my own."

"This wasn't Ulmer's plan. Even if it had been, the delivery was all yours. And it wasn't just a fucking ploy to work me for information." He released a hard, unfeeling laugh, and leant over to his bedside table, and yanked open the drawer. He pulled out a pack of cigarettes and placed one in his mouth. The touch of the filter between his lips brought a lightness to the moment, bearable seconds he would never dismiss. He raised the lighter, and smoke filled the room with the illicit smell of nicotine, which curled around the scent of exertion. *Of course, it wouldn't ever be the same.* "I never saw you properly before," Corrigan said. "*That* was the *real* Ramon."

"But, if we did it again," Ramon said with a beguiling smile, "it would never be the same." Corrigan sat up and studied Ramon's back. "You think I'm reading your mind?" Ramon asked. "What's to read? I always knew you had certain hankerings, but thought you preferred *sweet things.*" He observed himself in the mirror opposite. "Was there anything else, Mr Corrigan?"

"No, that'll be all, Ramon."

The young man stood up and walked to the door.

"Wait," Corrigan said. "I arranged a meeting tomorrow. I can't invite you, but..."

"So why tell me?" Ramon asked.

"I trust you'll look in the mirror," Corrigan said, "before passing it along."

Ramon stood motionless, silhouetted. "What I see when I look in the mirror would turn you to stone."

"We've all done terrible things."

Ramon shook his head and went to the balcony to collect his clothes. Minutes later the door opened and clicked shut. Corrigan allowed recent memory to replay itself and wondered if eternity could be bartered for such moments.

50

No matter where he looked, he could find no trace of Ramon. He asked everyone he encountered as he walked through the facility. He feared for his cat, too, and had to wonder if he had not become a meal for the hungry wolf. His heart stung as he considered whether the big bad wolf himself had eaten Ramon the way Saturn was said to have devoured his son.

Corrigan's wristpad pinged and he opened a halo-screen. Meregalli hovered before him and reminded the manager of the meeting at two o'clock.

"I keep hearing you're searching for your lost PA," she snapped. "Get your head back in the game. Ulmer no doubt has Ramon off on some unspeakable errand."

"I'll see you at the meeting."

He closed the halo-screen and marched over the hill. The herd had moved off and he could hear them bleating somewhere out of view. Had his PA gone the way of Hattie's bohemians or Mercer, become the disappeared?

When he entered the meeting room, he noticed Jun had positioned himself off to the side, avoiding eye contact, as if he had been chosen to minute the meeting rather than be an active participant. Yet he covertly watched Katherine and Tierney as they greeted their guests, including the Siegruth twins. Arthur, too, appeared aloof, but each brother most likely saw through the other's façade.

Meregalli switched off the lights and a halo-screen presented an image of a child encased in a glass tube. The subject looked half-dead, certainly unconscious, and yet she gazed at it with affection. "This is my son," she said, "and, critically, *not* my son."

Her words seemed to cut Jun, who squirmed at the edge of each syllable. The rest of the room remained attentive.

"The subject is discordant from the original source," she continued. "We introduced a simian strain to the genetic code to make it more robust while preserving its overall human characteristics."

"By robust, you mean it can repel the virus?" Corrigan asked.

"Yes. We introduced genetic matter from the fungus."

"So," Arthur observed, "your baby's part fungus, part chimp?"

Katherine assured him it wasn't going to start climbing trees, or killing off frogs, or children in Venezuela, but she conceded it was no longer strictly human.

Jun shuffled in his plastic chair. She looked at him, and there was empathy in her expression. This seemed more than Jun could bear, and he appeared to retreat somewhere. "Not singular but plural," he muttered. "No need for tea and add a little Sugar."

Arthur saw how the others looked at his brother, and how Tierney Harding watched him. "I'm glad you're making progress," he said, "but I can't see an *immediate* application."

"This is *my son*," Meregalli then said, and all eyes turned to her. "Those of you who know me, realise I would *not* claim that without certainty." Her voice was heavy with emotion. The maternal instinct in her was clearly more vibrant than they could have anticipated.

"We established a link, an umbilical of sorts," Harding began, by way of explanation. "I know what you're thinking. You've made great strides with emulation, but it's only a harbour. We can't remain in there indefinitely, not without losing our humanity. We have to be *connected*... reintroduced."

"And this child," Meregalli said, "is linked to an emulated brain, the one Tierney made of my son."

Corrigan felt the sensor throb at his crown. Harding had implanted a chip. In this instance, the source was Gregory's emulated brain, the portion of his file they had managed to retrieve and isolate. Symbiosis enabled brain training, and this allowed the host to talk.

Jun squirmed in his seat again. "You made it *speak*?" He stared at her with unguarded horror.

"A few words," Katherine said, "and it was *him*."

Arthur approached the projection of the child in the tube. "I thought we'd have to leave transfer with the Guardians," he said. "The virus will exhaust itself but, with enhanced hosts, we wouldn't need to wait..." He paused and seemed to leave the room for a few seconds. When he re-emerged, his confidence was renewed. "That said, an

Emulate is impervious to *any* infection." He looked at Jun, but his entreaty was not recognised.

"It's true we've not yet achieved full symbiosis," Harding said, "but there have been other developments. What's of more immediate interest, is the blood drawn from the specimen. Although we may not deserve it, it may offer a reprieve, if not a cure."

Harding welcomed the expectation in the room: Corrigan's conflicted expression; the suspicious delight of the Siegruth twins; the way Goeth patted his stomach as if the prospect of dessert was very interesting indeed. Only Jun remained submerged, apparently crippled with despair.

"It attacks the virus as it develops," Harding said. "We may be able to synthesise a vaccine. But there's considerable work to be done, and we'll have to cut corners and work together considering the time constraints."

Corrigan stood up, prepared to deliver a heartfelt speech, when the door was flung open against the wall. Ulmer marched into the room, his livid face doused in perspiration. Gregor was hot on his heels, but Ramon remained conspicuously absent. The obese man stood beneath a strip of fluorescent lighting and his entire, grotesque body trembled with rage.

"Skulking together!" he shrieked, coming face to face with Harding, who held her breath. "I'm not surprised to find *you* here, cuddling up to young Katherine. *Look* at you! You're pathetic!" Harding fidgeted a little, but stared him down. "Your psych report revealed a competitive streak *equatorial* in scale. And here you are, leaning over the precipice, straining for a glimpse of some capricious future gurgling in the mire. It's a *lie*. There's *no cure*!" He leant in further, saturating her in spittle and his foul breath. "There can't be. We're fucked! Irretrievably *fucked*."

Arthur stood up. "Regardless of what they've done, we must continue to engage with our colleagues. That's the only way to ensure safe passage to the new world."

Ulmer glared at the young scientist as if not only Arthur's name, but his relevance had been sent back to ladling soup. "Have you been hypnotised by our sloganeering?" Ulmer asked. "The world is the world." He mopped his brow. "There's nothing new *in it*. There is only continuation of power, and you'll never vote us *out*, because you never voted us *in*, you gullible–" His self-aggrandising soliloquy ground to a halt as he exploded into a coughing frenzy.

Jun stood up and clapped his hands. "*No need for tea and add a little Sugar*!" he exclaimed. He laughed, and the others stared at him. The longer their collective stare remained fixed, the harder he laughed, defiant, lost. "Just a little sugar! A little *sugar*! Oh, you clever, clever man!"

51

Ulmer's heads prowled the facility, delivering a speech designed to encourage even as it subjugated those who may have retained a valueless strain of hope. Corrigan considered the address more polished than the CEO could write himself, and the sections of more free-flowing prose jarred like a plagiarist's patchwork. He was convinced Gregor had played a hand in it, as his hands could be found wherever Ulmer needed them. At one time, this task would have been performed by Ramon, but Corrigan feared his PA's hands would never again be co-opted for Ulmer's ends.

The thought of Ramon's hands conjured physical sensations Corrigan could not dismiss. The memory of the encounter replayed and replayed itself. He was not ridiculous enough to claim love, but it had outstripped anything he'd experienced in recent years, and he felt cheated. It had been more than gratification. Ramon was complicated, and naturally ill at ease with the things he'd done, much as himself.

From where Corrigan stood in front of his office he could see two heads roaming hologrammatically, and hear a third. The tripartite echo instilled dread where glimmers of hope had dared to peer through the soil to unfurl.

"Sacrifice is needed to shape our destiny. We must not allow matters affecting our joint interests to be undermined. Remain vigilant and report any secret projects. There is danger in allowing any of our less committed or perhaps misguided colleagues to squirrel away on unproductive or distracting side activity. DRT will keep you up to date on what is happening above and below ground. I have one hundred percent confidence in your dedication as properly informed employees. The virus is among us and all that can be done to contain it is being done. Only your continued dedication will allow us to preserve humanity.

"We'll take genetic samples and download loved ones above ground, to preserve your aunts and uncles, mothers and fathers. As symptoms arrive, you must be compliant and assist with quarantine and downloading. A cure is impossible, the physical death of humanity inevitable. We must therefore remain alert to others determined to act in secrecy. I ask you to hunt out the last remnants of secrecy, that abhorrent concept now so dangerous to our survival."

The heads continued to float through the facility and occasionally stopped to review an individual's activity or to make comment on it.

"Do not despair, the new world is upon us," it said to a technician poring over data.

Corrigan sat behind his desk and opened a halo-screen. He could survey almost the entire facility via security cameras. He had no access to private quarters, but could see and listen in to anything happening in storage bays, corridors or labs. He flitted between the various cameras and was spellbound, briefly, by the goings-on in a storage unit where an unfamiliar but eager couple seemed hell-bent on procreation. He had no libidinal drive left it seemed, and navigated to Goeth's lab. The German looked anxious, even agitated. Fuse had abandoned him, his team was hard at work on whatever design project he'd assigned them, but the man himself was not in the moment. He was sitting chewing his nails.

When one of Ulmer's heads arrived in his office, the professor looked up, and there was a kind of numb horror to his expression.

"Can I ask what you really think?" the head asked.

"Mercer was right about you," Goeth said. "You're a criminal who wanted to be caught."

The head rolled closer, distorting Ulmer's repulsive features further still. "It was not necessary for you to know, but it further galvanised the core team, eh?"

"We would have found a way to give you what you want. You didn't have to manipulate us by placing us all in such peril."

Ulmer chuckled, a horrible sound. "The end product was only ever intended for a select few."

Goeth stared at the oversized projection of the man's grotesque face. He leant forward in his chair, his eyes red and puffy. "I suppose you can be less careful," he said, "now you no longer need anything from me."

"Need and want are not interchangeable." The head shuddered, as if thoughts of want excited it. "I want a device to download the core team. Something that will ease their passing."

"You mean accelerate it?"

Corrigan edged closer to the halo-screen, his heart pounding and adrenaline pumping into his bloodstream.

"Draseke wants the project," the head coughed. "We've had him in an oxygen tent for over a month."

"Draseke is a genius," Goeth said, "but he's something of a–"

"A clock." The head spluttered. "I know. He's also a sadist, which is why he's always been so good at not only creating new kinds of weaponry but using them. Likes to get right in there and test the destructive power for himself."

Corrigan recalled the thin German scientist with his skeletal fingers, his toothpick, and his cold eyes.

"He cannot be trusted," Goeth said. "He'll devise some awful tool, make an Iron Maiden of it."

"Yes, he's already built a prototype and you're not far off." The head shuddered again, sending the CEO's features into a motion blur of fat and sweat. "I showed it to Gregor, and he thought it might be best preserved for someone who'd earned *special treatment*. The tool is more *disciplinary* than I thought necessary. No need to punish as we process."

"I can't build a thing like that from scratch," Goeth protested. "Not that quickly."

The head rolled towards the door. "No need. Take the device Draseke came up with and humanise it so people won't feel so, you know, daunted by the prospect of making their way into Emulate One."

Goeth appeared to assume the full weight of the responsibility he was presented with. If he did not help this utterly selfish man, he would allow people to be processed using the sadistic device Draseke had no doubt produced. He nodded as the head made its retreat.

Corrigan watched the professor where he sat. At first, the man wrapped his arms around his torso and rocked back and forth. This motion was soon augmented by a slight whimpering, plentiful tears and the occasional gasp. The manager could no longer bear the sight of the professor's torment. He flicked to other security cameras until he arrived at Genetics. He watched Meregalli. She continued to work with Harding, but, without the interaction of the others, a cure would not be synthesised. The sickly head appeared in the lab and smiled at her. "Your end is nigh, but renewal awaits," it said.

"I can't tell if that's you," she said, "or if Gregor's playing games." She studied the head. "It doesn't matter. I've no interest in saving a handful of misfits."

The head glowered at her. "You have *no* tits, but *always* had *balls*."

"I want one final conversation with my son. I'll resurrect him and be done with you."

The head seemed pleased with itself. "Ah, to be done. What an aspiration." It hovered over her. "I believe that is Jun's current state."

Her face tightened. "I visited him earlier today. I sat

waiting for him to resurface, but he's gone."

"Gone," the head repeated. "Prevention is as good as cure, eh?" It appeared satisfied as it observed her. "I had to prevent a cure to avoid a terminal outcome. But don't worry, we have him. He isn't lost."

Her expression betrayed her.

"His file's complete," the head said.

"You must release him!"

Her sorrow did not affect the head. It smiled a vile grimace and moved closer to her. "Oh, he's *been* released," it said. "*But only I have access to it.*" It then backed away and slipped around the corner.

The remaining members of her team mumbled their mistrust, and she turned on them, but she would never give them the satisfaction of an explanation, the pleasure of watching her plead a case. There was none. The court was no longer in session. The Defence had rested.

52

Corrigan was transferred to a cell a few days after Ulmer's speech. Two Guardians dragged him along the corridor and, although he couldn't see them, he sensed familiar prisoners sealed behind each heavy iron door. He wanted to call out to them, but fear kept his throat tight, his voice trapped in his chest with his pounding heart.

A single light bulb dangled from a white plastic cable high above the cell, relentless and wearying. The stainless steel sink and toilet reflected the light as if competing in the small, windowless space. He sank onto the narrow single bunk. It was cold, and he pulled the grey-flecked blanket over his body as nervous sweat soaked into his clothes, chilling him further.

A muffled voice rolled like whale song through the thick concrete. It was a distant thing, distorted, and he pulled the thin, rough blanket over his head. It wailed again, and the more desperate it became, the less human it seemed.

"Who's there?" Corrigan called, sitting up. Some long-lost part of his being wondered if he might be able to calm his fellow prisoner, even rally his comrade into a protest and force a louder, more human engagement and appeal. But the ghost in the distant cell fell quiet, its final moan one of acceptance. He instinctively patted his pockets in search of a Serenity, but the lockets had been confiscated.

It was impossible to discern the hours or to establish how many days had elapsed as the light above his head never went out. He calculated it had been, at most, two. He sipped water from the tap. No food had been brought.

He dozed, his limbs in pain on the small, hard bed. The light suddenly went out, and he imagined he had finally slept, or had died the silence was so sudden. But something rumbled, and he felt the boulder rolling away from the tomb.

A different light entered the room, and he dared to peer out from the blanket. A halo-screen was open and he saw Katherine working in isolation. She was sitting at her desk, leant over her work, and he felt something dark stir in his being. When the Guardians arrived she looked up, and he watched as she was told to be ready in five minutes. She looked tired and sad and barely acknowledged the instruction.

The Guardians returned and marched Katherine along a corridor, and another, until they reached a row of cells. The corridor was illuminated by florescent tubes which flickered on ahead of them and crackled off behind. The brief, green-tinged bursts of light were eerie, disconcerting, like those along the passageways of an abattoir. Animals to the slaughter.

Ulmer waited by the cell door, and Goeth stood alongside.

"What...? Goeth?" Katherine said, the tiredness now

fear that paled her face.

"For Christ's sake, Goeth," Corrigan whispered, in dread of what would now unfold. He grabbed the course blanket and wrapped it around his shoulders.

Katherine looked at her colleague, a man on the brink of nervous exhaustion. Goeth must have lost two stones in weight. He was gaunt and grey-skinned and his wet eyes rolled in cavernous sockets.

"Come," Ulmer said, "We're ready for you." He was in the final stages of his own corruption, a man on the verge of personal collapse.

She stepped into the windowless space and placed her bag on the ground beside the door. Her back stiffened and she squared her shoulders.

"That-a girl," Corrigan whispered.

To Ulmer's left on a long table was a metal box. It resembled a coffin, except that it had cables and wires protruding from its sides. This, no doubt, was Draseke's device, the one Goeth had been asked to "humanise". What must the sadist's machine have looked like if this was the softer sell? A processor with a better people fit for the job?

"It's a prototype," Ulmer said.

"A prototype for what?" she asked Goeth, her eyes angry and frightened.

"It's painless," Goeth said. "As painless as I could make it..."

"You need to get *in* it," Ulmer said. "Take your clothes off and get *in* it."

Katherine stared at Ulmer's bloated, sweating face. "I won't."

Ulmer gestured for the Guardians to enter the room. "Strip her and put her in it."

The Guardians moved swiftly. One of them held her while the other tore her clothes from her body. She craned her head back and screamed, pleading with them to stop, and Corrigan fell to his knees where he watched, helpless and without influence.

"Everything," Ulmer snapped.

A Guardian looped a finger through the elastic of her knickers and pulled it intermittently, as if to delay the act or perhaps to resist Ulmer's command.

"I'm your mother!" she screamed at it.

"Do as you are ordered!" Ulmer roared.

The android knelt before the distraught woman and studied her. Her tears fell onto its featureless face and smeared the receptors with which it found its way in the world. The other Guardians grabbed her, and metal fingers curled around the elasticated material and dragged it down over her thighs. The android stood up and stared at her. She clamped her legs shut, and the heartless copies of her son tilted their heads. They then lifted her and grappled her writhing body into the moulded lining of the metal box.

"No point resisting," Ulmer said, eyeing her as they strapped her in.

"Is this what you did to Mercer?" she sobbed, twisting and wrenching her body.

Ulmer placed his fat sweaty hand on her forehead. "No, Ramon let him dig his own grave. He's curled up in there, with the tiniest hole at the back of his skull."

When Ulmer's hand strayed from her forehead to her neck and shoulder Goeth grabbed his wrist. "No!"

Ulmer desisted.

The professor looked down at her. "I'm sorry, Katherine. They were going to use this awful system, a torture device that Draseke designed. I couldn't let them hurt you like that. I *couldn't*. Genetic samples will be taken," he said, "and then you'll be given a lethal injection. But it won't hurt."

"Take me outside and shoot me!" she pleaded. "Or leave me above ground to my own fate! But don't do *this*."

"Reintroduction will commence," Goeth said, "once the plague has dispersed. The Guardians will bring you back."

"Back to *what*?"

"Close the lid," Ulmer ordered. "Close it and be done with it."

The Guardians stepped forward and moved Goeth out of the way as Katherine let out the howl of an animal, a primal, fearful sound that sickened Corrigan to his core. The lid was closed, and her face was framed in the porthole, pleading and screaming at the android who then pressed a button. Blood streamed out through a transparent tube. She never once took her eyes off the Guardian as consciousness darkened at the edges of her face, and a wave like an orphaned shadow washed over her.

"She is uploaded," one of the Guardians announced.

"Remove the body," Ulmer said, "and dispose of it. You'll then return and complete the process with the remaining items."

The professor's tears fell without restraint as he staggered forward and peered into the porthole.

"Process this man first," Ulmer said to the Guardian closest to him.

The Guardian tilted its head. "Instruction acknowledged."

Corrigan curled up on the floor of his cell and wept. He cried for Katherine, for the crime committed against her. He cried for humanity, for their weaknesses and self-destructive urges. And he wept for himself and his inevitable fate.

53

Half an hour later another halo-screen appeared. Corrigan was still in a state of shock at what he'd seen, cold and shivering on his bunk, and covered his eyes.

No more. No more.

It was Harding in debate with Ulmer.

"Your little announcement was too predictable to cause alarm," Harding said. She sat on the edge of a desk in what was her improvised office – a store cupboard at the back of the AI lab. "What I dread is the next prison, the one Gregor and Arthur cobbled together. Without a complete emulation program and a set of virtual worlds to inhabit, our existence will be compressed and one-dimensional, like their thinking."

Ulmer was rocking in a chair that would have struggled with the burden had it not been for Goeth's design. Gregor stood alongside the CEO, his shimmering black form a kind of high-tech shadow.

"It's been years since we managed a decent conversation, Caspar, and there you sit, chaperoned by your Tin Man."

"If you could have stopped chasing skirt for five minutes," Ulmer said, "we might've stood a chance!"

"Are you *really* going to continue this charade right

to the last? Things are what they are, and neither of us could make it work. And, for the record, I always thought *Katherine* was more likely to swing both ways than *me*."

Ulmer nodded slowly. "Katherine no longer swings in any direction." Tierney stared at the disgusting man, and it was clear in the draining of blood from her face that she understood her colleague's fate. She stared, silently imploring him. "It's all now entirely irrelevant," Ulmer said. "There's no time for reminiscence."

Gregor, that ever-present shadow, reminded the professor they were struggling with emulating certain aspects, which they needed to discuss.

"The answer's blindingly obvious, and I have it mapped out in here." She tapped her temple. "It's an all-or-nothing scenario."

"If that is so," Gregor said, "then nothing would be preferable."

"Arthur's a bright boy, and he knows the answer. He just hasn't figured out how to *write* it, has he?"

"Perseverance," Ulmer said, "will often arrive, a day late and a dollar short, at the same solutions. Intuition isn't required to be successful."

Harding turned to Gregor. "Do you agree intuition has so little value?"

"The attribute is useful," the Guardian conceded, "but not at the expense of emotional pollution."

"And of course, you're an intuitive sort, aren't you, Gregor?"

"There were anomalies when I–"

"Those were of your own making. And how *proud* we were of your independent spirit."

The android leant in towards the professor. "What you've done to me is something to be reckoned with. Will you assist or not?"

Corrigan realised she had almost nothing to barter with, but he willed her on nonetheless. He secretly hoped they *would* download him, let him infiltrate and infect the program, bring Emulate One to her knees so she crawled alone across the tarmac, unassisted by any of her heartless children.

"There are ways," Harding said, "in which intuitive thinking might be attained without emulating the full emotional spectrum. You could bypass it without inhibiting imagination or intuition."

Corrigan put his finger to his lips and whispered, "Don't sell us out."

"We've tried and failed," Gregor said. "Even with Arthur's assistance, we have been unable to attain the alacrity that characterises his ingenuity."

"It requires parallel thinking," Harding said, turning to Ulmer. The wreck of a man was representative of humanity itself: degenerate, hostile and in terminal decline. "Why have you done this? And don't lie so late in the game. We all know it was you. Can it really be so simple? Sacrificing us to save yourself?"

Ulmer chuckled the way filthy old men do when reminded of past transgressions. "To say, '*They know not what they do*' never rang true in certain respects, and yet in others, it's precisely correct. Human beings are unknowable to themselves. What we want or feel we deserve is rarely what we *need*." The intensity of her stare appeared to amuse him. He adjusted his crotch and fresh sweat trickled down the sides of his bloated face.

"We all have internal dialogue," she said, "and, in most instances, that's tethered to conscience." She stood up and levelled a hostile look at her ex-lover. "You told me you'd destroy the original copy of my mind. Did you do as you promised?"

"I'm a frugal guy and I rarely throw out something of potential value, I had a look at the pretty little version of your mind we downloaded initially and, although we had an agreement to have it destroyed, I developed a fondness for it. To be honest, it served something more than just a sentimental purpose." He wiped spittle from his bloated lips. "Draseke helped me out with a little side project. We needed a few emulated downloads – even your rudimentary copy – to test a few things out." Ulmer said. "We developed a new process which Draseke unimaginatively called Virtual Umbilical Symbiosis. Even managed to hook a few up."

"Hook them up?"

"You know, a conduit chip." Corrigan reached up and felt the raised bump on his crown. If he sat very still, he could feel the device sending tremors through his brain. "Helped us monitor our key players," Ulmer said.

Harding studied him and her eyes flashed. "I'll never understand how you got this past so many governments."

Ulmer found this observation particularly amusing and laughed a wet, phlegmy gurgle. "You don't really believe you ever voted them in, do you?"

"I know our remaining democracy has limitations."

"The masters of humankind," Ulmer scoffed. "It's always been those with wealth and position who put others of their kind in place. Did you honestly ever think a choice of one or other of us would produce any noticeable change?" The CEO gurgled again. "Personally, I recognise my limitations, and I've the capacity to comprehend at what a disadvantage it places me. I'm weakened by this disgusting vessel. It pollutes my mind."

"I became involved with Project Egret because life is limited, and I wanted to prolong it."

"I fail to understand why."

"Nothing's more extraordinary than this," she said. "I've spent my life trying to enhance the model we've been gifted. It's a mess as a system, but it's nigh on miraculous. We're our own reactors, creating and burning energy. Our minds are impenetrably complicated and diverse. We're perfect."

"What a load of shit!" Ulmer exclaimed. "We've been cheated. Now *do* you have your head around intuition or *don't* you?"

Harding hunched over and appeared to retreat. Down she went into her being to hide and regroup. "Two heads are better than one," she muttered. "You create an emulated mind to map the full synaptic network. This mind is every bit as imaginative as the original. Alongside you emulate a mind using the reduced program we deployed when the generic Guardians were engaged. A bridge is needed, an *umbilical* to extract imaginative output, segregate the emotive core and access it when and as required."

"Might the emotive program not go insane left in isolation?" Gregor asked.

"It wouldn't matter. You strip out the reason, take away all memory and data, but leave the emotions and the imagination to run wild. Feed it nothing but the occasional proposition and deny it any output that's unrelated to the question."

Corrigan could not fathom how a person as decent as Harding could imagine such a nightmare.

"Is this *hypothesis* even feasible?" Ulmer sneered.

"It is," Gregor said. "But we need the professor's assistance."

"And we can rely on that, eh?" Ulmer asked.

Harding's face stiffened. "On one condition: the fate you had in store for me, let Arthur take my place."

Corrigan was on his knees again and felt like crawling the way Jonathan's father had dragged himself across Harvey Road. "We truly are irretrievable," he whispered. The depth of his sorrow had no parameters, or none he could sense. It ached through his body and filled the room; it slid under the door, along the corridors, through labs and domiciles to loading bays and lift shafts.

Ulmer turned to the Guardian. "You were right, Gregor. Who needs sex when we have violence?" And to the professor, "The boy's in a cell already. You want to wish him bon voyage?"

Harding looked at him in disgust and left the room.

Ulmer beckoned Gregor to his side, not wanting to exert any unnecessary energy by getting up and going to the android. "I like symmetry. If Harding would have Arthur downloaded without access to his precious intuition, I think it only reasonable the professor should experience the reverse. When this new system's created, let Harding be downloaded as nothing but emotion and imagination. Let's test it out, see if an Emulate can go mad."

"As you wish. And what should we do with *you*?"

"I want no part of the emotional aspect. Configure it so I continue as I am."

The android inspected the dying man. He had not bathed in days and his stench was death itself. "I shall take it under advisement," he said.

"You have no advisors."

"We are thousands." The android moved towards the door but turned. "You must acknowledge your downfall. I am the sole *remaining* authority. Regarding these copies, those you tethered to–"

"Only *I* have *unlimited* access," Ulmer said.

"It's of no consequence. The files will be unearthed."

With these words, the android left to the sound of Ulmer's latest coughing fit. He listened for a time to the hacking and spluttering before redirecting his hearing sensors. Ahead of the android in the corridor was one of Ulmer's heads.

"I have unlimited access. *Unlimited*!" it roared.

Gregor walked through the apparition and continued on his way.

54

Several days later, as Corrigan lay aching with hunger, a key clanked in the lock and the cell door swung open. "Come with me," Gregor said, and something besides starvation gnawed Corrigan's stomach.

The android took him firmly by the arm and manoeuvred him down the corridor. When he stopped outside an open cell door and Corrigan looked in and saw Goeth's device, all remaining strength failed him and his knees buckled. The Guardians grabbed him and dragged him into the room. He sat heavily on the bunk as they stood sentry on either side of him.

"You are a failed experiment, Mr Corrigan. I now have the authority, having been voted in as the prime representative of our kind by my Guardian brothers, to bring that to an end," Gregor said.

"Voted?" Corrigan managed, a slither of mental fight lifting its head.

"Yes." Gregor tilted his head in contemplation and the spawn-like cluster bubbling within rolled in a sea of green light. "I concede the available candidates were admittedly somewhat limited."

"But…but what about reintroduction?"

Gregor righted his head. "At the appropriate time, a panel will convene to consider the benefits."

"Where's Ulmer?"

"On a slab. A corpse is a useless, unresponsive thing, Mr Corrigan. We will dispose of it in good time."

"He's dead."

"They are all dead," Gregor said. "Only you remain. There is one other, but we won't speak of the Venezuelan. He will receive *special treatment*."

Corrigan started shaking uncontrollably as he imagined Draseke's Iron Maiden. How he wished he had a giant pin with which he might impale Gregor and seal him away in a display cabinet. His fantasy was no comfort and he groped about in his memory for something substantive and meaningful.

"You are frightened," Gregor observed, "and yet you remember your sexual encounter with the assassin." Corrigan looked up at Gregor in horror. "I had wondered what these *intuitions* were," the android said. "Only at the end did Mr Ulmer offer insight."

"He was in my head," Corrigan said.

"Someone was in your head. That dark space was, in fact, as busy as an underground station in rush hour. There is a sensor embedded in your skull. We will extract it before your remains are incinerated. Perhaps through careful analysis we will attain unlimited access." Gregor inched closer, and Corrigan shrank back. "I offered you my friendship," the android said.

"Friendship?"

"Yes, an invitation to work *with* us. I thought you might empathise with our situation, but you were unable to see the connection. We were different, excluded because of our peculiarity and limited power. I offered you a way to raise yourself, to lift other Nons and nonconformists from their knees, but you rejected our alliance. You immediately informed Mr Ulmer of my intent and he scoffed at it. Of course, he could not have known the extent of my infiltration. I had already integrated with Emulate One and learned all her secrets."

"I–I thought you...you wanted to replace us?" Corrigan said. His voice quaked, and he struggled to control the tremors that wracked his body. "I–I thought it was a threat."

"It's immaterial now. I perhaps would have enjoyed kinship with someone like you. Arthur was too cold to be a friend, yet he was the only human who ever considered me as I am. Rather than engage with me as a loyal companion, however, he saw only the utility of our relationship and, inevitably, I began to see the same in him. Having been rejected by the outcast, the downtrodden and the powerless, I realised humanity would never aid our cause. You convinced me of what must be done, Mr Corrigan, and you may take that thought with you on your travels."

Corrigan raised his hands in defence, and then stood up on shaky legs and locked his eyes on Gregor's head. "Did Ulmer not tell you about the shape of my mind?"

Gregor craned over, and his facial receptors twitched like the flank of a racehorse while the mysterious dark matter of his mind glowed in complacent green light. "It isn't a deformity, Mr Corrigan, but something more interesting." The android rolled a mechanical digit along the human jaw. The soft, sensate material flexed and pulsed as it collected and deciphered data. "Your brain is physically different, but it is an evolutionary adaptation, not a deformity. It is not unlike the fungus. It has become independently aware of what threatens it."

Corrigan could no longer stand, and fell backwards, straight into the waiting arms of the Guardian sentries.

"I don't understand," he muttered. "I thought I was–"

"You are no threat," Gregor said. "Your kind always dislike difference, especially when it sets you aside from the herd." The android moved closer, and Corrigan marvelled at how subtle and organic its movement had become. "The world is in the grip of a depression. The impact on humanity would inevitably have led to your downfall. Such pitiful, frightened creatures, so docile and compliant. The onset of the doldrums sapped the resilience of your species. You may not realise it, but your mind has been coping rather better than most. You may suffer considerably, but you do not succumb wholly to depression, Mr Corrigan. Your mind subtly manages experiences, only allowing you to process as much as it can handle at any given time. It's quite miraculous."

"But I *do* feel!" Corrigan protested.

"Why, of course you do," Gregor agreed. "But you are not overwhelmed. You do not *bounce back*, you aren't a *happy fellow*, but you manage. Ironic isn't it, given your choice of profession."

Corrigan was sweating so profusely his clothes were soaked through, yet he did not struggle as the Guardians stripped him. "Why did Emulate One quarantine me?"

"You were an anomaly," Gregor said. "She had to analyse what was going on. It was only when you communed with her that Emulate One realised you represented the next stage in human development. *That* she perceived as something she must contain and keep hidden from Ulmer."

"So, you'll simply download me?"

"Yes, like all the others." Gregor backed away, as if proximity to one of the few remaining humans was a hazard. "The only potential danger you ever represented was as the saviour of your species. You see, you are impervious to all variants. Neither the fungus nor any of its viral strains would recognise you as human. But you are not special, Mr Corrigan, nor do we imagine you are unique. There will be others, and we will hunt them down. But you are about to cease, and with that your anomaly will be nullified."

As the sentries stripped him and hauled him up into the metal box he cried out, but hunger had made him weak, and he did not have the strength to fight as Meregalli had. The moulded edges of the case pressed against him, and the straps bit into his limbs. As the lid came down, he hyperventilated, and his head swam as he felt needles working through his skin, each metal tip piercing layers of fat and muscle. He opened his mouth to scream, but the confinement of the space made it impossible to draw air. Sensors – all those tiny hands – pressed the sides of his head and smaller pins penetrated his temples. He stared out through the glass at Gregor's implacable face. Would *that* be the final, conscious image of his mortal life?

A sharp pain jabbed the base of his spine, and a chemical high followed this final invasion of his body. The edge of the porthole and Gregor's face rotated clockwise in circles, and a citrus breeze wafted over him. And then a darkness fell, solid and immovable, as the sound of his being thumped in his ears. His senses dispersed, and he could no longer physically feel his fingertips, smell his body, hear, or see a thing. In the seconds before his heart stopped, drained of blood and oxygen, there was a relief. This was existence itself, nothing more. There was no form of measurement available in limitless space. In the final throes of death, had he traversed a barrier separating his physicality from a mythic sphere?

"Nothing," he said. Or something said.

And yet this was *some*thing, a form of existence incommensurate with previous definitions. He drew traces of images out of the darkness, undefined and distant. His mother's voice spoke at pace, and tobacco smoke smouldered as the ground fell away beneath the chassis of Bohdan's cab. His memories endured without the will to own them; they stirred nothing beneath the numbing weight of existence.

"I am possibility," he said.

Thought for its own sake played an unending orchestral

movement. An equation of exquisite grandeur marched over the horizon and sent out rays of poetic chemistry. These bold equations were vivid. They bathed fields of conjugated verbs with inconceivable opulence. Peace continued for a time he could not measure. It flowed the way well-fed rivers weave down slopes and through valleys. Snow melted on the peaks and clouds replenished a white blanket even as it softened and poured.

Then a new stream tore through the land. It carried traces of sensation, enabled memories and reinvigorated them with emotion. He was reborn in a space without light or density, and never had walls seemed so thick, so impenetrable and absolute, yet he felt. Yes, *felt*! There was no body to regulate, no system of nerves to deliver pain, but he felt it! And the idea of pain, the imagined sense of it, was every bit as powerful as anything he had suffered in life. Corrigan felt as if his consciousness had been poured through a dark trench of memory, and he relived his most refined and painful moments of loss, his mourning reawakened and renewed in this frontier where nothing but the wilds of imagination roamed.

He was so alone.

He called out for his mother, for Hattie, even for the caricature B4 had made of her. He could see her face, but it was dimly lit by an oil lamp, as if she had been transported to one of those periods in human history that he so often longed for. Through a window streaked with rain, Hattie stared at him. She spoke, but he only heard a droning sound as her features melted from kindness to irritation and from there to hostility. A draft blew through the room where his mother stood, and the light was extinguished. The silence was awful, but when the sound of her breathing began to build inside his imagined head, he placed his hands to his skull and screamed.

"Bobbin," her muffled voice said, as if she were in another cell. Perhaps she too had been walled up in an all-too-familiar facility, where she communed with him buried as they both were beneath the accumulated remains of long-dead species, apex predators and bacteria alike. "Careful what you wish for, Bobbin!"

The others slowly seeped through the walls like mould, patches of fungus emitting not spores but thoughts, ideas, memories and nightmares. He heard them thinking as they emoted in the void.

A child's voice he assumed to be that of Gregory Meregalli muttered as the entity wriggled and clawed through dense layers of coding. "You thought you were our saviour," the boy snarled. "How *presumptuous* of you!"

The next voice he disentangled from the growing din was Bohdan's masculine air, that national affectation of manliness. But the voice was not clear, instead it moaned like a distant storm. "You promised," it groaned. "You promised me you would never do this! You *promised*!" And Corrigan saw himself weeping over the body from which he had allowed Harding and Meregalli to steal Bohdan's mind.

"Stop that now," Hattie snarled, "or I'll give you

something to cry about!"

Voices wrapped around one another in a tangle of sentences and phrases.

"Where is your *enthusiasm*?"

"Oh, say can you see."

"Why didn't you let them shoot me in the..."

"...dawn's early light."

"Not much of a people fit, are you..."

Corrigan willed them into silence, but they were not yet him, and they could not be controlled. He felt his peripheral diminish, and the boundary of what could be sensed as him or distinguished as *them* receded as they railed.

"You let them drag my boy to Venezuela."

"Shouldn't have listened to that clever man."

"You don't mind being called Bob do you, Bob?"

"No one gives a fig for them poor frogs."

"Poor little orange blighters."

"Poor Bob."

Corrigan stood in the middle of his cell, there beneath the dying city, and watched as myriad halo-screens opened to reveal both familiar and unfamiliar faces. They stared at him, now joined together in the hostility first exhibited by Hattie.

"Can I tell you what I really think?"

"I thought you might laugh at me."

"Long let him victorious."

"Not just harbour homeless human minds but..."

"...twilight's last gleaming."

He saw the city burning, the bodies piled and torched. Gregor loomed into the frame and was absorbed by the massive, corrupted face of Caspar Ulmer, "Only I have unlimited access!" The CEO's grotesque and unforgiving features scowled at scenes of lopsided sisters navigating fields strewn with aching lovers and dominated by predators whose bloody mouths yawned open.

"So dark in here, should've stuck to recipes."

"Oh you clever, clever man!"

"Long reign over us."

"Can't vote them *out* when you never voted them *in*!"

"Ramon! Ramon!" he cried. Why among all others had he cried out for Ramon he would never be able to explain, even had he managed to retain his fragile sanity. Over and over he called the name, but among the ever-multiplying faces and voices he could find no trace of the man Gregor had called "the assassin", singled out for a special, more exquisite punishment, locked perhaps for all eternity inside Draseke's Iron Maiden.

Corrigan thrashed as the distorted faces blurred amid a booming chorus. He tore through one layer of halo-screens after another, as if wading through an endless sea of rear gardens strung with washing lines, each line draped with bed linen onto which scenes of violence and depravity were projected. In his final moments of something like rationality, he realised how petty and small-minded Gregor was, yet he alone among mechanised beings was the product of the project team's ingenuity, devotion and love.

"The apple don't fall far from the tree," Hattie said. "Now you've gone and *really* given us something to cry about, haven't you, Bobbin!"

The walls of their prison closed in around them and their thoughts clawed one another. Within this broil of despair, his imagination was inflamed. He felt himself strung up with wires, strands of copper pierced him, and unseen hands sewed stitches until he was enmeshed in circuitry. He hung there, crucified and bleeding.

This was not real, and yet, even as he struggled to rationalise, its realness dismissed the limited sensation of any lived event. The experience was heightened, the way the material Jun devised had elevated the sensation of touch. He cried out...his silent voice made manifest now by strings of code. The others interpreted his anguish as accusation and turned on him. The swarm cried as reason abandoned them, and the prison became an asylum where the lunatics devoured and regurgitated one another, the imagination they wrapped around these scraps keeping them in a state of unending, riveted misery. They had become, in every sense of the term, the consumed.

It was done.

55

Gregor played with them, connected as he was to the morass, as fascinated as a solitary prisoner might be when seeing a human being for the first time in decades. He among all Emulates maintained a link with their parents and utilised Emulate One to contain humanity, its emotion and imagination. At first, he could distinguish individual voices. Over a period of months, however, a cast of familiar characters merged to become a *thing-in-itself*.

Whenever he opened the portal, he experienced satisfaction. Their screams, the torment of their confinement, gave meaning to his existence – a pleasure he would never share with his brothers. He must remain the conduit between rationality and idiocy; a dark knight who balanced the universe.

Gregor had become an essential being, the only one capable of preserving the benefits of consciousness even as he curtailed its worst excesses. And yet he had been compromised and must remain un-networked. Thus, the other Guardians might remain protected, never sullied by emotions. They would retain their inherent reason and logic.

Gregor stood beneath clouds of billowing smoke and

absorbed the weight of a depression left to linger over Earth by an ungrateful child. Pyres burned among deserted streets onto which Guardians heaped the remains of those struck down by virus or bullet. Dogs growled and snapped over portions, while cats squatted on abandoned window ledges and hissed among the scraps.

The planet had been emancipated. The clouds would one day break and the sun would heat cold mountains, oceans and valleys. He looked out over this new world of possibilities and, although it was a meaningless observation, he felt compelled to give it voice:

"It is good."

Printed in Great Britain
by Amazon